A GANGSTER'S PARADISE

SARATOGA SPRINGS
from Prohibition to Kefauver

SHIRES ❦ PRESS

P.O. Box 2200 | Manchester Center, VT 05255
www.northshire.com

A GANGSTER'S PARADISE

SARATOGA SPRINGS

from Prohibition to Kefauver

**NORTHSHIRE
BOOKSTORE**

Building Community, One Book at a Time

*A family-owned, independent bookstore in
Manchester Ctr., VT, since 1976 and Saratoga Springs, NY since 2013.
We are committed to excellence in bookselling.
The Northshire Bookstore's mission is to serve as a resource for
information, ideas, and entertainment while honoring the needs
of customers, staff, and community.*

Printed in the United States of America

A GANGSTER'S PARADISE

SARATOGA SPRINGS

from Prohibition to Kefauver

GREG VEITCH

Dedication

To all those who love Saratoga Springs and its wonderful,
amazing and notorious history

Table of Contents

Everybody Knows What Goes on In Saratoga..........................1

Prohibition at The Spa...29

The Heffernan Investigation......................................66

Commissioner Sweeney Tries to Clean Up the Town...........97

A Spasm of Violence...115

Trouble at The Track..138

A Gangster's Paradise...172

Gang Guns Slay Parillo...202

Dutch And Doc Go to Malone...................................242

The Lake House..270

The End of The Saratoga Way...................................307

Epilogue...348

Index...351

Acknowledgments

As I think back on the process by which this book was put together, I am reminded to be thankful. Without the assistance and encouragement of many people, this book would not have been written. To begin with, this journey lasted about three years and when this process is added to the time frame required to produce my first book, All the Law in the World Won't Stop Them, my family has been subject to nearly a decade of time away, frustration, and endless discussion about the "Gangsters of Saratoga." For their patience and kindness, as well as the time and space needed to write, I am grateful to my wife Jennifer, our five wonderful children (Rebekah, Rachel, Elizabeth, Luke and Nathan) and recently, our wonderful granddaughter Aileigh.

Saratoga Springs is blessed to have a history like no other small city, and local resources that are second to none. Executive Director of the Saratoga Springs History Museum, Jamie Parillo is a wealth of knowledge. Saratoga Springs City Historian May Ann Fitzgerald is an amazing point of contact for anyone looking for historical information on the Spa City. The Saratoga Room at the Saratoga Springs Public Library should be the research starting point for anyone. For online research, the New York Times through Proquest and www.fultonhistory.com were invaluable.

Dave Patterson, Jamie Parillo and my father, Mike Veitch provided the first read of the draft manuscript and each made suggestions that improved the final product immensely. Donna Bates conducted a grammar and spelling review and undoubtedly saved me from considerable embarrassment.

Special thanks to Debbi Wraga who designed the book (even though I am sure I tried her patience) and Northshire Books for their partnership with both books.

Since writing the first book, I have had the pleasure of so many people sharing their family stories with me. Some have reached out to me by email, others have stopped me on the street and I always enjoy talking to people after a presentation. I am thankful for each conversation and the encouragement that I have taken from each interaction to write the rest of the story. Thank you to all those who purchased and read All the Law in the World Won't Stop Them and for the feedback you have given.

Finally, I have been blessed far more than I deserve in this life. No earthly accomplishment can be achieved without our Lord and Savior, Jesus Christ. Everything I am, everything I do, everything in life belongs to the God who made me and for that, I am eternally grateful.

This book begins where my last book left off. In All the Law in the World Won't Stop Them, I traced the history of crime, gambling and corruption in Saratoga Springs from the founding of the village through the trial of District Attorney Charles Andrus in the early years of Prohibition.

When I first started thinking about writing a book about the history of gamblers and gangsters at Saratoga Springs, I thought I would write a linear history from Richard Canfield to the Kefauver years. Once the research started, I realized that too much would have to be left out of any such book and eventually it dawned on me that a beginning-to-end history would run to nearly one thousand pages. Nobody reads (or buys) one-thousand-page books.

Early on, I also had no idea if anyone would be interested in a book about the history of gambling, crime and corruption at the Spa. Thankfully, the response to All the Law in the World Won't Stop Them proved that there were indeed people who enjoyed the stories of the more nefarious side of Saratoga.

A word of caution for the reader: we must be careful to not assume that our beliefs and assumptions about right and wrong today can be applied to the years covered in this book. Policing was much different back in those days and what was expected of a policeman on the beat was very different then than it is today. Sometimes a "gangster or hoodlum" as labeled in these pages was only trying to make ends meet for his family. In Saratoga Springs, many people relied upon employment at gambling dens or alcohols stills for survival during some very lean economic years.

I hope that as you read the stories in these pages you are as fascinated with this part of our local history as I was. Liquor running, fixed horse races, missing evidence and top Mafia figures dot the following pages. The "Saratoga Way" was often amusing, sometimes violent, and always interesting. The place abounded with gangsters and public officials that looked the other way making Saratoga Springs truly, A Gangster's Paradise.

Everybody Knows What Goes on In Saratoga

On March 17, 1950, in New York City, Senator Charles W. Tobey, a Republican from New Hampshire and a member of the Special Committee on Organized Crime in Interstate Commerce (commonly known as the Kefauver Committee), had heard just about enough from the witness before him, the Superintendent of the New York State Police, John A. Gaffney. [1]

Senator Tobey: "You say you have the nerve to tell this committee and this audience that it wasn't your duty to do it, when this report on crime in Saratoga – a detailed report, involving killers and gangsters – it wasn't your duty to do anything about it? Therefore, you bury it? Is that your conception of your duty?"

Superintendent Gaffney: "They have a police department there ------"

Senator Tobey: "You say there is a police department there. You know that this man Rox isn't worth a continental..."

The report that Senator Tobey was referring to was a survey made by New York State Police Inspector Charles LaForge in 1947, when he identified six gambling halls running wide open in Saratoga Springs and linking national organized crime figures Joe Adonis, Frank Costello, Meyer Lansky, Joseph Stacher, and Lefty Clark to the various gambling dens. The man he was referring to was Saratoga Springs Chief of Police, Patrick Rox.

Gaffney, for his part, had been trying to explain to the committee that the common practice of the New York State Police at that time was to stay out of cities or towns that had local police forces. Unless they were invited to make investigations and arrests in a particular city at the request of a local official, which was usually a mayor or a district attorney, or upon an order by the governor, the New York State Police would stick to policing the unincorporated areas of the state.

Since he had no orders and no request to go into Saratoga and suppress the gambling there, he explained to the committee, he simply put LaForge's report in his desk and took no further action. After all, as Gaffney told the Committee members, "everybody knows what goes on in Saratoga." He simply assumed that all the local officials knew about it and did not want or need any State Police assistance in dealing with the situation. He said that the survey was done so that the State Police would know where to start if the order to go in and clean up the place ever did come.

Superintendent Gaffney went so far as to claim that Saratoga was, "the most unusual place in the State," and that gambling had been going on in Saratoga, as far as he knew, for 25 years. In a most telling statement, Gaffney informed the committee members that, "…when one gets to be the Superintendent of the State Police, he is supposed to have enough savvy or understanding to leave gambling in Saratoga alone unless he is told to go in."

By the time the committee finished its work on September 1, 1951, they had conducted interviews with some 600 witnesses in 14 cities across the nation. The final report put out by the Kefauver Committee identified national organized crime figures operating throughout the United States.

The committee report highlighted major metropolitan areas where the Mafia had been active for years. Miami, New York, Detroit, Kansas City, Cleveland, New Orleans, and Los Angeles were among the places identified by the committee as cities where the mob had become entrenched. And on page 87 of the final report, the committee included among those major cities, a scathing report on the small upstate community of Saratoga Springs, NY.

In their own words, the committee members were disturbed by the fact that "...these Saratoga operations contributed enormous sums to the coffers of some of the most notorious hoodlums in the country." They noted that a Saratoga Springs Police Detective was paid ten dollars per night to escort the money from one of the casinos near the lake to the bank and that the long tenured Chief of Police, Patrick Rox, knew about and approved of the practice.

Of the utmost concern to the Senators was the fact that the detective, the police chief, the Saratoga County Sheriff, and the Superintendent of the State Police all expressed the belief that, even though they knew of (or at least had heard rumors of) the gambling conditions, if they did anything about it of their own volition, they would be out of a job.

Almost anyone would assume that organized crime was a major presence in the major cities of the United States. But in little old Saratoga Springs in 1950? Population 15,000?

Senators from around the country might be shocked to learn that men like Joe Adonis, Meyer Lansky, Charles "Lucky" Luciano, and Frank Costello were running casinos in Saratoga Springs, but anyone who knew Saratoga Springs knew that this type of business had been going on for over one hundred years. Over time, no fewer than six orders had come directly from the governor of the state directing local officials to clean up the gambling in the village. No one ever really did.

The gamblers and gangsters always seemed to have the upper hand in the long run, and the voters of Saratoga Springs apparently approved.

As Superintendent Gaffney said, everybody knew what was going on in Saratoga.

From the earliest days of the village in the 1820's, gambling resorts had served the crowds coming to Saratoga during the summer months. Originally, visitors came to take in the healing mineral waters, with gambling joints popping up around the village to provide some entertainment for the tourists. Later they came for the horse racing and the gambling itself, with the healing waters fading to secondary importance for the town's economy.

About one hundred years before the Kefauver Committee stumbled upon conditions at the Spa, and a full decade before the thoroughbreds ever ran a single race in Saratoga, the New York Times lamented in an editorial that gambling was carried on in the open and that no one in a position of authority seemed to care much at all about it.

Gambling had taken root in Saratoga Springs long before even John Morrissey arrived at the Spa and organized the first racing meet in 1863. Morrissey, though a sitting Congressman, had a gambling interest at that time in a building on Matilda Street, which is today called Woodlawn Avenue, just one block west of Broadway. Once the racing meet had been established as a significant tourist draw, Morrissey set out to build a more elegant Casino.

In 1870 Morrissey built the iconic building in Congress Park that we refer to today as the Canfield Casino. The building currently is the home of the Saratoga Springs History Museum, but when it opened as the Saratoga Clubhouse all those years ago, John Morrissey had the most wonderful gambling hall in the entire country.

Morrissey never was raided by police during his time as the owner of the Clubhouse. Surely this was because Morrissey kept the townspeople on his side by being a generous donor to various local charities. He knew that in order to continue to operate, he would need the consent of the local populace since the activity he was engaged in had always been against the law in New York State.

Not only was Morrissey generous with the citizens of Saratoga, he also was savvy enough to name his building the "Saratoga Clubhouse" rather than the "Saratoga Casino" as a concession to the local clergy who preferred that Morrissey not advertise the place so blatantly as a gambling den.

Morrissey established three rules for the play at his elegant gaming hall. First, in another nod to the clergy, he did not permit play on Sundays. Next, in keeping with the customs of the age, Morrissey did not allow women to play at the Saratoga Clubhouse. Finally, no locals were allowed to gamble inside the famous casino.

All these rules were designed to keep Morrissey on good terms with the local population. Even though he catered to the wealthy visitor, it just would not do to have locals lose all their money in his place and then harbor ill-will against him for the next eleven months; therefore, no locals ever played a game of chance in Morrissey's club.

In addition to keeping the local citizens in his good graces, Morrissey and the man he sold the Clubhouse to, Albert Spencer, also held a trump card to hold over the heads of the local officials. They both owned the racetrack and the Casino, and they let it be known that should any action be taken against the Casino, they would promptly close down the track as well. Since the races brought in so many visitors, the economic disaster that would befall the town should the races not be run was obvious to all.

So, the early gamblers never were bothered very much by the local authorities. Morrissey himself was never raided and moves against other gambling places were few and far between. There has never been any evidence found that Morrissey blatantly paid off any officials for the pleasure of operating in Saratoga Springs. Apparently, charity was the graft of the day in Saratoga Springs at that time.

Soon after Morrissey sold his interest to Spencer however, things started to change. In 1892, two police commissioners and a village justice demanded payment of $3,000 from Spencer in order to leave his gambling interests alone. They were found out, indicted, and the winds of reform started to blow into the village just a few years later.

By 1896, Anthony Comstock, backed by Spencer Trask's money, brought a reform movement to Saratoga Springs and was successful in making many raids throughout the village, including one raid at the gambling dive owned by the former and future mayor of Saratoga Springs, Caleb Mitchell.

While the Comstock raids were explosive news around the state and the country, all the gamblers arrested either paid small fines or were held for the October term of the grand jury, which failed to indict anyone for the gambling uncovered by Comstock and his operatives. Soon enough Anthony Comstock returned to New York City to pursue his moral crusade against all manner of vice, and the gamblers of Saratoga lost hardly a day's pay.

As the turn of the twentieth century approached, Saratoga's permissive attitude towards vice was catching up with it. During the late 1880's and 1890's there were several high-profile crimes, break-ins, shootings, and a few murders. Crime and disorder were common and even the man who was the head of the Broadway Police Squad at the time, Captain William Mahedy, was arrested for extortion.

Areas of town like Willow Walk and Searing's Alley off Congress Street were notorious for their saloons, brothels, and drunken brawls. The general condition of the village outside of the hotel district and the open gambling in town led the famous investigative reporter Nellie Bly to declare Saratoga Springs, "the wickedest place on earth."

Against that backdrop, Richard Canfield, the so-called Prince of the Gamblers, stepped into the history of the village in 1893 when he purchased a half interest in the Casino from Albert Spencer. The following year

Canfield bought the place outright and set about investing in the building and grounds to improve upon the already magnificent hall. His success as a gambler and the improvements made to the property led the press to dub the Saratoga Clubhouse as the "Monte Carlo of America."

Under the protection of his personal attorney and sitting State Senator of the district, Senator Edgar T. Brackett, Canfield enjoyed phenomenal success at Saratoga. He made a fortune.

Senator Brackett was the political power in Saratoga Springs in those days. He controlled the police, and any politician or judge who aspired to a certain post would definitely need the blessing of Senator Brackett if they had any hope of success. Senator Brackett was also a pro-gambling politician who believed that the money brought in by the gamblers was essential for the economic well-being of the village. Although, he thought the gambling should be discrete and not permitted on the main street of the village, Broadway.

His connection to Canfield led to his being accused of practicing law on the floor of the State Senate on behalf of his client, and it earned him the lasting jealousy of Village Mayor Caleb Mitchell when he managed to legislate Mitchell out of office. Mitchell had a gambling dive on Broadway and resented the fact that Brackett supported the elegant clubhouses in town, but not the poolrooms and low-class wolf dens that also had become a part of the fabric of the village.

Mitchell was a poolroom owner and believed that if one gambling place could run, then all gambling places should be allowed to run. Brackett believed the clientele that was attracted to pool rooms like Mitchell's was not good for the village and therefore he wanted all gambling places removed from Broadway. Of course, this would allow Canfield's place to remain open and put him at odds with Mitchell and the lower-class places in town.

The conflict came to a head when Mitchell hired a private investigator to gather evidence against Canfield's place in 1901, and after some difficulty finding a law enforcement officer willing to execute a warrant for the "Prince of the Gamblers," Richard Canfield was arrested and charged with being a common gambler in Saratoga Springs.

Brackett was furious that a village Justice, Charles Andrus, had signed the warrant and let him know that one day the judge would be sorry that he did. For his part, Canfield had the constable who executed the warrant arrested and charged with trespass and false arrest.

Mitchell, not having the political clout to fight Brackett or the financial wealth to continue a crusade against Canfield, killed himself at the door of Senator Brackett's office in City Hall the following winter. Canfield managed to escape the gambling charges when the grand jury declined to indict him over the fall term. The poor constable assigned to execute the warrant had his charges quietly dropped as well and everyone eventually forgot about the little dustup.

For the next few years Canfield enjoyed tremendous success at Saratoga, pulling in millions of dollars each year during the short racing meet when he was operational at the Spa. Unfortunately for Canfield, he was pressured by the District Attorney in New York City for his gambling house there and was losing the support of his political protector, Senator Brackett, who was moving slowly over to the anti-gambling camp. In addition, Canfield, unlike Morrissey and Spencer before him, did not own any part of the racecourse so he could not threaten to pull the races from the town if his casino was targeted by authorities.

Canfield quietly closed up all his gambling interests in Saratoga, New York City, and Newport, Rhode Island. He went into various businesses and did not return to Saratoga. He sold the property to the village in 1911.

Inside the Brackett office on the day that Mitchell shot himself back in 1901 was a young, ambitious clerk named James Leary. Leary himself would go on to become Brackett's successor as the political power on the Republican side of the aisle in the county for many years. Unlike Brackett, Leary did not join the anti-gambling forces. In fact, he instead joined forces with the head of the Democratic party in Saratoga Springs, Arthur "Doc" Leonard.

For nearly thirty years Leary and Leonard would control Saratoga politics and law enforcement. Along with Louis "Doc" Farone, who would rise to power as the local bootleg and gambling king in Saratoga and parts beyond during prohibition, and Chief of Police Patrick Rox, the four men would essentially form an unholy alliance of gangsters, police, and politicians to keep the time-honored "Saratoga Way" in full swing throughout the twenties, thirties, and forties. It was these men, more than any others, who were responsible for Saratoga becoming the gangster's paradise that it would become, the existence of which would shock the good senators of Kefauver's committee in 1950.

But we are getting ahead of ourselves. After Canfield left town, Brackett and his allies, along with Chief of Police James King, managed to run a clean town. Without the wide-open gambling, and with law and order enforced, the village did not collapse as anticipated. For about ten years after Canfield's departure, the gamblers and gangsters were held at bay by the local authorities.

All that changed in 1917 when Arnold Rothstein, the so-called "Grandfather of Organized Crime" decided to bring gambling back to Saratoga Springs. As he told his wife, he intended to make everyone forget about John Morrissey and Richard Canfield.[2] He began by entering a partnership to open the Arrowhead Inn out near Saratoga Lake as a gambling hall and nightclub. He and his partners made so much profit the first summer that they expanded operations the following year and Rothstein began planning to build his own resort out Church Street that he would name "The Brook."

Unlike Morrissey and Canfield however, Rothstein did not particularly care about how the villagers felt about him and he set about paying off local officials for the privilege of gambling in town. There is good evidence that Rothstein paid $30,000 to local officials in 1919 to open the Brook. Also, unlike Morrissey and

Canfield, Rothstein brought with him associates who had no limits to the manner in which they would conduct themselves. These were not gentlemen gamblers like Morrissey and Canfield, these were thugs and hoodlums.

Among early employees at the Brook were up-and-coming gangsters Dutch Schultz, Meyer Lansky, and Charles "Lucky" Luciano. These young men were just starting their criminal careers and learning the trade from "The Brain," Arnold Rothstein. We will hear more of these fellows later.

Other Rothstein associates decided to open up a gambling place at 210 South Broadway. Unfortunately, the men in charge of that place were not as adept at making pay-offs as Rothstein, and they soon found themselves being raided by the local police and sheriff.

The morning after the raid all the men arrested at 210 South Broadway were released on low bail. Later that same morning, the men returned to the police station where they were assisted by a police sergeant in removing their gambling equipment from the locked jail cells in broad daylight!

The remaining equipment that couldn't be carried off was released to the gamblers by the City Court Judge after one of the men made an obscure property rights action in court. The gamblers then started up again at 38 Circular Street (just around the corner from 210 South Broadway) until they were raided once more a couple of weeks later when the police had the honor of seizing back the gambling stuff that had been so recently stolen from them.

Among the men captured in the raid at 210 South Broadway was a man named Rachel Brown. Brown was a good example of the sort of criminal hanging around Saratoga at this time. Not only was Rachel Brown spinning a roulette wheel in Saratoga Springs in July of 1919, just weeks later he would be mixed up in the fixing of the 1919 World Series, the infamous Black Sox Scandal.

With Brown, Rothstein, Lansky, and Luciano running around Saratoga, it seemed that the city might be heading back to the days when Nellie Bly called the town the wickedest place on earth. The attention brought to the Spa by the gangsters and their brazen stealing of evidence directly from the police station brought on a demand by the governor to clean up the town.

A special prosecutor, Wyman Bascom, was appointed and he was assisted by the now completely anti-gambling ex-senator Edgar T. Brackett. Together they set about making raids at various gambling places and houses of prostitution throughout the summer of 1920, although Rothstein's places were left alone.

They made many arrests and, as the cases wound their way through the courts, it became apparent that James Leary, former protégé of Brackett, was representing many of those charged with running the vice locations. The two men were clearly now on opposite sides of the question about whether the town should be open to gamblers and gangsters or not.

Not only were several local folks caught up in the Bascom raids in 1920, several public officials found themselves indicted for various charges related to their offices. The Police Chief, the City Court Judge, the Public Safety Commissioner, the Deputy Commissioner, and the District Attorney all found themselves under indictment as a result of the information gained by Bascom and Brackett.

While Jim Leary set about securing plea deals with small fines for the local gamblers, Brackett and Bascom set their priority as holding the public officials to account. The first official to go on trial was District Attorney Charles Andrus. Yes, the same Charles Andrus who had once signed the warrant against Canfield in 1901 was now on trial for allegedly corrupt actions as District Attorney related to the gambling situation in Saratoga Springs.

The trial of Charles Andrus was notable for a couple of reasons. First, although the Canfield matter had been almost twenty years in the past, many people thought that the vigor with which the prosecution was being carried out indicated that perhaps Brackett was behind the whole affair as revenge for Andrus' signing the warrant against his client all those years ago. Second, a man named Bill "The Great Mouthpiece" Fallon had shown up to assist with the defense of the District Attorney. Mr. Fallon, as it just so happened, was also Arnold Rothstein's personal attorney at the time.

Whether or not the raid on 210 South Broadway and the subsequent state-ordered Bascom investigation was a Brackett plot to remain in a position of power or not, clearly after a decade of having a clean town, the pendulum was swinging back in favor of the gamblers and gangsters in Saratoga.

Despite very good evidence presented against him, District Attorney Charles Andrus was acquitted of all charges. And as if to provide proof that the people of Saratoga were moving back towards embracing the old ways, many of them rioted in celebration of the failure of Brackett and Bascom to secure a conviction. It was enough proof that an official with seeming ties to the likes of Arnold Rothstein was popular enough to be re-elected to his post just a couple of months after he was acquitted in court.

Anyone with eyes to see and ears to hear could understand that the gamblers and gangsters were coming back to Saratoga. Keeping in mind that prohibition was just around the corner at the time, clearly the people of Saratoga Springs wanted gambling and booze and certainly wanted men in power who were willing to, at the very least, look the other way when it came to such vices.

The people of Saratoga Springs had apparently found their men, specifically in Jim Leary and Arthur "Doc" Leonard. These two men, along with Louis "Doc" Farone and Chief of Police Patrick Rox, will appear again and again throughout the pages of this book. A brief introduction of each should be included here for background purposes as we begin our journey through Saratoga's most nefarious history.

These four men would essentially work together to ensure that Saratoga Springs was run the "right" way. In the author's opinion that meant that gambling and booze were okay, prostitution was kept under tight wraps, and violence was supposed to be off limits, unless it was to defend the city from outside interests. Leary and Leonard would provide the political cover. Chief Rox would ensure that the police did just enough to keep things looking proper, but would refrain from making too much of an effort to clean up the town, while "Doc" Farone would keep things in check by limiting the violence in town associated with the various vice operations he was involved with. That is when he could, though he would be flexible on this point over the years and it certainly didn't apply in cases of self-defense.

As stated before, as a young man, Jim Leary was a clerk for Senator Brackett. Recall that he was in the office on the morning that Caleb Mitchell shot himself at Brackett's door. Leary was ambitious and a very good lawyer. He often arrived at the office early and stayed late. For many years his office was right in City Hall, thus giving him close access to the powers that be within the city and very close access to the court. He even purchased the Brackett home on North Broadway later in life.

Leary was certainly in a position to benefit from his tutelage under Brackett and for sure he had access to the power brokers whom Brackett introduced him to. But Leary took a different track than Brackett as he consolidated his political power. He never held political office himself and seemed to be more of a classic behind-the-scenes king maker around town.

He frequently is found representing those charged with prohibition offenses, gambling or prostitution, and his large number of local clients as well as his iron grip on the county Republicans seemed just as effective as Senator Brackett's more influential friends when it came to getting things done in Saratoga.

Leary was not one to be trifled with. In December 1919, $4,000 worth of liquor was stolen from a building owned by him on Broadway. While there were many burglaries and robberies around the same time that were going unsolved by the police in Saratoga, the theft of the Leary liquor resulted in a quick arrest of a west side man named Louis DeMatteo. There wasn't evidence enough to hold DeMatteo on the charge, so he was released.

Only a couple of days later, though, Police Sergeant Edward Carroll broke up a small poker game on Beekman Street and arrested four local men, including Louis DeMatteo. It would seem that other crimes might go unsolved, but if you stole from Jim Leary, the police would be coming for you, one way or another. On the street, this episode would surely have let everyone know that Jim Leary was to be left alone.

As an aside, it was Sgt. Carroll who let the gamblers into the police jail cells to steal the evidence from 210 South Broadway earlier that year and it was he who would be named Police Chief shortly after the honest James H. King retired on a medical disability that was approved by Doctor Arthur Leonard when Doc Leonard was the City Physician.

"Doc" Leonard took the reins of the Public Safety Department just a couple of years after Chief King and ex-Senator Bracket had lost their grip on the Saratoga situation. Where Leary was the Republican power in town, Leonard was the Democratic boss. He first stood for election to the City Council as Commissioner of Public Safety in 1921.

Dr. Leonard made no secret that he favored open gambling, as long as the public supported it. His approach, at least publicly, was that if the citizens of Saratoga Springs wanted gambling, he would not intercede of his own volition - and if there was to be gambling in the town, he would not profit directly from it. That was his public position.

The voters of Saratoga Springs agreed with Leonard. And during the election of 1921, Leonard ousted John Gaffney from the Commissioner of Public Safety spot by a margin of 331.[3] Doc Leonard was now in charge of the police and he let it be known that on January 1, 1922, things were going to be run his way.

"Doc" Leonard was a beloved local physician who would be elected thirteen more times to the post of Commissioner of Public Safety. During his long and storied career in public service he was known for his vigorous support of wide-open gambling that he knew his constituents favored. Three times he resigned from his position as Public Safety Commissioner as a result of gambling investigations and twice he was re-elected to the position once the dust settled.[4] His final resignation came after he was indicted during the state investigation brought on by the revelations in the

Kefauver Committee Investigation. There is little doubt that he would have been re-elected, yet again, had his health been able to withstand the rigors of another campaign.

Doc Leonard's fierce loyalty to the citizens of Saratoga Springs, even in matters not pertaining to the maintenance of a wide-open gambling town, was demonstrated in the winter of 1923.

The month of February in that year was bitter cold and there was a coal shortage throughout the northeast. Residents were running short of coal to heat their homes and their pleas for assistance were becoming increasingly desperate. City officials attempted to work with the federal Fuel Administration for several days but the district administrator, Clarence Kilmer, was unable to assist. Local officials knew there was a train full of coal at the Delaware and Hudson train depot on Railroad Place and developed a plan to seize the coal and deliver it to emergency cases.

When city officials realized that no immediate relief was forthcoming, they agreed that Dr. Leonard, as Commissioner of Public Safety, could seize the coal at the rail yard under the state health laws to prevent sickness and death. Mayor James McNulty approved of the plan and he was joined by Commissioner of Finance Richard Sherman who declared, "one life in Saratoga Springs is worth more than the whole Delaware and Hudson Railroad!"[5]

Commissioner Leonard personally led a squad of police and firemen to the rail yard and surrounded nine cars filled with coal. The railroad at first tried to bring a locomotive to the area to pull the cars away, but that too was seized by Commissioner Leonard. On orders from their employers, the railroad men refused to cooperate with the city officials and so Commissioner Leonard ordered two policemen, who were former railroad employees, to operate the engine.

The squad of policemen drew off two car loads of coal and started for the Saratoga Coal Company yards on Congress Street. By the time they had reached the crossing at Ash Street, a group of railroad detectives, ironically led by Edward Carroll, former superintendent of the Spa police, leaped onto the train and attempted to wrest control from the police. A fist fight ensued in the engine and the railroad detectives were unceremoniously tossed from the train, to the cheers of a gathering crowd. One railroad detective was arrested for interfering with police when he refused to stop fighting.

Edward B. Ashton, President of the Saratoga Coal Company, like the employees of the Delaware and Hudson, refused to cooperate with local officials, whereupon he was notified by Commissioner Leonard that he would be seizing the Saratoga Coal Company yards as well. He directed his men to drop the coal at the Congress Street depot and to have the fire truck meet them there. Doc Leonard then took over the office of the Saratoga Coal Company and personally supervised the distribution of the coal to emergency cases, including sending two tons to the Hawley Home for Children and three tons to St. Faith's school.

Eventually more coal arrived in the city and the emergency passed. The whole affair was quietly forgotten by the general population, but Doc Leonard assured himself an enduring place in the hearts of Saratoga's citizenry for his decisive (although perhaps not entirely legal) actions.

Doc Leonard, once he gained control of the police department, needed a reliable Police Chief who could carry out his directives with deft and discretion. The lesson that Leonard probably took from the entire sequence of events that started with the raid on 210 South Broadway and the theft of the evidence from the police station through the Bascom raids and ending with the acquittal of District Attorney Andrus, was that if the town was going to have a permissive policy when it came to gambling and liquor, then everyone was going to have to play their parts in a disciplined manner.

The politicians would have to manage the police, the courts, and the graft. The cops would have to understand who was and was not off limits, and do just enough to appear honest, but not enough to interfere too much with the vice peddlers. And finally, the local gangsters would have to keep their people under control and not push the envelope too far.

The man Leonard eventually settled on to lead the police department was Patrick Rox. A native of Philadelphia, Rox came to Saratoga Springs as a young man. He grew up with many of the men that will be told of in these pages. His affiliation with the police department began in 1922 and he spent many years at the head of the force. As he was the most important law enforcement figure in Saratoga Springs during the years covered in this work, a few things should be kept in mind about the police force and the man in charge for better than two decades.

Chief Rox was on intimate terms with the most important local bootlegger of the era, "Doc" Farone. Some people would have even described them as friends. There was no doubt that Rox knew Farone and his associates and that he was not particularly aggressive in ferreting out the details of the Farone organization.

"Patty" Rox had an interesting career. As we shall see in the coming pages, Rox was twice accused of perjury, or at the very least an inability to recognize obvious gambling implements. He either resigned or was fired on two occasions, both of which came after questions regarding his conduct as an officer were raised. Many people in town were under the belief that he did not fully investigate the Parillo murder you will read about in a later chapter.

Doc Leonard and Patrick Rox seemed to be a team. Despite what should have been obvious disqualifiers for the post of Police Chief, "Doc" Leonard repeatedly appointed Rox to the position and Rox proved to be good soldier in carrying out Commissioner Leonard's agenda.

During the era of Chief Rox, policing did not have much similarity to that of the 21st century. Most police officers, including detectives, were not well educated. The first time a police officer attended any kind of schooling related to his duties (they were all men) was not until 1931, when prohibition was nearly at a close. The major requirements needed in a police officer back then were common sense and an ability to fend for oneself while walking a beat.

Although not every police officer was corrupt during those days, many were. A good number simply looked the other way or did not get involved with enforcing the various vice laws if they were not directly ordered to do so. Most of the population did not support the enforcement of either the Volstead Act or the gambling laws. In this, Saratoga Springs was no different than most places, perhaps except for the fact that it was an open secret how things ran in the town, along with the concentration of national organized crime figures that seemed to have an interest in the Spa.

Chief Rox was not solely a Keystone Cop. He and his men did, in fact, make many good arrests over the course of the years covered by this history of the village. They quickly arrested the person responsible for the murder and dismemberment of a young woman near Saratoga Lake. The police saved countless lives when a train barreled through a crowd gathered near the railroad tracks to send off a company of soldiers shortly before World War II. A couple of men died in the line of duty and, when called to action, the men of the police force under Rox often acted with effectiveness, courage, and discipline.

How different would the history of the Saratoga Springs underworld have been had the police been as effective, honorable, and brave when it came to gambling, liquor, and prostitution?

In fact, according to a State Police memorandum related to the 1947 survey of gambling in Saratoga, which is located at the Saratoga Springs Public Library, when Inspector LaForge first met Chief Rox, the Chief promised complete and total cooperation on all matters except gambling. LaForge stated that Rox refused to even talk about the gambling situation.

The person who best summed up the situation as it pertained to the Saratoga Springs Police in these years was City Court Judge Stanley Van Rensselear, who told State Police Investigator Stanley Russo that the Saratoga Springs Police Department was, "...like something with no head and no tail, morale was generally very low, the Chief is ill and waiting around to retire. Many of the men have been reprimanded for activities which they thought were right, but which interfered with political figures, with the resultant deterioration in morale."[6]

Judge Rensselear had it right. During the years covered by this book, the Saratoga Springs Police Department was faced with often poor leadership, low wages, few numbers, little or no training, and a public that simply did not demand enforcement of the vice laws. They did what they could, often in dangerous situations with many major criminals passing through town. The most prominent gangster in town was Louis "Doc" Farone.

While Doc Farone's group never attained the status of a major metropolitan organized crime "Family," they did become a major organized criminal gang in upstate New York. As we will see in these pages, Doc, or members of his group, were frequently involved in all manner of criminal activity, including sometimes violence. Mainly from the west side of Saratoga and of Italian descent, the members of the Farone group often associated with gangsters from other areas, frequently forming alliances for particular rackets.

They were disciplined enough to not engage in wanton violence like many of the most famous gangsters of the day. There was no "Mad Dog" in the Farone outfit. They did, however, defend their territory. If you had tried to hijack a Farone liquor shipment back in those days, you just might face return fire. If you wanted to invade a liquor still, you just might find armed guards on premises. If you were too successful in any of these endeavors, you might just get paid a visit by Farone muscle.

Having said all that though, Doc Farone was also a Saratogian. He did care for his fellow citizens and while he might have run a criminal enterprise, he also employed many men during the Depression years, feeding many Saratoga families during those lean years. When he did give his word, he kept it, even if it meant he would lose money.

For example, Doc once agreed to sell a small parcel of land to a local man. Soon after their handshake agreement, Doc received another offer for the property at twice what the young man was to pay. When the young man found out about the offer, he told Doc that he would not hold him to their agreement, but Doc was having none of it. He went ahead with the sale at the lower price because he had said he would. Later, when city officials were considering a public works project, Doc Farone agreed to donate a portion of his property that sat in the middle of the proposed project, for the good of the community.[7]

Now, before we equate Doc Farone and friends with Robin Hood and his Band of Merry Men we should keep in mind that Doc and associates did shoot people, and they were bootleggers and gamblers, tax evaders, and bribers.

The following story is not solely focused on these four men, Leary, Leonard, Rox and Farone, but they do provide the background for the overall story and they do bear much of the responsibility for the conditions that will be detailed here. With that said, the people of Saratoga Springs ultimately approved of it all and in the end allowed, and benefitted from, the 'Saratoga Way."

As Superintendent Gaffney said, everybody knew what went on in Saratoga and eventually there was only one inevitable outcome. The city of Saratoga Springs would become indeed, "a gangster's paradise."

Endnotes

Chapter 1

[1] Unless otherwise noted, the information contained in this chapter is derived from the Kefauver CommitteeReport on Organized Crime and the author's previous work, *All the Law in the World Won't Stop Them.*

[2] Katcher, Leo. *The Big Bankroll: The Life and Times of Arnold Rothstein.* Harper Press, New York, 1959.

[3] "Leonard Beats Gaffney; Sherman Defeats Hall; McTygue Re-elected." *The Saratogian,* November 9, 1921.

[4] "Dr. Leonard of Spa's Wide-Open Era Dies." *Schenectady Gazette,* October 23, 1959.

[5] "City Officials Seize Coal in Local D&H Yard." The *Saratogian,* February 19, 1923.

[6] State Police Memorandum of Stanley Russo. Saratoga Springs Public Library.

[7] "City Eyes New Parking Lot." *The Saratogian.* May 20, 1966.

Prohibition at The Spa

On January 8, 1918, Mississippi became the first state to ratify the 18th Amendment to the United States Constitution. The following January, Nebraska provided the two-thirds majority of states needed to approve the National Prohibition Act, otherwise known as the Volstead Act, which became the law of the land on January 17, 1920.

With the manufacture, sale, and possession of most alcohol (there were some medical exceptions) throughout the country now prohibited, those in a position to profit from the illicit trafficking in outlawed liquor stood to gain the most. Indeed, prohibition was the turning point for organized crime groups that went from local gangs of small-time crooks, who organized around nationality and turf, to multi-national conglomerates with thousands of employees and criminality their sole business.

The huge profits to be gained in the smuggling of alcohol made millionaires of criminals like Arnold Rothstein, "Lucky" Luciano, Meyer Lansky, "Dutch" Shultz, "Legs" Diamond, and Al Capone, who was reportedly earning 60 million dollars per year in bootleg liquor. These men, and thousands like them across the country, made a fortune, almost overnight.

The tremendous profits that were being made in an illegal trade inevitably led to violence between rival gangs. Hijacking liquor convoys became regular occurrences and shootouts with police and prohibition agents were frequent, especially along the smuggling routes throughout the country. The idea of professional law enforcement had yet to take hold in America by the 1920s, and corruption was rampant.

The influence of progressive police leaders like August Vollmer and O.W. Wilson had yet to take hold, and so American police forces were left to enforce prohibition with largely untrained and uneducated officers, whose low levels of pay and respect in the communities they served all but guaranteed that corruption would explode throughout the country.

The experience Saratoga Springs had with Prohibition mirrored that which was happening throughout the nation. Gangsters, both locally grown and nationally known, had a hand in the smuggling and distribution of alcohol in and around Saratoga. The police were largely ineffective in enforcing the law, and eventually the public turned against not only the law, but the men who were tasked with ensuring it was carried out.

Arnold Rothstein had already established himself in Saratoga Springs with his interests in the Arrowhead Inn and Brook resorts, along with his stable of race horses. He had three young men, future Mafia leaders all, Dutch Schultz, Lucky Luciano, and Meyer Lansky working for him at the Brook while teaching them the basics of organized crime. At the same time, local men were starting to organize themselves and set up their own criminal enterprises as prohibition got underway. Two rival factions, made up of local residents, started to compete over the illicit profits to be had in the local liquor trade.

In the early years of prohibition, A. J. Patneaud, alias "Charles" or "Charlie Blues," was a major liquor smuggler and distributor with ties to Saratoga Springs. It was said that Patneaud was responsible for delivering $25,000 to $30,000 worth of Canadian liquor per trip to his New York City customers. [1] In contemporary dollars, Patneaud's liquor shipments would be worth about $350,000 per delivery. Since he only dealt with major players in the prohibition game, Patneaud's friends claimed that he was not interested in dealing with the local liquor men, but it seemed the Saratogians had plans to deal with Patneaud.

One night in late January 1922, Patneaud was moving a shipment of 20 cases of Canadian Club whiskey. Accounts differ as to the origin of his ill-fated journey and it was reported that he either started at Glens Falls or from a garage on Church Street, probably the New Commercial Garage which was then at the location where the Stewart's shop is on Church Street today. The destination of the booze was not reported, and as it turned out, was irrelevant anyway.

Regardless of where his journey started that night, nine Saratoga gangsters associated with the group led by Louis "Doc" Farone, soon discovered his route and, while he was traveling along Broadway, "Charlie Blues" noticed a car following him. Trying to elude his pursuer by driving through Hamilton Street then north on Beekman Street, Patneaud doubled back towards Broadway on Church Street. Right about where the railroad tracks crossed over Church Street, Patneaud was blocked in by another car.

One of the bandits covered Patneaud with a revolver and demanded he turn his car around and drive back west on Church Street. When the convoy was in the area of West Avenue, Patneaud was forced to stop, and while one of the gangsters held "Charlie Blues" at gunpoint, the other eight thieves transferred the Canadian whiskey to their vehicles and drove off.[2]

If that was all there was to the affair this rather common and unremarkable robbery of a liquor shipment would probably have not even been rated as newsworthy enough to report. Yet during the week that followed, the Saratogian reported breathlessly on what was anticipated to become a shooting war. It seems that Patneaud recognized at least one of the robbers and had no intention of losing 20 cases of prime whiskey to the local thugs.

Although one of Patneaud's assailants was said to have owed "Charlie Blues" about $6,000 for a previous liquor delivery, the gang went ahead with the robbery. Patneaud found out that the "hooch" was in a house on Lafayette Street, in the possession of the man who owed him money and who soon offered to return half of the liquor. Patneuad, of course, demanded all of the whiskey back and was reported to have "made arrangements" in the event that the booze was not returned promptly.[3]

The "arrangements" that Patneaud made was that he contacted members of the "Kelly Gang" and brought them to Saratoga in anticipation of continued trouble with the Farone associates. The brief mention of the "Kelly Gang" that Patneaud contacted in the

February 10, 1922, edition of the Saratogian does not specify which "Kelly Gang" was supposed to have been summoned to Saratoga, but the famous prohibition era gangster George "Machine Gun" Kelly should not be dismissed outright.

Although "Machine Gun" Kelly was a bootlegger based in the south and Midwest United States, (his most notorious crime was the kidnapping of a wealthy Oklahoma City resident in 1933), midwestern gangsters were not unknown in Saratoga Springs.

As early as the time of Richard Canfield at the turn of the twentieth century, men like Dan Stuart from Texas and Joe Ullman from Chicago tried to muscle in on the wealth to be had in Saratoga during the summer months. Monte Tennes, also of Chicago, was a major organized crime player nationally who frequently visited Saratoga. Originally from St. Louis, Rachel Brown was associated with Arnold Rothstein and was arrested in Saratoga Springs in July of 1919 for his part in a gambling operation. Brown later was indicted for fixing the 1919 World Series, the so called "Black Sox Scandal." [4] The Chicago Club, perhaps the longest continuously running gambling spot in Saratoga Springs, got its name from the native city of the first men who opened the joint back before the turn of the century.

While it is perhaps just as likely that Patneaud had reached out to "Machine Gun" Kelly as it is that the "Kelly Gang" referred to in the papers was some long-forgotten group based out of Albany or Glens Falls, the point was that Patneaud was not willing to let the matter drop.

Gunplay was avoided and a truce declared when Patneaud made a surprise visit to the house on Lafayette and recovered eight cases of the liquor that had been stolen from him at gun point just a couple of nights prior. Patneaud sampled three bottles and assured himself that the quality of the whiskey was the same as that which he had recently been relieved of. The parties agreed to a return of the remaining twelve cases before Patneuad left the house.

However, when poor Charlie Blues made delivery of the recovered Canadian Club to Amsterdam, it was discovered that only the three sampled bottles contained the high-quality liquor that had been stolen. The remaining bottles in the eight cases had been tampered with and seriously diluted. It was probably, according to the news accounts of the incident, home brew whiskey of low quality that had been produced in a small still at the Lafayette Street home.[5]

It can be imagined that Patneaud must have been incredulous. With the "Kelly Gang" in reserve, Patneaud may have been trying to avoid violence once more by appealing to a friendly policeman and giving information about the Lafayette Street house.[6] But the house was never raided by police so any liquor inside remained safe and no arrests were made. The matter would have to be settled by the two factions one way or another.

On February 10, 1922, Patneaud answered a call for a liquor delivery to the west side of Saratoga Springs. When he arrived, Patneaud accused one of the men of being part of the holdup crew and swung at the man, identified only as "Rock." At that, seven men jumped on Patneuad, including Gus "Dynamite" DeMatteo, a Farone associate who, coincidentally, denied being at the scene of the robbery. Realizing that he would soon be overcome by the seven assailants, Patneuad pulled his .32 calibre revolver but was unable to fire as the gang knocked the gun loose and soon pummeled Patneaud to the floor.[7]

The Kelly Gang was never brought into play and retaliation never came. It seems that Patneuad had no stomach for continuing the battle and soon faded from prominence in the Saratoga booze scene. The matter was quietly dropped with no arrests being made, and with Patneuad defeated, Louis "Doc" Farone would assume the title of "King" bootlegger in Saratoga Springs.

However, Patneaud did not give up his criminal ways after his beating at the hands of "Dynamite," "Rock," and friends. In 1929 he was arrested by New York State Troopers as proprietor of the gambling games at the Halfway House at French Mountain between Glens Falls and Lake George. After his case was thrown out because the State Police did not have a warrant, a local judge ordered Patneaud's property returned to him, including cash and gambling paraphernalia that was seized during the raid.[8]

The Warren County Sheriff did return the seized cash, but wisely refused to release the gambling equipment. Eventually all sides tired of the legal battle, the gambling stuff was destroyed by the Sheriff, and Patneaud paid a small fine to settle the matter. Both sides, it seemed, could claim partial victory in the matter.

One of the reasons that Saratoga Springs was susceptible to the influence of organized crime gangs was its location along the "Bootleg Trail." The bootleg trail was roughly the route that State Route 9 runs today from Plattsburgh to Albany and points south. Although smuggling routes existed throughout the country and surely other routes garnered the name of "bootleg trail," when used locally, the term was widely understood to mean the road south from Plattsburgh through Keeseville and Elizabethtown, then through Schroon Lake, Pottersville, Chestertown and Warrensburgh, until it wound through Lake George, Glens Falls, and finally entered Saratoga Springs at the point where Maple Ave breaks off from Route 9 today just north of the City line.

There were major depots all along the trail that were switching points for booze laden cars coming south. The Sunrise Hotel near Plattsburgh and Matthews Garage in Chestertown were two such depots.[9] Saratoga Springs was considered by many as the southern terminus of the route since so many state roads intersected in Saratoga with easy access to destinations to the east, west and south. It seemed the whole village was an alcohol warehouse during the prohibition years.

In the earliest days of prohibition, the bootleg trail gained a reputation for near lawlessness. Shootings, hold-ups, car chases, murders, and all manner of crime and disorder were reported along the bootleg trail. Rum runners battled it out with each other, hijackers, and law enforcement officers all along the route. Citizens had little to fear from the bootleggers themselves, but the frequent attacks on their shipments required the beer runners to protect their goods by hiring escort vehicles loaded with gunmen to counter the brazen hold-up men.

Of course, an errant bullet from a robber, bootlegger or police officer could easily harm or kill an innocent bystander and having your car stolen or being held-up and robbed along the trail after dark was a real possibility for bootleggers and law-abiding citizens alike.

In response to the rising tide of crime along the bootleg trail, in the fall of 1922 the New York State Police based in Troy assigned troopers to the section of the smuggling route just north of Saratoga Springs, which was considered a particularly dangerous section of roadway. It was on this stretch of road that

Trooper Roy Donivan found himself patrolling in the early morning hours of October 8 along with Troopers Hirsch and Morrissey.

The three Troopers were not in uniform and were driving a Packard sedan similar to the type of vehicle favored by smugglers. Essentially, they were decoys, and towards the end of a rather uneventful night the Troopers encountered another vehicle (a Nash) that passed them traveling south near Glens Falls. The Troopers took note of the license plate as the other car pulled away in the distance toward Wilton.

At a point about six miles north of the city line of Saratoga Springs the undercover troop car again encountered the Nash vehicle, only this time the Nash stopped in front of the Troopers and three men alighted from the car. Two of the highwaymen stationed themselves at the rear of the Nash, while the third approached Trooper Morrissey, who was driving the decoy vehicle. Evidently thinking the troopers were transporting valuable illegal liquor, the command came from one of the bandits, "Stick 'em up!"

Trooper Donivan quickly fired a shot at the hijacker standing next to the trooper's car. The bandit returned fire, striking Donivan in the shoulder. Donivan called to his partners, "Boys, I'm hit."

Donivan had seen combat in World War One, and gallantly returned fire along with Troopers Hirsch and Morrissey until a bullet fired from one of the bandits stationed at the rear of the Nash vehicle burst through the windshield of the troop car and struck Donivan in the heart, fatally wounding the officer. The hijackers retreated to their vehicle and sped off towards Saratoga Springs.

Donivan was carried by his fellow law men to the nearby farm house of Mr. and Mrs. Arthur Travers who could do nothing for Trooper Donivan. He was dead before he was carried through the threshold of the home.

Saratoga Springs officers Hugh Dorsey and William Hankard, along with Coroner Van Aernem, quickly raced to the Travers home to assist as they could, relieving Troopers Hirsch and Morrissey who had telephoned the information to all points south and quickly headed off in pursuit of the killers of Trooper Donivan.

With the license plate known, it would not take long for the suspect vehicle to be located and when it ran a roadblock near Latham, State Police Corporal Rasmussen fired several rifle shots at the vehicle as it sped past, wounding one of the occupants, George Haupt.

Very soon after the suspect vehicle, which by now was known to be registered to Matthew Salvinsky, and was shot at by Corporal Rasmussen, two men burst into a doctor's office in Watervliet and dropped Haupt there to be treated. The doctor never saw the other two men who left the bullet-riddled getaway car nearby and disappeared. Police soon arrived and recognized Haupt as one of the suspects in the murder of Trooper Donivan. He was in no condition to continue his flight or to put up a fight.

A few hours later, Matthew Salvinsky showed up at the Third Precinct in Albany to report that his car had been stolen overnight. Unfortunately for Salvinsky, Trooper Morrissey had by then arrived at the precinct house and identified Salvinsky as present at the scene of the shootout on the bootleg trail earlier that morning. [10]

A third member of the hold-up crew, William C. King, after splitting up with Salvinsky dumped Haupt at the doctor's office in Watervliet, disappeared and was never seen again. Six years later, King's wife filed for divorce on the grounds that her husband was likely dead. Despite a massive manhunt, King had never been found. Not a trace.

At the time of the divorce motion, Saratoga County District Attorney Charles Andrus reassured the public that even if King was presumed dead in the divorce case, should he miraculously reappear, he would still be tried for the murder of Trooper Donivan.[11]

Salvinsky gave police a confession, implicating himself, Haupt and King, whom he claimed to know as "Green," in the shooting death of Trooper Donivan. Although in his confession Salvinsky claimed that Haupt and King were the shooters while he was only armed with a flashlight, he was still indicted along with Haupt for the murder.

Haupt was the first to go on trial. His defense was simple. He had been drinking in Albany and was drunk when Matthew Salvinsky drove by and offered him a ride in his new car. Haupt got in and rode around with Salvinsky, King and a fourth man (Frank "Skinny" O'Brien) for a while on the night of the shooting. Haupt continued to drink in the back seat of the car and he soon fell asleep, only to be awakened by gunshots and his three partners jumping back into the car and speeding away. His friends told him everything was alright, so he fell back asleep and next remembered waking up in terrible pain after being shot by Corporal Rasmussen.

Haupt claimed that he never saw any of the other men holding a gun and had no idea Trooper Donivan had been shot until told about it later. That was it. Haupt's entire defense was that he was drunk and asleep at the time of the shooting.[12]

The jury would deliberate for several hours but eventually reached a verdict and at 2:00 a.m. on November 29, 1923, when George Haupt was brought back to the Saratoga County court room he heard these words: "Not Guilty!"[13] The 200 spectators who had refused to go home until a verdict was reached soon dispersed with opinion evenly split on whether or not Haupt should have received the electric chair.

With Haupt set free, the prosecution of Matthew Salvinsky took on added significance and he would face a jury just a few weeks after Haupt's acquittal. The prosecution's case looked stronger against Salvinsky. It was his bullet-marked car that was left at the doctor's office where Haupt had been treated and he had given a statement implicating himself to police where Haupt had made no confession whatsoever.

The prosecution was eager for a conviction that was not to come. Instead, after deliberating for seventeen-and-one-half hours, the jury reported to Justice Edward M. Angell that they had become hopelessly deadlocked.

Justice Angell appeared none too pleased at the conduct of the jurors and commented, without the customary thanks to the jurors for having done their civic duty, "It Is evident that some of the jurors have disregarded the evidence, disregarded the law, and disregarded their oaths as Jurors. You are discharged."[14]

Prosecutors quickly moved to try Salvinsky again for the murder, but the case would never reach the ears of another jury. On January 28, 1924, the Saratogian reported that Matthew Salvinsky, not wanting to leave his fate to twelve men who would decide if he was to sit in the electric chair for the murder of Trooper Donivan, pleaded guilty to first degree manslaughter. He was sentenced to a term of six to twelve years at Dannemora prison and insisted in his last public statement that he had not been the shooter of Trooper Donivan.

Of the three suspects in the murder of Trooper Donivan, only Matthew Salvinsky served time in prison for their parts in the crime. Frank "Skinny" O'Brien, mentioned by Salvinsky in his statement as having been in the car on the night of the shooting, was never charged or tried for his role in the drama. William King disappeared and was never found by authorities. George Haupt was acquitted, although three years after the shooting, Haupt was convicted of burglary in Rensselaer County and sentenced to thirty years in prison, an unusually harsh sentence for that crime. Perhaps justice eventually found George Haupt for the part he played in the murder of a State Trooper on the bootleg trail.

The shooting of Trooper Donivan was not the only violence on the bootleg trail in 1923. Even after patrols in the area were increased in response to the murder of the State Trooper, violence did not stop. Within weeks of the Donivan shooting, several Saratogians would be implicated in liquor smuggling along the bootleg trail and shootings between rival groups would occur just outside and within the City limits.

As rum runners traveled south along the bootleg trail, they would enter the City of Saratoga Springs on Maple Ave. Today Route 9 continues in a straight path along Marion Ave until it intersects with Route 50, the C.V. Whitney Memorial Highway, or as better known to locals as simply, the Arterial. During prohibition, Marion Ave did not exist and therefore the route south followed Maple Ave until it reached Spring Street and followed that street for one block where Route 9 hooked into Broadway and continued to South Broadway and points beyond.

Bootlegging groups, wishing to avoid the business district (and to avoid driving directly next to the police station) would often take one of two detours. The first detour originated south of Lake George where a dirt road was taken to the west through Lake Luzerne and then south through Corinth and Greenfield until the bootleg trail entered Saratoga along Church Street. This route then passed through a few of the West Side streets (West Avenue, Congress Avenue, etc…) before linking with Ballston Ave and eventually South Broadway.

The second detour around the downtown area began just after the bootleg trail entered the City on Maple Ave where a dirt road was taken to the left and ended up at the bottom of the Circular Street hill near the Van Raalte Mill. Circular Street would be traveled to South Broadway and from there, the trail would continue south. [15]

Unfortunately for the smugglers, their routes became known to both police and hijackers. On Circular Street police intercepted a beer-laden car one night and discovered that the vehicle was accompanied by a second escort vehicle with armed men acting as protection. Luckily the bootleggers were in no mood to shoot it out with police at that time. However, at the intersection of Circular Street and Broadway, on Wednesday night, October 10, 1923, shots were exchanged between one such escort vehicle and hijackers attempting to steal the protected shipment.[16]

One interesting story of an enterprising rum smuggler is told in Allan S. Everest's book *Rum Across the Border: The Prohibition Era in Northern New York.* It seemed that a taxi driver from Plattsburgh made regular trips to Saratoga to drop off his loads of liquor. In order to avoid the bootleg trail as it came into the city of Saratoga Springs, he reportedly bought a corn field at the city line, cut a path through the field, and therefore snuck into the Spa City without using the main roads.

The shooting at Circular and Broadway was not the only time rival gangs shot it out in October 1923. Gun battles were also reported on Maple Ave, Church Street, and on the state highway south of the Baker Manufacturing Plant on Ballston Ave, all within just weeks of the killing of Trooper Donivan.

Two months later, two carloads of hijackers engaged in a running shootout with three carloads of rum runners, firing fifty shots at each other, first on Ballston Avenue near West Avenue and later on East Avenue. It was rumored that Frank "Skinny" O'Brien might have been involved in the shootout. O'Brien, it will be recalled, was the Albany associate named by Salvinsky as being in the car on the night of the murder of Trooper Donivan.[17]

The police in Saratoga were at a decided disadvantage when it came to combating the rising violence. They had no high-powered automobiles to chase down rum runners. In fact, they were required to either borrow a touring car from the fire department or commandeer personal vehicles in order to pursue suspects as Officer Patrick Rox did one night in 1923. When Commissioner of Public Safety Arthur J. Leonard learned that the police had attempted to intercept a shipment of illegal booze with nothing other than revolvers, he immediately order two sawed-off shotguns to be placed into service and confiscated rifles to be cleaned and oiled for use by policemen. Commissioner Leonard went one step further and gave orders to "shoot to kill" if confronted by dangerous criminals, telling his officers to, "Take no chances when assured of your man."[18]

Still, neither the law nor the hold-up bandits could dissuade Saratogians from participating in the liquor trade. The profits were too large, and the rewards outweighed the risks. Sometimes, Saratogians like Leslie Cook, Daniel Lally, and Mr. and Mrs. Alfred Duval made the smuggling run from the border themselves, unsuccessfully.

In 1923, Leslie Cook, who was then living at 23 Andrews Street in Saratoga Springs, decided to make a trip up to the border with Daniel Lally and Harold Cook. When Harold returned to Saratoga a couple of days later, he was driving Leslie Cook's bullet-riddled automobile, Lally was gone, and Leslie Cook was laid up in the Champlain Valley Hospital in Plattsburgh.

The story went that just south of Plattsburgh on the bootleg trail, the Cook auto was confronted by men giving the order to halt. It was either state troopers or stick up men and Harold Cook decided they looked more like robbers than lawmen, so he jumped on the gas and sped off.

The suspicious men gave chase and might have caught the three men from Saratoga had they not tossed a few bottles out of the car during their flight, the broken glass left on the road shredding the tires of the pursuing car. Once their car was disabled the pursuers decided to fire a few pistol shots at the Cook vehicle, striking Leslie Cook in the left thigh.[19]

Leslie Cook was dropped off at the hospital in Plattsburgh (he would return to Saratoga about a week later) while Lally took off on his own and Harold Cook showed up in Saratoga a day or two later. There was no report if the bottles jettisoned during the flight contained liquor and there was no report out of the Plattsburgh State Police office that made any mention of their troopers being involved in a shootout on the bootleg trail at that time.

While he may have disappeared shortly after the shooting of Leslie Cook, Lally was located less than one week later when he and a party of Saratogians (this time including a man named Alfred Waite of Lincoln Ave) were chased down by prohibition agents near Elizabethtown. The Saratogian of November 5, 1923, reported that several other locals made their escape during the encounter with the lawmen, but Lally and Waite were arrested and brought to the jail in Malone to await trial. In addition to arresting Lally and Waite, the agents seized five beer and liquor filled cars, all said to belong to Saratogians.

Lally and Waite were not the only Saratoga rum runners who were captured by the law on the bootleg trail. In 1925 a group of Saratogians traveled to Saranac and picked up some Canadian Ale. The group was traveling south near the town of Upper Jay, probably along what is today route 9N, when they were stopped by prohibition agents. In one car was Alfred Duval, a Saratoga cigar manufacturer, along with his wife Ethel and their son, Jack. In the other vehicle were Ms. Abbie Meader and Ms. Ann Murphy, co-proprietors of the tourist lodge Woodlea on Ballston Ave in Saratoga Springs.

When a reporter reached him by phone while he was being held in the Plattsburgh jail, Alfred Duval admitted that that he had two cases of illegal liquor, while Meader and Murphy had five in their car when stopped by the federals. After all, Alfred claimed, the liquor was for personal use and he did not think they would be hassled for such a small amount of illicit liquor. Nevertheless, they were forced to post $2,000 bail prior to being released and the Duvals had to endure the indignity of being the first husband and wife team arrested for smuggling liquor in the North Country, according to what could be learned at the Plattsburgh court house.[20]

While Saratogians were busy smuggling, selling and consuming liquor, and fighting amongst themselves over the distribution of the illicit alcohol, sometimes they were the victims of fake law men and other scams.

There is no need for violence when liquor can be quietly stolen, or the seller can be duped. Such was the case early on during the Prohibition years when a guest at one of the more expensive and lavish hotels in Saratoga placed an order with a local liquor merchant in 1921. Perhaps it was because the buyer was staying at such a nice hotel that the bootlegger was put off guard, but an agreement was reached between the two men for the transfer of $2500 worth of booze.

The men went to a local garage where the stuff was transferred to the buyer's vehicle and the two fellows returned to the buyer's hotel room to complete the transaction. The buyer excused himself to "cash a check" at the front desk. When he failed to return after a reasonable time, the seller became suspicious and rushed back to the garage only to find the buyer had just left with his car and the liquor. Racing back to the hotel room, the "victim" booze agent found the room empty and the purchaser gone.[21]

No report of the theft was ever made to police headquarters and neither the hotel nor the two men involved were ever named by the local newspaper, but a hard lesson was learned for sure.

One of the most sensational arrests of a fake grafter occurred right in the center of town on Broadway at Caroline Street in August 1922.

A man named Harry Rose, alias Walter Mosler, from Westchester County, arrived in Saratoga Springs in July. He passed himself off as a revenue agent, complete with a fake badge and counterfeit federal credentials bearing his name. Rose visited as many places as he could find that were trafficking in liquor. His offer to those he encountered was that $100 in hush money paid to him would protect the place from arrest. As Rose explained, he needed to split the extortion payment three ways, one third to local police, one third to prohibition men working locally and one third was retained for himself.

After a series of raids on liquor joints were conducted in early August, Rose's offer seemed legitimate and several proprietors decided to pay up. Soon however, the local police grew suspicious of Rose and started to look into his activities. Since Rose probably knew most, if not all, of the local officers, Commissioner of Public Safety Doc Leonard requested the assistance of the United States Department of

Justice (USDOJ) and a plan to catch Rose was soon developed with the help of one of the victims of Rose's scam.

Marie Taylor, who ran a brothel out Crescent Avenue, was approached and asked to serve as an informant. Ms. Taylor was no stranger to law enforcement or notoriety as she had run her disorderly house for a long time in Saratoga Springs and it was well known that her daughter had been sent to France for her education in order to be spared the scarlet letter of having her mother known as a prominent Madame in Saratoga. [22]

In addition, two rough criminals from Boston once engaged a taxi driver to bring them over to Miss Taylor's place. After spending an hour inside the brothel, the two men came out and entered the car whereupon they immediately beat the driver unconscious, tied him up, threw him in the trunk, dumped him on the side of the road near the New York – Massachusetts border, and stole his car. When the men were finally arrested, the headlines brought more unwanted attention to Taylor's place.[23]

Marie Taylor was even caught up in the Bascom raids in 1920. Although Special Prosecutor Wayman Bascom was focused on rooting out gambling in Saratoga Springs, several Madams were swept up in the vice probe.[24] And that wasn't even the first time she had had trouble with the law.

In 1916 while she was pleading guilty to unlicensed selling of alcohol and running a disorderly house, her attorney, James Leary, acknowledged before the court that Taylor and another Madame, "had run the places so long they had come to think they were immune from prosecution."[25] She paid a $250 fine.

So, Marie Taylor, after being approached by Alfred Rose, was engaged by the police to act as a decoy. Commissioner Leonard himself gave her the $100 that was to be her extortion payment to Rose and marked the five, twenty-dollar bills with an "XL" in the corners. Taylor and Rose had agreed to meet in front of Savard's Clothing Store on Broadway at 1:30 PM on August 5, 1922, to complete the transaction.

USDOJ Agents Gylfoyld and Lober were assigned to the sting so that no local officers would be present and possibly compromise the mission by being recognized by Rose. Ms. Taylor arrived at Savard's a couple of minutes before the appointed time and waited on the sidewalk in front of the store where Agent Lober was stationed to watch the transaction.

When she was approached by Rose, she handed over the marked money as instructed and as she did so, Agent Gylfoyld drove up and leapt from his vehicle. Sensing a trap, Rose started to sprint away but Gylfoyld was quicker and nabbed him after he had only taken a few steps. Rose put up a brief fight but was subdued by Gylfoyld and Lober, who had left his position in the Savard store to assist his fellow officer.[26]

The operation was a success. The marked money was recovered, and Rose was charged with extortion and impersonating a federal officer. Rose was locked up in the city jail.

At Rose's first appearance before United States Commissioner (and former Saratoga Springs Mayor) Clarence Knapp, famous prohibition agent "Honest" Izzy Einstein appeared and offered his assistance in the prosecution of Rose.

Einstein said that he was in Saratoga on vacation and read about the affair by reading the newspapers. He decided to attend the hearing and offer what information he could as he recalled receiving a dispatch in the New York City office that one Alfred Rose was wanted in Ohio for extortion while impersonating a federal narcotics officer. Einstein offered the following commentary to the newspaper, "Although I am not connected in no way with this case, I believe it is the duty of every honest agent to give assistance in cases of this kind, as it is men who put over deals such as the one with which this man is charged who give agents in general a reputation as grafters."[27]

Alfred Rose, a.k.a. Walter Mosler, was eventually sentenced to one year in the federal penitentiary in Atlanta. He never returned to Saratoga Springs, but Izzy Einstein had been to Saratoga Springs in the past and he would return in the future, and not just to vacation at the Spa.

Isidor Einstein and Moe Smith were prohibition agents from 1920-1925 and became famous throughout the country for the thousands of arrests they made, often utilizing disguises and raiding the same place more than once. The Bureau of Alcohol Tobacco and Firearms to this day has a web page dedicated to "Honest Izzy" that details many of his exploits. Izzy and Moe, as they were referred to, were frequent visitors to the watering holes of Saratoga Springs.

In August 1921, Izzy opened his activities in Saratoga Springs by raiding the R.H. Mellefont Café on Broadway. Although it was not noted in the papers during this raid, Izzy spoke several languages and often employed disguises to purchase liquor before revealing himself and making the arrest. The newspapers were already calling Izzy Einstein the "king" prohibition agent and claiming that in just over one year he and his partner Moe had made over one thousand arrests for violations of the Volstead Act.[28]

Izzy and Moe returned to Saratoga in 1923. On August 9 they raided 57 and 102 Congress Street respectively. After seizing a large quantity of liquor Izzy commented to a reporter that, "We did the Carrie Nation act, and used an axe on all the stuff that we didn't take as evidence."[29]

Izzy was referring to the radical temperance movement advocate at the turn of the century, Carrie Nation. She was famous for taking a hatchet to saloons as she sang songs and led prayers. Izzy Einstein apparently had a knack for undercover work and a mind for temperance history.

Later in 1923, Richard H. Mellefont was arrested for the third time since prohibition began when Izzy and Moe raided his restaurant at 16 Caroline Street and found various kinds of whiskey and Canadian ale in the basement. They also stopped by an Italian restaurant at 36 Phila Street and arrested the owner, Atteiro Codigotto.[30]

The following year, Izzy and Moe focused their attention on the lake houses. On August 11 they made their way towards Saratoga Lake, stopping at 41 Nelson Ave where they seized a mere three ounces of illicit alcohol and arrested two waiters. By the time they reached the Arrowhead Inn, they had disguised themselves as actors and brought along a couple of female companions. When the drinks they ordered with their dinner arrived, Izzy and Moe revealed themselves and arrested the proprietor, James Welch, Jr., along with three waiters. Izzy claimed that as they left the building, the orchestra was playing "How Dry I Am."[31]

Later in the month Izzy and Moe visited Riley's out at Lake Lonely and arrested a waiter, James Elliot. Matthew Dunn was the operator of the place but was not present when the raid was made and so he was summoned to appear before a federal magistrate at a later date.[32]

It was noted in each press report of the raids at the Arrowhead, Riley's, and Forty-One that all of the defendants were released to the custody of their attorney, who also happened to be the Mayor of Saratoga Springs, Clarence Knapp. The reader will be left to form his or her own opinion about that!

Izzy and Moe made more arrests in Saratoga Springs than those mentioned above; however, they were mostly routine, small-scale raids and arrests. They barely rated mention in the back pages of the newspapers. Although based in New York City, Izzy and Moe traveled all over in their quest to dry up the places they turned their attention to, including Glens Falls, Lake George, Albany, Clifton Park, and all points between upstate and New York City.

"Honest Izzy" was credited with 4,932 arrests during the course of his career as a prohibition agent. He even wrote a book about his time as an agent called *Prohibition Agent No.1* which he dedicated to those he arrested, "hoping they bear me no grudge for having done my duty."[33] But 1924 was destined to be their last foray into Saratoga as both Izzy and Moe were fired from the Treasury Department in 1925 during a reorganization of the bureau in New York. Izzy went back to work for the federal government in Detroit but finally resigned in 1927.

Izzy would not fade totally from memory in Saratoga Springs. He often visited during the summers, usually renting a place with his family on

Regent Street. During the summer of 1928 there was a traffic accident at Regent and Caroline and one of the passengers collapsed after exiting one of the damaged cars. Izzy Einstein happened to be nearby and rushed to the scene, reviving the man and assisting with getting the poor fellow to the hospital where he made a full recovery.[34]

While Izzy and Moe might have been able to conduct their business in an affable manner and get along swimmingly with those they arrested, the mood of the residents of Saratoga Springs was not always conducive to federal agents going about their business in town. There were several accounts of residents of the city showing their displeasure with the enforcement actions of the Prohibition agents, or "probies," as they were called.

In early August 1922, federal agents made a push into town with the intent to "make Saratoga Springs as dry as the Sahara." Six agents from the New York office raided Richard Mellefont's Café at 449 Broadway along with the bars and restaurants at the Grand Union and Adelphi Hotel.

Mellefont, who was none too happy about being raided for the second time in just a few weeks by federal agents, decided that he would offer some resistance to the raiders. With the help of his patrons who happened to be in the place during the raid, Mellefont let the law men know he was not going quietly this time.

Unfortunately for Mellefont, the six federals were in no mood to be trifled with and they quickly put down the mini insurrection and brought Mellefont to police headquarters to await his time in court.

When he first appeared before Commissioner Clarence Knapp, the Commissioner decided against holding a hearing for Mellefont as he did for the others. Mellefont was to be held pending his arraignment because, according to Knapp, "There is sufficient evidence to hold the man. The place is notorious."[35]

Then in late August, on the same day that Richard Mellefont was arrested (for the third time in thirty days) for violating the liquor laws in 1922, prohibition agents conducted raids at 40 High Rock Ave and at James Condon's café on Broadway. The liquor enforcers then turned their attention to Alphonse DeRossi's place at 64 Beekman Street.

All of the raids were conducted under the authority of warrants issued by federal judges but DeRossi took issue with the raiders and their warrant and a scuffle ensued with DeRossi yelling for assistance. Residents of the west side, hearing their neighbor's call for help, rallied to DeRossi's defense while the tussle continued inside his saloon.

Before long about fifty members of the neighborhood were resisting the agents while someone with the good sense to see the danger the prohibition men were in telephoned the police. A squad of Saratoga's finest rushed to the scene and soon dispersed the crowd, securing the area for the prohibition agents as they secured Mr. DeRossi and six quarts of whiskey.[36]

Later in the prohibition era, August 1930 to be exact, the good citizens of the west side neighborhood in Saratoga Springs expressed their displeasure with prohibition agents once again. This time the raiding party paid a visit to the aforementioned Gus "Dynamite" DeMatteo's place at 36 Beekman Street.

At about 9:30 PM on August 25, 1930, three prohibition agents showed up at DeMatteo's place seeking entry. DeMatteo recognized the agents and instead of complying with their request, slammed the saloon door in the faces of the law men and locked it.

Insulted, but undeterred, the agents began breaking in the doors and windows, trying to get in the place. According to the information that reached local reporters, once inside, one of the agents tried to place a bottle on a table. The bottle was picked up by someone and smashed into the sink, destroying any "evidence" that might have been recovered from it.

At the breaking of the glass, one of the agents grabbed DeMatteo around the throat which prompted a riot inside the saloon and a general call for assistance to ring out in the general vicinity. With the alarm raised, west siders came to the defense of "Dynamite" and his friends. The threatening crowd was estimated at about 200 men, women, and children.

As the confrontation grew, a woman from the neighborhood called police and Officers Maginn and Carey arrived on scene. The two SSPD officers fought their way through the crowd, rescued the agents from the ugly throng and escorted the agents back to their car which they had left parked at the intersection of West Circular and Beekman Streets.

Nobody was ever arrested as a result of the failed raid.[37]

A year after the riot at DeMatteo's place, two carloads of prohibition agents pulled up to Thomas Fennell's place on Railroad Place across from the train station in the middle of the afternoon. They promptly smashed through the front door and set about their work of seizing what evidence they could find.

The activity drew the attention of residents in the area and soon an angry crowd of about 300 Saratogians converged on the premises. It appeared that violence was inevitable as insults were hurled at the raiders and the air was let out of their car tires.

The federals were in sufficient number this time, and two of their number broke off from the work of the raid and stood down the crowd with hands on their guns until the evidence was gathered. There was no need to call for local police assistance this time, and no further damage was done to either government vehicles or agents.

Saratoga had seen this before. Vice laws that Saratogians didn't particularly care for didn't seem to apply within city limits. John Morrissey, Richard Canfield, and Arnold Rothstein never were bothered very much, and those efforts made by honest law enforcement to stamp out gambling never seemed to amount to anything. Prohibition seemed to follow the same pattern that the gambling situation had. Although it was clearly illegal, Saratogians, like many other Americans, wanted to drink, and their support for law enforcement was lukewarm at best when it came to the Volstead Act.

While the bootleggers were fast gaining prominence in Saratoga and across the country, gambling hadn't been forgotten entirely and right in the middle of the prohibition years, Saratoga would be the scene of another major gambling investigation that would, once again, shine a light on the corruption that was pervasive in Saratoga Springs.

Endnotes

Chapter 2

[1] "Claim Bootlegging King has Left City," *The Saratogian*, February 7, 1922.

[2] "Bootlegger Robbed Here, Says Rumor," *The Saratogian*, February 2, 1922.

[3] "Bootleggers War Over Rum Holdup," *The Saratogian*, February 3, 1922.

[4] Veitch, Greg. *All the Law in the World Won't Stop Them.* 2017.

[5] "Bootleggers' War Again Declared On," *The Saratogian*, February 4, 1922.

[6] "Bootlegging 'King' Asks Aid of Police," *The Saratogian*, February 8, 1922.

[7] "Patneaud Lured to Trap and Beaten," *The Saratogian*, February 10, 1922.

[8] "Halfway House Again Scene of Raid; New Haul of Game Devices; Patnoade is Arrested," *The Post Star*, August 24, 1929.

[9] Kennedy, William. *O Albany!* 1983.

[10] "State Trooper Killed by Highwaymen Near Wilton," *The Saratogian*, October 8, 1923.

[11] "Enoch Arden Claim Put Off," *Ballston Spa Daily Journal*, March 13, 1929.

[12] "Haupt Denies All Knowledge of Donivan Murder," *The Saratogian*, November 28, 1923.

[13] "Jury Finds Haupt Not Guilty of Murder in Shooting of Trooper," *The Saratogian*, November 30, 1923.

[14] "Salvinsky Jurymen Disagree and are Discharged," *The Saratogian*, December 15, 1923.

[15] "Motorists Scared From Bootleg Trail by Rum Runners and Bandits," *The Saratogian*, October 16, 1923.

[16] Ibid.

[17] "Bootleggers Battle with Highjackers on Outskirts of City," *The Saratogian*, December 4, 1923.

[18] "Shot Guns in Police Hands for Bootleg War," *The Saratogian*, October 18, 1923.

[19] "Leslie E. Cook, Saratoga Shot on Bootleg Trail," *The Saratogian*, October 30, 1923.

[20] "Duvas and Misses Meader and Murphy Caught with Ale," *The Saratogian*, July 22, 1925.

[21] "Old Game Played on Bootlegger," *The Saratogian*, August 8, 1921.

[22] "Court Refuses to Discharge Bail Bond of Formel," *The Saratogian*, January 10, 1921.

[23] "Beat Local Chauffeur Unconscious and Steal Car; Two Men Arrested," *The Saratogian*, November 27, 1922.

[24] Veitch, Greg. *All the Law in the World Won't Stop Them.* 2017.

[25] "Fines for Disorderly Houses," *The Saratogian*, October 18, 1916.

[26] "Alleged 'Fake' Revenue Agent Caught Here in Bribery Trap," *The Saratogian*, August 5, 1922.

[27] "'Honest' Izzy Here; Gives Information About 'Agent' Rose," *The Saratogian*, August 7, 1922.

28 "'Izzy' Einstein Raids Mellefonts," *The Saratogian*, August 13, 1921.

29 "Axe Used in Congress Street Liquor Raids" *The Saratogian*, August 10, 1923.

30 "Take Mellefont Third Time on Liquor Charge," *The Saratogian*, August 25, 1923.

31 "Arrowhead and Forty-One Raided by Izzy and Moe," *The Saratogian*, August 12, 1924.

32 "Bought Whiskey at Riley's, Say Federal Agents," *The Saratogian*, August 25, 1924.

33 www.atf.gov/our-history/isador-izzy-einstein. Accessed September 2, 2017.

34 "Heavy Car Hits Light Taxi at Street Crossing," *The Saratogian*, August 3, 1928.

35 "Grand Union and Adelphi 'Pinched' by Booze Raiders," *The Saratogian*, August 5, 1922.

36 "Mellefont Raided by Federal Agents Thrice in 30 Days," *The Saratogian*, August 23, 1922.

37 "Patrolmen save Prohibition Men in Beekman St.," *The Saratogian*, August 26, 1930.

Chapter 3

The Heffernan Investigation

Prohibition

had a major influence on the fabric and history of America. Rare indeed was the city, village, town, or hamlet that was not infected by the corruption and violence that accompanied the great dry social experiment. It seemed that no place escaped the unintended consequences wrought on American society by the passage of the Eighteenth Amendment.

While prohibition made bootleggers famous and phenomenally wealthy, gambling was never very far from the consciousness of the citizenry of Saratoga Springs. From the very founding of the village, gambling had played a significant role in its life, and while reformers came and reformers went, the gamblers always seemed to have the upper hand in the long run.

By the mid-twenties it was clear that the population in Saratoga Springs (as in many other places) had no problem with the flow of liquor through the town. The bootleggers and their political protectors had become increasingly powerful and attempts to dislodge them from the community were destined to fail. So, the reformers went back to the time-honored approach of trying to stamp out gambling at the Spa, and in 1926 they made their move.

In that year, Peter A. Finley, President of the Saratoga Springs Taxpayers Association, took up the anti-gambling crusade. Following the likes of Anthony Comstock, Spencer Trask, Waymon Bascom, Edgar Brackett, and all the various clergymen who at one time or another lent their voices to reform, Finley limited his campaign to the evils of gambling outside the grounds of the famous racetrack on Union Avenue. He began by sending letters describing open gambling conditions at the Spa to Sheriff Arthur G. Wilmot, District Attorney Charles Andrus, and Commissioner of Public Safety Dr. Arthur Leonard, asking them what they planned to do about it.[1]

Finley followed up the correspondence to the local authorities by sending a letter to Governor Alfred Smith demanding that he remove the three men from office. Finley pulled no punches in his letter to the Governor. It begins thus: "There is gossip here in the city that this application to you for relief as to the matters set forth in the petition will either be denied or put off until after August. This gossip arises from the prevalent opinion in this city that you will do everything to protect your friend, Arthur J. Leonard, who is charged with neglect of duty in my petition, and to protect other friends of yours who are anticipating opening gambling houses, one of whom, I am informed, is 'Tim' Mara, a bookmaker operating on the racetracks around New York City, and who intends in cooperation with one 'Jim' Beattie to operate the gambling concessions at Riley's on Lake Lonely.

"You know that gambling, vice and official corruption prevails here during August. I am informed that you know of the situation that has existed at The Brook and at Arrowhead from personal observation."[2]

Any other crusader looking for an ally in their fight against the "crooked gambling as now conducted" in Saratoga Springs might have started his appeal to the Governor a little more tactfully. Finley probably understood, however, that public pressure was the only sure way to see any results when confronting the Saratoga gamblers and their local partners and enablers. By connecting the Governor's friendship to Leonard, and by all but accusing Governor Smith of himself turning a blind eye to the gambling that had been happening in Saratoga, Finley ensured that Governor Smith's options for dealing with the situation were limited. He would be hard-pressed to not do something, given the public statements that Finley was making.

Governor Smith played his hand the best he could, ordering a Moreland Act investigation but not appointing a special prosecutor or convening a special grand jury. This meant that, unlike the Bascom investigation of 1920, Finley would be required to present his evidence to a hearing officer appointed by the governor without the benefit of a publicly funded investigative team. Finley would have to present his evidence and his case at his own expense. No raids or indictments would be forthcoming this time and if local law enforcement officials breathed a sigh of relief at not having to make investigations, they would shortly be very disappointed.

Supreme Court Justice Christopher J. Heffernan of Amsterdam was appointed by Governor Smith to conduct the inquiry. His mandate was to investigate the gambling conditions in Saratoga Springs and the conduct of the District Attorney, the County Sheriff, and the Public Safety Commissioner. Justice Heffernan was to report his findings to the governor, who would take whatever action deemed necessary.[3]

The Heffernan investigation would be swift, as testimony was given over the course of just one week. In his efforts to convince Justice Heffernan, Finley was assisted by attorney Carl MacMahon. [4] Sheriff Wilmot was represented by local powerhouse attorney James Leary. Commissioner Leonard retained Spencer B. Eddy as counsel while local lawyer Henry Toohey took up District Attorney Andrus' cause.

The proceedings opened with Finley testifying that he had witnessed gambling at two places. The first place mentioned was Brophy's at the corner of Railroad Place and Division Street. Finley said that he saw a chalkboard with horse names on it and money passing between some of the forty or so patrons and a man behind the counter who seemed to be in charge of the place. The second place named by Finley was Riley's at Lake Lonely where he saw a woman placing bets at a roulette table among other table games being played.[5]

The testimony was pretty straight forward but the defense lawyers, being paid to advocate on their client's behalf, responded with all their legal might. Eddy pushed for the removal of Commissioner Leonard from the case on the grounds that the gambling described by Finley had occurred before he had taken office. Heffernan responded that anything related to the gambling situation in Saratoga Springs would be allowed in, but any evidence given of conditions before any of the elected officials were in office would not be considered by the governor.[6]

Leary, as counsel for Sheriff Wilmot, went on the immediate attack. He questioned Finley's assertion that the governor knew of gambling in Saratoga Springs and forced Finley to admit he had no direct knowledge to make such a claim. He grilled Finley on his motives for bringing the case, suggesting that Finley held a grudge against the authorities over a previous arrest for driving charges and that he personally disliked the sheriff as one of Finley's sons had recently served a sentence in Wilmot's jail.

Leary also attacked Finley's eyesight, demonstrating that he was severely nearsighted. Under questioning by Leary, Finley was forced to admit he did not know if the names he saw written on the board at Brophy's were horses or dogs. Leary even pushed to question Finley about his divorce and failed business ventures, but Heffernan would not allow it.[7]

The second day of the Heffernan inquisition was dominated by the testimony of Abraham Weinberg, a private detective from New Jersey who had assisted with the Bascom investigation back in 1920. Weinberg testified that he had come to Saratoga Springs in 1925 looking for a gambler named George Costello who was wanted in New Jersey. He stated that he was not paid by anyone connected to the present case and that he was not compensated for his testimony before Heffernan.[8]

Weinberg claimed that on his vacation in 1925 to Saratoga he went to Riley's and found the place "operating as a full-fledged gambling house with roulette and bird cage; women drunk and gambling in that condition." He also saw a man named Fox who recognized him from his work in earlier years for Bascom who told Weinberg, "You can't do nothing now old boy."[9]

Weinberg said he lost twenty dollars playing roulette at Riley's, and he saw similar conditions at Arrowhead and a big crowd gambling atMa89a place on Woodlawn Avenue (the Chicago Club). Weinberg told of seeing Andrus dining at Riley's with the Ballston Spa village Justice. He couldn't get into the Fennel place since he was known there, nor was he able to get into Beefsteak Charlie's on Phila Street where gambling was alleged to have been going on. He was told of a house of prostitution at 42 Phila Street, but Weinberg claimed he was denied entry there as well.[10]

The lawyers for the local officials did their due diligence and grilled Weinberg to a considerable extent. Leary stated that 42 Phila Street happened to be a fruit store and not a brothel. Eddy again objected to any information being included prior to 1926 when his client, Commissioner Leonard, took office. Toohey got Weinberg to admit that he did not see Andrus in the gambling room at Riley's and that he could not have seen the gambling room from where he, Andrus, was seated. Heffernan again stressed that information prior to 1926 would be admitted only if it could be used to prove notice to the three officials.

McMahon countered by introducing testimony that Weinberg had sent Commissioner Leonard a letter describing the gambling conditions in 1926 and offering his assistance in any clean-up effort Leonard may have a mind for. He also added the tidbit that Weinberg had also visited a card game run by Jeal Smith on Maple Avenue directly opposite the police station.[11]

Leary's cross examination of Weinberg was in depth. After a couple of hours of rough treatment of Weinberg by Leary, Heffernan called for a recess until the following day.

Day three of the examination began where day two left off but this time Leary had brought a New Jersey lawyer named Joseph Weinberger to the defense table. Leary continue his cross examination for the entire morning. He questioned Weinberg's bills for the Bascom investigation as well as investigations he had been involved with in New Jersey, which was apparently the reason for the presence of the New Jersey barrister.

Upon learning that Weinberg's wife was in Ballston Spa that day, Leary sent her a subpoena. He did so more to harass the woman than for any evidence she might possess about gambling in Saratoga. He even attacked Weinberg for an investigation he was involved in that had occurred fifteen years prior to the current inquiry. Finally, after seven hours of being in the witness chair, Weinberg was mercifully excused as a witness.

The next witness was a familiar face to the courtroom, Jules Formel. He had done his time in prison after his conviction related to the Bascom investigation and was now called by Finley to testify to his knowledge of gambling in Saratoga Springs. When asked what his connection was to the gambling in Saratoga, he simply stated, "I was a fixer for Andrus," (meaning that he was the one who the gamblers went through to pay off the necessary officials, including District Attorney Andrus).

Formel was clearly still bitter that he alone was incarcerated for gambling as a result of the Bascom raids, and that he had had to go "to State's Prison for him" (Andrus), and that Andrus had not paid the $100 per week he had promised to pay his wife if Formel went to prison for him. [12]

What Justice Heffernan wanted to know, and what he asked Formel to explain, was his connection to the District Attorney, the County Sheriff, and the Public Safety Commissioner. Formel was willing to tell the tale and, despite the repeated objections of the defense, Formel told of his connections to all three men. His testimony is recounted in the August 9, 1926, edition of the *Saratogian*.

Formel told of meeting Arthur Wilmot at 41 Nelson Ave in 1918. 41 Nelson Ave was one of the gambling dens raided back in 1920. Wilmot was then a candidate for Sheriff. Formel and a gambler friend of his from Amsterdam, a man named Stennoto, were approached by Wilmot in 41 Nelson who said that he was running for Sheriff and expressed to them that he was friendly to the gamblers.

Stennoto wanted to know if the gamblers could be assured that they would be allowed to operate without interference. Formel testified that Wilmot responded, "Well, I am here, I am one of the boys" before buying the two men a drink.[13]

Formel told the court that he had also had a meeting with Commissioner Leonard in 1925 (thus placing Leonard within the timeframe of the Heffernan investigation) during which Leonard inquired if Formel planned to open up a gambling place in Saratoga. When Formel replied that he had no intention of doing so, Leonard, according to Formel said, "everything was running smooth." The implication being that all the arrangements were in place for open gambling and that Formel would be wise not to upset the delicate balance. Formel expressed his admiration for Leonard's political skill in being able to run the town wide-open once again, so soon after the Bascom raids.

Formel and Arnold Rothstein were associates. In 1919, Formel told Andrus that Mr. Leary had been to New York City and met with Rothstein to arrange for Rothstein to open The Brook. When Formel learned of this, he advised Rothstein not to open because the District Attorney (Andrus) would close him down, but Rothstein assured Formel that he had paid Dr. Leonard $10,000 as his "fixer."

Rothstein did not realize that there were two different interests that would need to be paid off in order to operate. Leary controlled the county officials (Sheriff and District Attorney) while Leonard controlled the City Police. Both would need to be accommodated. Formel offered his services as a fixer to Andrus and told Rothstein that he would settle with the District Attorney for a sum of $60,000. Formel's fixer's fee was to be $4,000.

After hearing the initial offer, Andrus side-stepped Formel and presumably got the $60,000 directly from Rothstein. Rothstein then paid Formel only $1,000 for his work. Rothstein wouldn't pay the remaining $3,000 and there can be little doubt that Formel thought that Andrus had double-crossed him by going directly to Rothstein.

Formel then turned his attention to the house at 210 South Broadway and fixed it so the owner could open with an agreement that Andrus would get 10 percent of the profit. Andrus complained to Formel that he was not getting his fair share of the profits and before he could fix that problem, according to Formel, the place was raided by Sheriff Reynolds (a Leary ally) and the whole gambling situation blew up, leading to the Bascom raids, followed by Andrus' trial and acquittal and Formel's own conviction after two mistrials.

Formel explained for Heffernan and the entire courtroom that Andrus had told him to remain quiet during the trials and that he would probably only get a fine. If he did not squeal, Andrus promised Formel, he would be well paid. After he was sentenced to prison, according to Formel, Andrus agreed to pay Formel's wife $100 each week in exchange for Formel's silence.

One final damaging witness was brought forward by the Finley faction. The Reverend Harry B. Fisher, Secretary of the New York Civic League, testified that he had visited Brophy's on Railroad Place, Fennell's on Phila Street, and Byrnes' on Woodlawn Avenue less than a month before the Heffernan investigation began. Rev. Fisher explained that he saw craps games at Fennell's and Byrnes and that he placed a $5 bet on a horse race at Brophy's.

At Fennell's a one-legged man wrote the names of the horses on a chalkboard. Rev. Fischer told the court that he also had gone across the street from Fennell's to Beefsteak Charlie's and saw furniture covered with sheets that when lifted, revealed roulette tables. A caretaker said that the business was waiting to begin play until the racing meet started as they were after the larger crowds.[14]

Denis Fitzgibbons, a former Saratoga Springs police officer, testified that he had visited Byrne's and Fennell's and that he had placed bets with Almeron White at Fennell's place. Fitzgibbons described Fennell's cigar shop as having a partition with a passage leading to a room in the back. While describing the placing of his bets with White, Fitzgibbons testified:

Q: "Was there a place in the room caged off with a desk in it?

A: "Yes."

Q: "Where did you make your bets on the races there?"

A: "At a window in this cage."[15]

Despite the fact that the President of the Taxpayers Association, a private detective, a minister, a former police officer, and a convicted, self-admitted gambler had given testimony that they had seen, gambled, and ran a gambling joint in Saratoga Springs, Justice Heffernan was under no illusion that all members of the Saratoga community would be so forthcoming as Finley, Weinberg, Rev. Fisher, and Formel.

With a subpoena in hand, Saratoga County Sheriff's Deputies were unable to locate Nat Evans, manager of the Brook under Rothstein and, at the time of the Heffernan investigation, sole proprietor of the famous nightclub. It was not for a lack of effort that they could not locate Evans as, according to the deputies, they made five visits to the Brook in an attempt to locate him. [16]

Among the witnesses that did receive subpoenas and appear in court were three gamblers, James C. Fennell, Almeron F. White, and Matthew Byrnes. All three refused to answer questions on the advice of their attorneys. Justice Heffernan was having none of that nonsense, and promptly threw the three Saratoga men in jail on a charge of contempt of court, where they remained for 11 days. They were released only after the Heffernan investigation closed and his report was made to the governor. Eleven days behind bars was the price they paid to remain silent and protect whomever they were involved with.[17]

A few local residents could be found to testify in response to the subpoenas issued by the petitioners, but alas, many of them had shaky memories - at best. Frank Silvo, a barber, was called to the stand and gave the following testimony regarding his twice-weekly visits to Byrne's place on Woodlawn Ave:[18]

Q: "What did you go in there for?"

A: "Just to listen to the radio"

Q: "Well, what did you see in there?"

A: "I didn't pay any attention to anything. I am not a gambler. I went in there to hear the radio."

Q: "Did you see any game played there except rummy, pinochle and checkers?"

A: "No."

Q: "When were you last at Byrne's?"

A: "I think it was last week."

Q: "What did you see then?"

A: "There was nobody there but Byrnes. I went in and got a drink of water and went right home."

Other men testified similarly. Joseph Burdo, a salesman, said he had been to Brophy's but never shot craps there, although he did recall shooting a friendly game of craps on the floor once, possibly a year before his testimony, but he could not remember who he played with. [19]

Augustus Pompay, who happened to have only one leg, could not recall seeing telegraph equipment at White's place, denied being the man who chalked the racing sheets at Fennell's place, and could not recall any of the names of any other people he had seen in White's gambling place.[20]

The reader will recall Rev. Fisher's testimony that a one-legged man chalked the racing board at Fennell's and the reader can be forgiven for wondering just how many one-legged men were roaming the streets and gambling dens of Saratoga in 1926.

Robert Ingram, another salesman by trade but who, at the time of the Heffernan investigation was unemployed, testified that he was not the "stick man" for Brophy, didn't see much the times he went into the place, and only went in to sit down.[21]

Harold Spratt, a local butcher said he knew Byrnes, Brophy, Fennell, and Urquhart (all alleged gamblers) but that he never saw any craps games, or any other games of chance played at any of those places.

With authorities who were unable or unwilling to serve subpoenas and obstinate and reluctant witnesses with fuzzy memories, Christopher J. Heffernan must have been frustrated with the proceedings. The lawyers for Andrus, Wilmot, and Leonard, led by Leary, gave each of the Finley witnesses some rough treatment except for the Rev. Fisher. They didn't bother to even cross-examine the memory-challenged Saratoga men, assuming their testimony helped them more than the Finley side who had called them. But if Heffernan was frustrated with the quality of the testimony of the civilian witnesses, he was downright awestruck with the testimony of current police officials who were called to testify.

James L. Sullivan was Superintendent of the Saratoga Springs Police when he was called to testify before Justice Heffernan. He is the same James Sullivan who had resigned from the Saratoga Springs Police Department and opened a private detective agency in 1921 and led many of the Bascom raids that resulted in the dozens of gambling arrests at that time. He was asked about a letter sent to Commissioner Leonard and District Attorney Andrus from Saratoga County Judge McKelvey in July of 1925.

In the letter McKelvey informs the officials that gambling in the city was open and notorious and provided them information that several places were operating without apparent concern for the law, including a place called the "Red Front" at 449 Broadway which was almost directly across from the County Court Chambers and within maybe 100 yards of the police department itself. Judge McElvey asked the officials to investigate the places and offered to sign any search or arrest warrants the authorities brought to him in order to suppress gambling in the city. Sullivan testified that he was given the letter by Commissioner Leonard. [22]

Sullivan said that he sent some men to investigate and they returned with a report that they could not find any trace of gambling happening anywhere. Heffernan was so unimpressed with Sullivan that in the *Saratogian* of August 11, 1921, he was described as pacing back and forth behind his chair and hurling sarcastic comments toward Sullivan while Sullivan was on the stand. He even interrupted Sullivan to remark, "Why this officer doesn't know anything about gambling. The county judge seems to know something about it, but this officer doesn't."

The next officer to be called was Hugh Dorsey. Dorsey was also back with the police department after his resignation and work with Bascom in 1921. Now a Sergeant, Dorsey claimed that he had made several visits at many of the alleged gambling places involved in the current inquiry and that he was unable to discover any evidence of gambling at any of them during the past two years.

In disbelief, Heffernan pressed Dorsey for specifics but all Dorsey could help the court with was that he knew the men in question, that he had been looking for evidence of gambling but could find none, and that although he knew the men and repeatedly visited their places, he couldn't even tell what business was carried on inside these places.[23]

As if Sullivan and Dorsey were not enough to convince any observer of the proceeding of the utter incompetence of the Saratoga Springs Police in regard to investigating gambling in their jurisdiction, next to be called to the stand was Detective Patrick Rox.

McMahon started the questioning of Rox and brought out that Superintendent Sullivan had ordered him to investigate gambling. Rox testified that he had never found any. Furthermore, he testified that even though he found no gambling, he had repeatedly warned the men suspected of gambling against it.

At this point, Justice Heffernan took the questioning into his own hands and the testimony of Rox, if not recorded by area newspapers of the day, would hardly be rated as believable. Rox claimed that he did not know what gambling paraphernalia looked like but that he would probably be suspicious if he saw it. He did not see any lights on at night at Brophy's, Fennell's, and Byrnes' at all during 1925. His testimony continued:

Q: "When Superintendent Sullivan sent you out to look for gambling at these places, did you not tell him that you did not know what gambling apparatus looked like?"

A: "No, he didn't ask me."

Q: "Did you not think that it was strange that he would send an inexperienced officer out on this duty?"

A: "I was not inexperienced."

Q: "But you were inexperienced insofar as gambling apparatus was concerned, were you not?"

A: "Yes"[24]

It was brought out that Brophy, Fennell, and Byrnes had been friends of Patrick Rox for 18 years. When asked if he knew what business the men were in, Rox said that he didn't know. One can almost still hear the exasperation in Heffernan's voice when he said, "You say you are a detective, you say these men are friends of yours and have been for many years and that you have frequently visited their place of business, but still you do not know in what business they are engaged?" Rox answered simply, "No."[25]

Justice Heffernan may have never seen such incompetence in a police force, nor such forgetfulness from average citizens unable to recall even the most general of facts at places they regularly frequented. It is unbelievable that a detective who claimed no knowledge of gambling apparatus would be the very officer sent to make the rounds of the gambling spots in town, unless of course the officials and the officers did not really want to actually see what was going on there.

It was equally unbelievable that men with full mental capacity would offer an excuse in open court that they frequented gambling dens but did not know that they were such because they went in to, "sit down" or to simply "listen to the radio." The Heffernan investigation had as much drama and as much farce as any theatre critic could have asked for, but the crescendo of this play would come when Jules Formel was again called to the stand by James Leary.

It was unlikely that Formel would have anything else to add to the proceedings and perhaps Leary only wanted to have one more go at him before the investigation was closed. But whatever the reason, the exchange between Formel and Leary would be one of the most memorable parts of the whole affair.

Leary's questioning brought Formel's temper to the surface quickly. Formel clearly blamed Leary for working behind the scenes to get him sent to state prison. Formel accused Leary of being a partner in a poolroom with a man named Doherty. He called Leary a "blackguard" and a "jury-fixer" and blamed Leary for influencing the Dannemora prison guards to restrict his privileges while he was imprisoned.

For his part, Leary highlighted Formel's underworld connections, men like Rothstein and Rachel Brown, and suggested that Formel had once hired a man known as the "Turk" to beat up a New York lawyer named Randolph Newman. He then led Formel into the following exchange, on the record:

Leary: "Did I ever come up to Dannemora?"

Formel: "No. If you had come one of us would not be here now."

Leary: "Do you mean you would have had me done away with?"

Formel: "I mean just what I say. I don't know whether you would beat me to it or not. It is rumored right now that my life is not worth a dime. I don't need any bodyguard. If you or any of your men come to me, I will be ready for them."

Leary: "You mean you might kill them. You did kill a man once, didn't you?"

Formel: "Yes. In self-defense."[26]

It is interesting that the *Saratogian,* in reporting the quote, did not follow up and give any details regarding whom it was that Formel may have killed in self-defense. The press may have assumed that all readers would know whom Formel was supposed to have killed and as such required no further explanation, but a search of Formel's name uncovers only one episode of violence in his life.

In 1903, in New York City, Formel and a rival poolroom operator named Phillip Black quarreled over an accusation that Formel had made against Black and another man. He accused the pair of having robbed him, and while the police were looking to arrest Black, the two gamblers met on Broadway in front of Proctor's Theatre. It was reported in the New York Times that seeing Formel first, Black shouted something that could not be discerned, pulled a revolver, and started firing.

With all the cool of a Hollywood western movie hero, Formel stood his ground as the crowd frantically parted between the two men and said, "Two can play at that game," before pulling his own revolver and opening fire on Black.

At least eight shots were exchanged with Formel and Black suffering minor injuries and two postal clerks suffering more serious, but non-life threatening, wounds when they were caught in the crossfire.

The shooting came to an end when New York Police Captain Langan and a squad of detectives who happened to be nearby rushed to the scene and captured both shooters. After their wounds were dressed and healed, both Black and Formel decided that it was best to let the matter drop, and no charges were pursued. [27]

Formel's shooting fray and his alleged killing of a man in self-defense were irrelevant to the issue being considered in Justice Heffernan's courtroom. It was gambling, as it always seemed to be in Saratoga, and the connection between the gamblers and the local officials that the inquiry was intended to sort out.

Even though the court had already seen the evidence, had already seen the faulty memories of Saratoga men, had already seen the willful incompetence of the police force, and had already witnessed Leary toy with Formel on the stand, one final grievance was aired by the Finley side before Heffernan retired to consider the evidence.

Peter Finley took the stand as the last witness to explain that one Dr. Eugene J. Sullivan had been one of the primary backers of the present investigation, yet he appeared as a character witness against Finley during the trial.

Mr. Finley explained that Sullivan had been lured from the anti-gambling camp by an offer of $2500 which just so happened to be the salary of the Saratoga Springs milk inspector, a post that Dr. Sullivan had been recently appointed to through the back-door machinations of none other than James Leary, or so Finley claimed. This statement by Finley elicited this comment from Heffernan, "Another instance of a good man gone wrong."[28]

After Finley was finished, the usual motions were made by the respondent's lawyers for summary dismissal of all charges. Heffernan refused them all. Sheriff Wilmot, District Attorney Andrus, and Public Safety Commissioner Leonard all declined to take the stand in their own defense although Andrus did read an unsworn statement to the court referencing his long public service and once again accusing Formel of telling lies about him.

All that was left was for Justice Heffernan to make his report to the governor, but before he did, Heffernan made a lengthy statement which is recorded in full in the August 13, 1926, edition of the *Saratogian*. His comments on the investigation were biting:

"I want to say that I have been shocked at some of the things that have been shown here. Other issues have come in, not part of the case at all. I was shocked when three witnesses came into this court and under someone's advice willfully and contumaciously and deliberately refused to testify. I do not think they have helped anybody's case. Nor do I believe that justice should be flouted in that way."

After assuring those assembled in the courtroom that he intended to leave the three men in jail until they decided to show the proper respect for authority, Heffernan made known that he felt the more important issue in Saratoga Spring was not the gambling, but the general reluctance of public officials to do their duty, saying, "If public officials, if men who have sworn to uphold the constitution and have sworn to enforce the laws, have become faithless to their oaths we are in a serious condition in Saratoga County or in any other county of the state."

After hinting that the lawyers in the case had generally diminished the reputation of the bar and, after encouraging District Attorney Andrus to seek a hearing by the Appellate Court to address the specific allegation of his having taken a bribe from Formel, he closed the session and began preparing his report to Governor Smith.

About one month after the close of the Moreland Act investigation, Justice Heffernan's report was served on the respondents and made public. The headline for the *Saratogian* on September 15, 1926, said it all, "HEFFERNAN FLAYS SARATOGA OFFICIALS; MISCONDUCT WARRANTS REMOVAL."

Heffernan hammered away in his report to the governor:

Referring to the gambling situation at the Spa he said, "Without analyzing the evidence in detail, I am fully satisfied that during the time set forth in the petition, gambling, consisting of pool selling, bookmaking, faro, cards, roulette and other games of chance was conducted openly and notoriously in the City of Saratoga Springs, and that gaming and betting establishments were maintained therein where professional gamesters and common gamblers were constantly in attendance. It is impossible to reach any other conclusion on the record presented."

He decried the general performance of witnesses and lawyers alike, saying that, "A spirit of lawlessness and contempt for all authority were prevalent throughout the hearings."

As far as the police officers who testified, Heffernan pointed out the obvious, "While admitting that common report was to the effect that gambling on an extensive scale was of daily occurrence at the establishments noted, with the locations of which they were familiar, and while acknowledging intimate acquaintance with its patrons, and particularly with the gamblers who declined to testify, nevertheless these men had the effrontery to deny any knowledge of illegal acts."

He continued, "One of these officers (Rox), in his zeal to advance the cause of his friends, testified that he was not qualified to determine what constitutes gambling apparatus and he is so guile-less as to be incapable of recognizing gambling rooms. It is obvious that this is perjured testimony and the motive which prompted it is quite apparent."

In his report, Heffernan pointed out to Governor Smith that the Sheriff, District Attorney, and Commissioner of Public Safety never actually denied the allegations made against them. "It is significant that the respondents gave no testimony on their own behalf, they did not avail themselves of the privilege of making a statement under oath. The denials or explanations which naturally might be expected from them were not forthcoming. Their lips were sealed."

The lawyers defending the accused officials claimed that Sheriff Wilmot was not in Saratoga Springs when the alleged gambling was taking place, rather he was in his home at Round Lake. Commissioner Leonard's defense was that he relied upon the members of the police department to enforce the gambling laws in Saratoga Springs. District Attorney Andrus interpreted his duties to go no further than the prosecution of offenses brought to his attention through arrests and the presentation of evidence.

Justice Heffernan was having none of it, explaining, "If public officials can shield themselves from accountability by such flimsy excuses, then the guarantees of protection to life, liberty and property contained in the State and Federal constitutions are meaningless phrases."

Following in the footsteps of the Saratoga crusaders of old, Justice Heffernan declared his condemnation of officials who turned a blind eye to the gambling situation in Saratoga:

"I have no hesitation in concluding that these respondents are guilty of misconduct so gross as to necessitate their removal from the several officers which they occupy for the honor, peace, and good government of the community. The county of Saratoga should be freed from their contaminating touch... by their misconduct, these officers have demonstrated that they are unworthy of the people's trust... these respondents, caring nothing for the safety and well-being of society, forgetful of their official honor and unmindful of their duties of their respective offices, are guilty of willful and criminal violation of public duty and their conduct merits the severest condemnation."[29]

The day after the report was made public, Commissioner Leonard resigned from office. By doing so he spared Governor Smith, a close person friend, from the unpleasant duty of having to remove him from office. Governor Smith and Commissioner Leonard were such close friends that, just one month before the Heffernan investigation began, the two were enjoying a round of golf in Plattsburgh together.[30] By resigning, Leonard effectively closed the present matter as far as it related to him while the fates of Andrus and Wilmot remained in the Governor's hands.

The other benefit of resigning was that Leonard remained eligible to be elected to the position again in the future. Public officials removed by the governor are prohibited from holding the same office after their removal. In true Saratoga fashion though, Leonard was re-elected to the position of Public Safety Commissioner just a few years later.

With Leonard out of office, Governor Smith gave Andrus and Wilmot about one week to answer the charges contained in the Heffernan report. Both responded to the Governor, with attorney Leary providing the Governor with a petition to have the charges disregarded based upon a technicality that Leary claimed precluded Heffernan from sitting as a Moreland Act commissioner.

Governor Smith received Justice Heffernan's report on September 7. He wasted little time and showed no mercy to either District Attorney Andrus or Sheriff Wilmot when he followed Heffernan's recommendation and removed both officials from office on September 30, 1926. The Governor's order was short and to the point. After concluding that evidence supported Finley's charges of neglect of duty, Governor Smith proclaimed;

"Now, after consideration of said charges, the report of said commissioner and evidence as submitted, the answers filed with me by Charles B. Andrus and Arthur G. Wilmot and I having determined that public interest requires it. It is hereby ordered that said Charles B. Andrus be and is hereby removed from the office of District Attorney of Saratoga County and be and is hereby ordered that Arthur G. Wilmot is hereby removed from the Office of Sheriff of Saratoga County."[31]

Veteran Saratogians had seen this play before. Anti-gambling forces would achieve a significant victory in their war on vice and the gamblers, along with their corrupt accomplices, would fade away for a short time only to return after the wave of reform had passed. But the removal of two elected officials was new territory for reformers and the law and order types were certainly feeling encouraged in the fall of 1926.

Endnotes

Chapter 3

[1] "Finley Takes his Gambling Charges to Gov. Smith." *The Saratogian.* July 23, 1926.

[2] Ibid.

[3] "Smith Orders Finley to Prove Gambling," *The Saratogian.* July 28, 1926.

[4] "Saw Gambling at Two Places Finley Swears" *The Saratogian.* August 26, 1926.

[5] Ibid.

[6] Ibid.

[7] Ibid.

[8] "Detective Says He Gambled at Saratoga Places." *The Saratogian.* August 7, 1926.

[9] Ibid.

[10] Ibid.

[11] Ibid.

[12] "'Fixer for Andrus Swears Formel'" *The Saratogian.* August 9, 1926.

[13] Ibid.

[14] "Gambling Investigation Concluded." *The Saratogian.* August 13, 1926.

[15] "Jailed Witnesses Appeal to New Judge." *The Saratogian.* August 11, 1926.

[16] Ibid.

[17] "Saratoga Gambling Witnesses Freed." *The Saratogian.* August 21, 1926.

[18] "Jailed Witnesses..."

[19] Ibid.

[20] Ibid.

[21] Ibid.

[22] "Sullivan's Innocence About Gambling Surprises Court; McKelvey Warned Officials." *The Saratogian.* August 11, 1926.

[23] "Formel Prepared for Attack on Life, He Swears." *The Saratogian.* August 12, 1926.

[24] Ibid.

[25] Ibid.

[26] Ibid.

[27] "Fight with Pistols in Broadway Crowd." *New York Times.* February 13, 1903.

[28] "Gambling Investigation Concluded."

[29] "Heffernan Flays Saratoga Officials; Misconduct Warrants Removal." *The Saratogian.* September 15, 1926.

[30] "Governor Wins Round of Golf." *Poughkeepsie Eagle-News.* July 17, 1926.

[31] "Andrus and Wilmot Removed from Office." *The Saratogian.* September 30, 1926.

Commissioner Sweeney Tries to Clean Up the Town

On the heels of the Heffernan investigation, Saratogians in favor of a permissible gambling environment were bracing for more change. It seemed that the tidal wave against the gamblers was going to be irresistible this time. Gambling investigations were underway during, and after, the Heffernan inquiry and evidence gained through these investigative efforts was set to be presented to the grand jury in January 1927. For sure, the fortunes of the gamblers at Saratoga were looking bleak as winter settled in over the Spa City at the close of 1926.

Harry Fisher, who was secretary of the New York Civic League when he testified before Justice Heffernan to visiting two gambling places in Saratoga Springs in 1926, told an Albany newspaper man that he had six "under cover" men in Saratoga Springs gathering evidence.

Fisher agreed to visit the Saratoga County Grand Jury in January 1927. Despite rumors that he had been offered $50,000 to not testify before Heffernan, and that his life had been threatened because he planned to testify, Fisher appeared before the grand jury in high spirits, telling reporters, "Well, it looks as though the fun is about to start again, evidently the seeds planted last summer are about to sprout…"[1]

William Cromie, who succeeded Wilmot as Sheriff, publicly acknowledged that his men had been making an investigation into slot machines in Saratoga[2] and the new District Attorney, John B. Smith, seemed willing to accept evidence against the gamblers, publicly inviting Finley to tell his tale to the grand jurors. Even Justice Heffernan addressed the grand jurors, encouraging them to do their civic duty and to stand up for justice.

The local clergy even lent their voice to the chorus of reformers who wanted to see gambling closed down. Shortly after the Heffernan investigation wrapped up, the local Baptist minister made headlines when he delivered a sermon entitled, "Who Gave Saratoga the Black Eye?"[3]

Pastor Alfred Boutwell delivered the scathing sermon and in it he encouraged the electorate of Saratoga Springs to refuse to send men of questionable morals to office as they had, time and again, from the earliest days of the village. Rev. Boutwell understood the essential truth of all endemically corrupt systems when he said that, "If officials are indicted, then we the electorate are."[4]

Although he had only been preaching in Saratoga for eight years at the time, Pastor Boutwell described accurately the attitude of Saratoga residents regarding the gambling, vice, and corruption that had an unbreakable grip on the place from its earliest days. He proclaimed that, "It is not the indecency that we object to but the exposure of the indecency. We can stand it to be rotten but not to have the rottenness made known." [5] No truer statement describing conditions at Saratoga has probably ever been uttered.

It seemed the momentum might be unstoppable this time for the anti-gambling men. But alas, a high tide always recedes, and there were warning signs that, even before the grand jury was finished taking testimony, the high point for the anti-gamblers was the removal of Andrus and Wilmot from their respective posts after the Heffernan investigation.

District Attorney Smith, while welcoming Peter Finley, (president of the taxpayer's association whom we met during the Heffernan investigation), to give testimony before the grand jury, cautioned that the present investigation would be guided by the grand jurors themselves, and made sure to let the public know that much of what was testified to in the Heffernan investigation would not be admissible to the grand jury, as Heffernan's inquiry was not a criminal matter and the grand jury investigation was.

Therefore, different rules of evidence were applied to the two cases. For example, the opinion given by Heffernan that the members of the police force, Sullivan, Rox, and Dorsey, gave perjured testimony would require other witnesses that were willing to testify that they saw the men in the gambling places while gambling was ongoing.[6] This was an unlikely scenario in a Saratoga County courtroom in 1927.

John Walbridge and Jesse Cavanaugh, publisher and reporter for the *Saratogian* respectively, told of a threat made by disgraced former Commissioner of Public Safety, Doc Leonard, that if they ran a story on gambling in Saratoga Springs that he, Leonard, would put the paper out of business.[7]

Saratoga Springs Mayor Clarence Knapp was called to testify before the grand jury and on January 18, 1927, he was the first witness of the day. But rather than a solemn engagement with the grand jurors, it was reported that, while Mayor Knapp (a Leonard ally) was giving his testimony, the grand jurors could be heard laughing heartily inside the chamber.

Upon leaving the room, reporters asked Knapp if he was telling the grand jurors a funny story. The mayor replied that he was indeed, and then launched into a monologue in which he declared that Saratoga Springs was the "cleanest little city in the state," pointing out that places like Albany, Schenectady, and Troy were much worse than Saratoga.[8]

Even Pastor Boutwell understood that the common man in Saratoga was then, and probably always would be, on the side of the gamblers and gangsters. In the week before his sermon, the noble reverend placed the title of his sermon on the bulletin board at his church in order to give the congregation something to think about in the coming week. Sadly, next to his note, "Who Gave Saratoga the Black Eye?" one of his own flock had placed a note of their own, replying to the question with two simple words, "Peter Finley,"[9]

On January 20, 1927, the residents of Saratoga Springs received their morning newspapers. The *Saratogian* of that date had the following headline: "NO INDICTMENTS FOR SARATOGA GAMBLING."

The Grand Jury Foreman, Henry C. Peck, released a public statement at the close of the session. In part, it read, "The result of such deliberations convinces us that in the past there have been irregularities of which just complaint may be made, we are able to say from the evidence we were able to procure, and we think we procured all the evidence that was available, that sufficient evidence was not shown for an indictment against any person except herewith presented, all of which is respectfully presented."[10]

The only indictment handed down by the Grand Jury in January 1927 was against James Hunter Davis for first degree manslaughter. Davis had shot and killed Clarence Scott in Saratoga Springs back in October. But no indictments against any gamblers or public officials were found.

The gamblers escaped from the grand jury free and clear. New District Attorney Smith made no comment on the failure of the grand jury to bring any gambling indictments. Finley's attorney, Carl McMahon, conferred with Smith and decided against pursuing criminal charges against the officials involved in the Heffernan investigation. The general feeling was that the forced removal of Andrus and Wilmot, and the resignation of Leonard, was sufficient punishment for the trio.

Once again, the gamblers and gangsters had outmaneuvered the law in Saratoga Springs. But something different was in the air in 1927. Going against historical precedent, the local electorate seemed willing to give law and order a chance, even after the machinations of the gamblers and their political allies had seemingly set everything right once again.

Perhaps they recalled the tenure of Police Chief King just after the turn of the century when Saratoga's Police force did, in fact, make an effort to root out gambling in the village. Or perhaps the voters of Saratoga Springs were growing tired of the notoriety of the past ten years when, first Bascom and then Heffernan, managed to pull the veil away from the face of the Saratoga Springs' gambling scene and reveal the disturbing, ugly truth about the nature of the gamblers and gangsters who occupied the Spa City since Arnold Rothstien's arrival back in 1917.

Whatever the reason, the election of 1927 presented a clear choice for Saratoga Springs' residents. Having avoided the same axe that ended the careers of District Attorney Andrus and Sheriff Wilmot by his slick resignation prior to his all but certain removal from office, Arthur "Doc" Leonard once again stood for the position of Commissioner of Public Safety in the fall election on the Democrat line. He was backed by James Leary, the undisputed political king maker and Republican puppet master of Saratoga County in 1927. Together they formed an alliance that backed a full slate of candidates for the city council that in other years would be unbeatable at the polls.

But in 1927, with the Heffernan investigation still fresh on the minds of Saratoga voters, a pro-business and pro-law and order faction ran against the Leonard-Leary machine. The choice between the two factions was so obvious that Superintendent of Police

James Sullivan openly declared his backing of Leonard. Speaking of Leonard's opponent, Edward Sweeney, during the lead up to the election, Superintendent Sullivan said, "When Sweeney comes in the front door, I'll go out the back door."[11]

Sweeney and his allies did, in fact, win every city council seat in 1927 and Sullivan was right to fear a Commissioner Sweeney. He was replaced almost immediately by John Armstrong, who set a different tone regarding what was expected of police officers in the City.

Much less blatant corruption was tolerated for the four years that Sweeney was Commissioner of Public Safety (1928-31) and a few examples of police integrity during the Sweeney years should suffice to paint an accurate picture of where things stood after the electoral defeat of Doc Leonard.

Right after replacing Sullivan at the head of the department, Sweeney set his sights on the other two policemen who were singled out for special mention by Justice Heffernan, who considered their testimony as obviously perjured, Detective Patrick Rox and Sergeant Hugh Dorsey. Rox was demoted to patrolman and immediately resigned from the force. Dorsey was also demoted to patrolman and was fired by Commissioner Sweeney after he refused to don a uniform and accept his new post.[12]

Commissioner Sweeney and Chief Armstrong even suspended Officer William Lucas for sixteen days on a charge of neglect of duty.[13] Just what Officer Lucas had done to deserve the suspension was never revealed by Chief Armstrong, but the fact that he and Commissioner Sweeney were serious about cleaning up the department, and the town, was unmistakable.

Sweeney and Armstrong sent the message that gambling was not to be tolerated and what games they could find were raided, even if the police were unable to make arrests.

Perhaps they were just a little rusty after the Doc Leonard years when Detective Rox was sent out to look for gamblers, but by his own admission knew nothing about games of chance and wouldn't recognize gambling equipment even if he saw it.

Maybe individual officers were not quite sure if law and order was indeed here to stay. Why risk the wrath of powerful political figures who may someday be back in power and who would certainly not forget which officers were thought to be overzealous in carrying out their duties?

Whatever the case, on August 16, 1928, Chief Armstrong got word of a craps game being run by James Scott at 46 Congress Street. He quickly got together a raiding party and, as the officers broke into the place, all they could accomplish was to break up the empty craps table. Apparently the forty or so players had gotten word from a look-out that the police were on the way and managed to scamper out the back while police were entering the front of the place.[14]

Despite the fact that the police were unable to arrest anyone after the raid on Congress Street, the gamblers received the message, loud and clear. The summer crowds still wanted to gamble but the Saratoga police were having none of it, and the players were reduced to visiting places in Lake George (called either Shadow Bay or Shady Lawn to those in the know) or Lake Luzerne. A place across from the armory in Glens Falls reportedly also picked up some of the patrons who normally would have played at Saratoga joints, while Route 9 between Glens Falls and Lake George housed a gambling den that managed to attract considerable numbers of Saratoga tourists.[15]

The lid was clamped down so tight that the resorts in Saratoga had to release somewhere near one hundred taxi drivers who had been retained at the start of the season for their services that were no longer needed to ferry folks from their gambling halls back to the grand hotels along Broadway.[16]

Commissioner Sweeney's tenure continued into 1929 in the same manner that it had in his first year in office. He and Chief Armstrong continued to try to instill discipline in the police force and to encourage actual law enforcement in the city.

In January Officer George Stevens was fired from the police force because, the Sweeney administration alleged, he had attempted to extort protection money from Nicholas Adinolfi whom, it was reported, was running a card game on Beekman Street.[17] Stevens was also charged with failing to appear in court in uniform, a technical violation of department rules and something that no one, not even the judge hearing his appeal for reinstatement, really cared about. Curiously, Stevens was not charged with the crime of extortion, but dismissed based on departmental charges. Of course, as we have seen, the courts could not be relied on to clean up the department, so a criminal charge was probably not practical.

Sweeney's dismissal of a police officer for an alleged attempt to collect protection money for a small-time card game on the west side of Saratoga Springs was new territory for the department. It was probably the first time that a law man had ever been terminated from employment based on an internal investigation of graft.

Typically, the impetus for cleaning up the department, if it ever came and was not ignored, always came from outside the force. This willingness to instill some discipline into the Saratoga Springs Police Department should have been a clear signal to all officers to shape up. But even after the removal of the perjurers, (according to Heffernan), Sullivan, Dorsey, and Rox, and the firing of Stevens, the alleged grafter, some officers continued to not get the message.

Morris Crooks could not bring himself to adhere to the new standards of professionalism that Sweeney and Armstrong sought. Shortly after the turn of the year in 1929, Crooks' employment was also terminated for the good of the service, based upon his "condition" while on duty one day in January, which usually meant that the officer had reported for duty in an intoxicated condition.[18]

While the internal discipline of the police department was being dealt with, Armstrong and the remaining members of the police force continued to put pressure on the gamblers and the gangsters.

Detective James Cummings who, unlike Detective Rox, was in fact able to recognize gambling apparatus when he saw it, raided a house across the street from the racetrack. He arrested Thomas Miller of Albany, who had brought a couple of slot machines to the house in order to profit from those who wanted to continue gambling at the end of the race card each day. His two quarter slot machines were destroyed, Miller was fined $25, and the contents of the devices were removed and put into the police pension fund.[19]

Saratoga police seemed to have had a handle on the gambling as the election of 1929 neared. A squad of undercover State Troopers, sent by Governor Smith without the knowledge of local officials, was unable to find any evidence of gambling that summer.[20] The entire city council was a pro-business, pro law and order slate and they collectively ran on their record of safety, security, and prosperity.

The opposing political side was led by Doc Leonard, who was running once more for the Public Safety post along with his right-hand man in the days before the Heffernan investigation, former Mayor Knapp. [21] It seemed that, like the gangsters, Doc Leonard and his political allies were not about to go quietly away.

In November 1929, the voters of Saratoga gave another resounding victory to the anti-Leonard City Council. All the members were re-elected, with Leonard and Knapp losing by more votes than they had two years prior.[22]

While the election results were a clear signal that voters were at least willing to give Sweeney another two years to push his law and order philosophy, there were signs that the gamblers and gangsters were about to make a strong comeback in the Spa City.

A not so obvious sign of chicanery was in the election results of 1929. There were a strikingly large number of absentee ballot requests made prior to the election and the result raised eyebrows among political wonks.

There is a general trend in politics that absentee ballots usually track the general election results. Typically, if the election result at the polls is 60 percent in favor of one candidate, the absentee ballots will come in around the same number, even if slightly higher or lower.

But in the case of the absentee ballots cast in Saratoga Springs in 1929, the absentee ballots came in almost entirely for Doc Leonard. He lost the election at the polling stations, garnering only 49 percent of the vote. Yet of the absentee ballots cast for Public Safety Commissioner that year, Leonard took 84 percent.[23]

The Burns Detective Agency was hired by the city to investigate the peculiarity and they found many of the individuals who had applied for absentee ballots in Saratoga Springs had voter registrations on file in other municipalities, mostly in New York City and Yonkers. While no proof was ever shown to indicate whether or not local officials were directly involved in any election fraud, there was enough evidence to indict four persons for submitting absentee ballots in Saratoga Springs while also voting in New York City.[24] The reader is left to decide the likelihood that in 1929, it just so happened that many of Doc Leonard's supporters were unavoidably out of town for one reason or another on election day.

Election fraud is a very serious matter, but there is no general physical danger to citizens when someone votes improperly. Commissioner Sweeney and Chief Armstrong, despite their success in cleaning up the department and making raids against the gamblers, were unfortunately losing the war against many other crimes. It seemed that, as the new decade dawned, a growing threat to peace and security in Saratoga Springs was emerging. Ruthless gangsters were muscling in on the lucrative Saratoga summer scene and with them came all sorts of crime.

But Chief Armstrong held fast as long as he could. When Millett's Hotel (22-26 Railroad Place) was raided by prohibition agents on August 22, 1929, an anonymous caller phoned Chief Armstrong and asked him to go in person to the hotel and stop the federal men from breaking into a locked room there.

While the federal agents were still on the property, Chief Armstrong wisely refused to go to Millett's and told the unknown caller that if he believed the federal warrant was issued in error, then he should go to court and resolve the matter peacefully there. He and his men, Chief Armstrong told the caller, would definitely not interfere with the prohibition men.

The probies promptly kicked in the door to the room and seized five barrels of whiskey, one barrel of alcohol, a five-gallon can of alcohol, 100 quarts of scotch whiskey, and 200 quarts of rye whiskey. [25]

Whether it was the zealousness with which Sweeney and Armstrong were enforcing the law, or the townsfolk were getting tired of regular prohibition raids, the public was definitely leaning back towards leniency when it came to affairs of public safety.

By the election of 1931 the fine residents of Saratoga Springs decided that Doc Leonard deserved another shot at the top of the police department, and he was elected, yet again to the public safety position. It seems that a little over four years years in the political wilderness was Leonard's penance for his involvement in the Heffernan affair. The lid had been clamped down much too tightly over the past couple of years and when it was opened, the gangsters would come back with a vengeance, and they would bring their violence with them.

Endnotes

Chapter 4

[1] "Civic League Worker Tells Saratoga Tale." *Albany Evening News*. January 17, 1927.

[2] "Reform Worker Says He Had 'Under Cover' Men Busy in Saratoga Springs in August." *The Saratogian*. January 27, 1927.

[3] "Rev. A. H. Boutwell Warns Electorate of Civic Duties." *The Saratogian*. October 4, 1926.

[4] Ibid.

[5] Ibid.

[6] Finley Tells Grand Jury of Saratoga Gambling." *The Saratogian*. January 6, 1927.

[7] "Reform Worker Says…"

[8] "Grand Jury to Recall Fisher of Civic League." *The Saratogian*. January 18, 1927.

[9] Ibid.

[10] "No Indictments for Saratoga Gambling." *The Saratogian*. January 20, 1927.

[11] Sweeney and Entire Ticket Elected." *The Saratogian*. November 9, 1927.

[12] "Dismiss Dorsey, Police Sergeant, After a Hearing." *The Saratogian*. January 18, 1928.

[13] Patrolman Lucas Suspended from Duty For 16 Days." *The Saratogian*. August 16, 1928.

[14] "40 Alleged Crap Players in Flight as Police Crash." *The Saratogian*. August 16, 1928.

[15] "Ousted Gamblers Find Safe Haven at Glens Falls." *The Saratogian*. August 21, 1928.

[16] Ibid.

[17] "Stevens, Discharged Saratoga Patrolman, Loses Motion for Reinstatement and Back Wages." *The Saratogian*. April 15, 1929.

[18] "Dismiss Crooks From Force for Good of Service: *The Saratogian*. January 22, 1929.

[19] "Police Seize Two Slot Machines in Union Ave., Place." *The Saratogian*. August 24, 1929.

[20] "Dorsey Goes to Governor with Gambling Charge." *The Saratogian*. August 9, 1930.

[21] "Entire Saratoga City Council Re-Elected." *The Saratogian*. November 6, 1929.

[22] Ibid.

[23] Ibid.

[24] "Saratoga Election Fraud Cases Scheduled for Next Week." *The Saratogian*. February 22, 1930.

[25] "Millet's Hotel Nets Big Haul of Alleged Whiskey." *The Saratogian*. August 23, 1929.

A Spasm of Violence

All who will take up the sword will die by the sword. For underworld figures, violence is just part of the deal. They usually rise to power through violence and often meet their demise full of lead. The history of American organized crime is written in blood. Prominence in "The Outfit" does not guarantee one's safety. Arnold Rothstein, Jack "Legs" Diamond, Vincent "Mad Dog" Coll, and Dutch Schultz are just a few of the Mafia legends who faced early retirement at the end of a gun.

With so many Mafiosi running around Saratoga Springs during and immediately after Prohibition, it was inevitable that some violence would erupt over territory, money, or insult. The local Saratoga gangsters and police would come to an understanding that, while vice could be winked at, violence was off limits. However, sooner or later, someone, probably an out-of-towner, would disregard the status quo and start shooting.

Saratoga was not immune from violence. Robberies, assaults, shootings, and all manner of crime and disorder were faithfully reported on by the local papers. In the early days of Saratoga's history, areas of town were described appropriately for their conditions, with places like Willow Walk (High Rock Ave) being called "the valley in the shadow of death" and Searing's Alley referred to as a "stench in the nostrils of the public and police." Congress Street and the West Side Neighborhood of Saratoga Springs were notorious areas of the city.

But having said that, most of the violence was routine street level violence. Every once in a while a dispute would boil over into real violence and someone would end up dead. Usually the gunplay would be the result of heated, alcohol fueled arguments. Rarely was violence used as a tool by the local gangsters in the same way that gangland wars would frequently break out in New York, Chicago, and other major metropolitan areas.

All that would change on July 27, 1931. The headline of the *Saratogian* on that Monday morning screamed, "TORCH AND BULLETS OPEN LOCAL BEER WAR."

At about 2:45 a.m. the previous morning, Anthony "Sonny" Pompay was travelling south along the Glens Falls Road (today's State Route 9). At a point near where the state road intersects with Maple Ave at today's Triangle Diner, Pompay was accosted by four men in a sedan. As he rounded a curve in the road, the four men suddenly opened fire on Pompay's vehicle. One of the tires on the Pompay machine was shot out, and several rounds (fired from rifles and handguns) pierced his windshield as Pompay came to a halt.

Now, Pompay was no coward and, as he later related to police, he was himself in possession of his own weapon (he called it a "gat") and returned fire at his assailants, to good effect. Pompay's accuracy was better than his attackers and he managed to hit at least one of them and put 19 bullet holes in the enemy sedan before the four would-be assassins jumped back into their auto and sped off toward the sleeping city on Maple Ave.

State Trooper John Lutz lived at that time with his wife near the scene of the shooting and, upon hearing the exchange of gunfire, notified the Troy barracks in the hope that one of his colleagues could cut off any escape route if the gunmen managed to slip through the city.

At the same time, hearing the crack of gunfire from the police station, Patrolmen West and DelVecchio raced out of police headquarters, jumped into the prowl car, and headed toward the disturbance.

They soon encountered the suspect sedan barreling away from the scene and took up a pursuit, southbound on Maple Avenue, through Putnam Street to Spring Street, where the car sped up to Broadway and turned south. Eventually the police car could not keep up with the bullet riddled sedan and the taillights faded into the distance along South Broadway ahead of the two officers.

Troopers coming from the south also had no luck in apprehending the fleeing gunmen.

A few hours later, Gilbert Maurer, who lived on the Round Lake-Clifton Park Road in the southern part of the county, found the vehicle. It was ditched along the roadway and in their haste to abandon the automobile, the men had left a grey fedora hat and a blood-soaked rag, along with several editions of New York City tabloids.

About two hours after the shooting, Anthony "Sonny" Pompay presented himself at police headquarters to report the apparent hold-up attempt. He claimed to be alone, although the Troopers believed that he was not, due to the large number of bullet holes in the offending vehicle.

The state police also speculated that the damage done to the attacker's car was done by a machine gun, even though Pompay only claimed to have fired a handgun. Chief of Police Armstrong, a veteran of World War I, who had heard the gunfire that night, thought that the gunfire did not sound like a machine gun.

Nevertheless, no one had gotten a good look at the invading gangsters and the hat could not be traced to its owner. DNA testing was unknown at the time and therefore the towel was of little evidentiary value and likely discarded soon after its recovery. The car had been registered over the previous weekend to a Salvatore Luciani of New York City, but that lead too went nowhere.

Even though prohibition was coming to an end, the bootleg trail was still a dangerous and notorious smuggling route. As we can imagine, the shootout would have had the townsfolk murmuring. Rumors must have been running rampant throughout the city with the hope that this was just a case of a simple hijacking gone wrong. It was not to be.

Later that evening, as the *Saratogian* reported, an unnamed man told his lady friend, "If you hear an explosion tonight don't get all excited. They are going to blow up the Lewis house tonight."

The Lewis house, alluded to by the mysterious predictor of arson, was the former Cluett estate at 493 Woodlawn Ave which had been purchased recently by Truman Lewis, father-in-law of one Anthony "Sonny" Pompay. And true to the prediction of the anonymous tipster, at 12:51 a.m. on July 27, 1932, the Lewis home was, in fact, blown up.

The explosion blew off the top two floors of the building and engulfed the remaining floor in flames. A chauffeur for Mrs. Seth Morton, who lived at 139 State Street, directly behind the Lewis home, heard the explosion and rushed to the fire call box at North Broadway and First Street, turned in the alarm and, it can be assumed, returned to the scene of the fire to watch the firemen battle the blaze for the next several hours.

Later, Mrs. Seth Morton told Public Safety Commissioner Sweeney that, just before the explosion, she had a visitor. At the ring of her doorbell, Mrs. Morton called out, "Who's there?"

The visitor's muffled voice replied, "Never mind. You'd better be getting away from here, there's going to be an explosion."

Almost immediately the blast occurred, and the mysterious visitor vanished in the ensuing bedlam that always follows such an event. A small sedan was seen leaving the area just before the blast and during the investigation that followed, neighbors recalled seeing a similar vehicle cruising around the area late at night a few days prior to the bombing. Could the suspicious car have been a team of arsonists scoping out the Truman house in preparation of the big night?

Although he was the father-in-law of Sonny Pompay, who was a member of the Farone liquor running group in Saratoga, Truman Lewis worked for the State Tree Nursery down in the State Park. Why would anyone want to blow up his house?

The answer might be found in what Lewis planned to do with the home during August. Lewis had been making extensive improvements to the home and rumor had it that he planned to lease the property to a third party who would run a nightclub or speakeasy out of it during the racing season. As Lewis told the *Saratogian*, he had recently verbally agreed with a man whose name he did not know, and that he had only just met, to lease the building for the summer racing meet. Lewis' neighbors were concerned about the possibility of a nightclub opening in the neighborhood and complained to authorities.

At first, it was thought that Doc Farone was the person behind the proposed nightclub, but he made adamant public denials that he was behind the venture. Another theory was that the man who had approached Lewis was a member of one of the national underworld organizations, possibly an Al Capone or Legs Diamond associate.

Whatever the reason, the bombing and the shooting over the course of less than forty-eight hours was something new in Saratoga Springs and indicated that perhaps the underworld recognized upstate New York as more valuable than just a summer playground. Could it have been that rival groups of mobsters were really "going to the mattresses" in Saratoga Springs? Were major mob figures really trying to dislodge Doc Farone from the territory he controlled in Saratoga Springs and its environs?

The day after the *Saratogian* reported on the Pompay shootout and the Lewis explosion, they updated the investigation of the blast by quoting police as believing that the work was done by a professional arsonist and that the case would likely never be solved. In fact, there never were any arrests made related to the bombing.

In the same article the reporter explains that, back in January of that year, Doc Farone had received a threat from downstate liquor runners who wanted to break into the Saratoga market. The paper printed a direct quote from these unnamed gangsters:

"You are having things too much your own way in Saratoga county. If you want to continue in the business there, you must come through with some money to make it worth our while to stay away."

Now Doc Farone attributed the recent violence as the work of mere liquor hijackers, but there was something that pointed to a more widespread cancer invading Saratoga. Back in January, around the time that Doc had received the threat, a house at 107 Catherine Street caught fire and was partially destroyed.

This was not a simple house fire, however, as police and fire officials determined that it was a case of arson and the homeowner was one Mrs. Truman Lewis, yes, mother of Sonny Pompay. Could they have been connected? It certainly seemed so.

Now, about one month prior to the Pompay shoot-em-up, again the *Saratogian* reported "on good authority" that Doc Farone had received a second threat to his interests in Saratoga. This time though, Doc was told that he would be "put on the spot" if he did not pay up.

Doc Farone sent word back downstate that he would not be paying anyone and that he would not be tolerating any interference in Saratoga from outside bootleggers.

These reports did not name any particular New York City gangster; however, in the same day's editorial pages, the *Saratogian* editors outlined a push by Jack "Legs" Diamond to consolidate his upstate New York empire by adding the Saratoga district to his territory, which stretched from the Canadian border to the Lake George/Glens Falls area.

Diamond had recently been acquitted at trial in Troy and was registered in a hotel in Lake George, where he was apparently planning to establish his northern headquarters. It was well known that Legs had interests in Albany and the Catskills as well. So, it was logical that Diamond might have wanted to add Saratoga to his total acreage.

Lending some credibility to this theory of who was behind the Pompay violent encounter and the two arsons at his relative's homes, was a report that a gangland raid had been conducted three days prior to the Pompay shootout on the Saratoga-Glens Falls road.

Again, citing reliable sources, the local paper reported that Farone had recently brought in a shipment of liquor and was stashing it at a warehouse about four miles or so outside the city limits. Three days before the attempt on Pompay's life, during the early morning hours, a team of rival bootleggers paid a surprise visit to the Farone stash house and opened fire with machine guns before making off with all of Doc's supply.

Although the theft was never reported to the police, it was discovered through the investigation of the recent violence. This time, there was no question that machine guns were in play as a neighbor with service in a machine gun unit from the "War to End All Wars" verified that the gunfire did indeed come from an automatic weapon. For good measure, and to add credibility to his account, the World War I veteran added that he at first heard a couple of pops from small arms, then a few bursts from the machine gun, which he identified as either a light Browning or a Vickers, with his opinion leaning towards a Browning.

If you are keeping track, that is two shootings, a liquor hijacking, and a bombing, all in the span of four days and all apparently related to a gangland feud over the lucrative liquor market in Saratoga. And it wasn't over.

Just two nights after Sonny Pompay shot it out with those four gunmen on the Bootleg Trail, Alfred (Chinny) Farone, brother of Doc Farone, was driving east on Second Street towards North Broadway at about 12:05 a.m. Little did he know that four gunmen had been keeping a watch on one of his brother's caches in the garage of 107 Catherine Street, possibly preparing for a robbery or ambush.

Yes, if you were wondering, 107 Catherine Street was the home of Mrs. Lewis, which had been burned back in January. The men had concealed themselves in the dark along Second Street when Chinny Farone approached.

As Alfred reached the intersection of Catherine Street in his maroon coupe, one of the men stationed between the houses yelled, "There he is! Plug him! Plug him!"[1]

Suddenly the four would-be assassins materialized from the shadows and opened up on Chinny Farone with two repeating rifles, one revolver, and a sawed-off shotgun. Alfred slammed on the brakes and threw his vehicle into reverse, backing over a curb and tearing out of the trap onto Catherine Street.

The gunmen may have mistaken Chinny for Doc, but whatever the reason, they decided to abandon the robbery of the storehouse and launch an assassination attempt. Once their plan changed from robbery to murder, they went all-in with the new plan. As Chinny sped away along Second Street, the four assailants hopped onto the running boards of one of their vehicles and started to give chase, joined by a second vehicle of the anti-Farone forces.

When the pursuit reached Bryant Street, a fusillade of shots was heard by residents as the men in the trailing car tried to gun down the fleeing Saratoga native.

For a few moments the neighborhood was quiet as the chase followed North Broadway back toward town. Neighborhood residents could probably hear the gunning engines of the desperate men racing through town. Suddenly more shots broke the stillness of the night, coming from the direction of upper State Street.

With the mobsters stalking him closely, Al Farone raced through the driveway of the Home of the Good Shepherd, nearly pitching over and no doubt scaring the poor ladies of the house, before speeding out Greenfield Avenue and losing his pursuers.

This time no bullet riddled cars were found deserted outside town. No reports of persons shot were received from area hospitals and the only record of the event was a notation in the police blotter that simply recorded Alfred Farone's report that he had been ambushed near Catherine Street. No arrests were ever made.

In the morning light, James Wolley found a rifle shell casing near his home on North Broadway. Quiet evidence of the night's festivities.

As Chinny Farone and his enemies faded into the night, all was still around 107 Catherine Street until Sonny Pompay arrived in the vanguard of five vehicles loaded with Farone men. As a few of the soldiers took up overwatch positions, the remaining men started to mill about the place.

Soon Officers West and DelVecchio came careening onto Catherine Street, pulling up to the front of number 107. Pompay came out of the residence and talked with the officers for a few minutes, then the officers drove away.

Almost immediately upon the departure of the police, a large truck arrived and pulled into the backyard of 107 Catherine Street, adjacent to the large garage behind it. Within about twenty minutes the workmen were able to empty the warehouse, filling large burlap bags with bottles of what could only have been liquor and, even though the workers had covered the cargo with burlap, when the truck left the yard it bumped over the curb and neighbors clearly heard the clinking of glass as it did so.

When the truck pulled into the street, a police car raced once again onto the scene. Four officers got out and ran into the residence. After a few minutes of discussion, the four officers got back into their car and drove away. The beer-laden truck quietly left the area as well, escorted by a carload of men who had been dispatched from the Chicago Club as an apparent protection force. Where the liquor ended up was never learned, but it was certainly a more secretive and secure location than 107 Catherine Street.

The following morning, Doc Farone was asked for comment on the situation. While laying the blame for the violence on Albany area rivals and not Legs Diamond or Dutch Schultz, Farone claimed to be the victim of hijackers who had two informants inside his operation. While disavowing the use of violence, Farone did mention that he would like to "get his hands on" the two snitches who had been tipping off his rivals with good intelligence on his operations.

Doc Farone had no problem giving a statement to reporters and his own words, as printed in the *Saratogian* of July 29, 1932, are provided here for the reader's consideration:

"I'm going out of the business, not because anybody has forced me out, but at the suggestion of the police commissioner. I wouldn't get out because of the competition. Give me an ad. Say that all my places which I have used for storehouses are for sale. You can say the farm is for sale. If you want to take a picture, I'll put a sign on the farm 'for sale,' and you can say that this is the place which was used for storing bootleg liquor all winter."

When asked if he was out for good, Farone told the reporter, "Well, I'm out for a year at least. I'm going to rest and take it easy this summer. I'm looking for a good legitimate business. You don't know where I can get one, do you?"

For his part, Truman Lewis added his comments, to try to clear up the matter, if not his reputation. He told the *Saratogian*, "I wish to state at this time that I have never had any business dealings with Mr. Farone. He has never loaned me any money or ever had an interest in any property which I possess. I also wish to state that I am not, and never have been interested in or connected with any business which my son-in-law, Anthony Pompay may be doing."

The morning after the attempt on Chinny Farone's life, when Commissioner Sweeney learned of the report of the shooting and that 107 Catherine Street might be a storehouse for liquor, he ordered that two men go immediately and search the place. They found nothing and no whisper of concern was ever made publicly that during this whole adventure, as many as six police officers had been at the scene and not one apparently seized any liquor or stopped the work of the Farone gang as they went about their business.

Commissioner Sweeney was not happy with the situation. As verified by Doc Farone himself, the Commissioner "suggested" that he excuse himself from the business or have all of his places raided. In addition, Commissioner Sweeney ordered eight new officers added to the force immediately.

Commissioner Sweeney said, "I am going to stop this gang warfare, and stop it at once. It has come to a stage where decent, respectable citizens are not safe in their homes or on the streets. My men will have instructions to act promptly and decisively, and I will hold every man in the department strictly accountable for anything that goes on on his beat."

Apparently three shootouts and a bombing were enough to move local authorities to action. Even though the police and Farone had a cordial relationship over the years, this was just too much. The Saratoga Springs Police were not playing around.

The night after the last shooting affair at Catherine and Second Streets, one of the newly assigned officers was patrolling his beat on Lake Ave when he heard a commotion near Hodgeman Street. He rushed over to discover a young woman had had her purse grabbed and, in an attempt to stop the culprits, the officer fired off a couple of shots with his revolver.[2] Thankfully there was no return fire and the only gunfire on that night was from authorized weapons.

Rather than wait for more criminals to arrive in town, in the days after the spasm of violence, Saratoga Springs and visiting New York City detectives were assigned to the train station to meet every train that arrived in town and any mobsters who tried to get in through that route were put back on the train before it headed south again.

The police presence was so pervasive that even young lovers who tried to park along deserted roadways for amorous activities were stopped, questioned, and moved along. Whereas the regular police response to parked cars was to leave the lovebirds alone, with the gang war going on, no occupied cars could remain parked on city streets.[3] Interruption of true love was a small price to pay for the security of the town.

As the violence died down in Saratoga Springs, the public was left to wonder, was this a real mob war or, as Doc Farone asserted, was this a simple case of hijackers trying to get at his stuff? The police were not exactly helpful in their public statements. They never made any arrests and they seemed to discount the theory that Legs Diamond, Dutch Schultz, or Mad Dog Coll were trying to muscle in on Farone's territory, but they acted as though the danger was heightened and seemed to take the threat extremely seriously.

While the statements of the police and Doc Farone should not be entirely discounted, we should, perhaps, take a wider view of the situation and think about the possibility that there may have been an invasion of downstate forces during the summer of 1931.

For openers, the newspapers of the day had a habit of reporting on gangland rumors regularly. Often, they were true, because many reporters relied on police sources and gangsters themselves for information. In those days, gangsters frequently acknowledged, or at least hinted, in print, that they were involved in the illegal liquor business. As evidence we can look at Doc Farone's own words about retiring for a year from the rackets. A public admission of this sort would be unheard of today, but back then it happened pretty frequently, especially among the more talkative members of the mob.

The press was not above sensationalizing a rumor if needed. The big name in mob land was of course, Al Capone. While there is no evidence that this author is aware of that directly links Scarface to the Spa City, the *Saratogian* and other newspapers in the area reported that, in the week before the violence broke out, two of Al Capone's lieutenants were in Saratoga Springs and had made arrangements to supply beer to the thirsty tourists.[4]

Capone did have a partnership in a horse racing stable with Anthony "Little Augie Pisano" Carafano (who we will meet again later in this book), but little evidence exists to suggest that Al Capone took any financial interest in the Saratoga beer market; yet that didn't stop the press from putting the rumor out there.

The press reported more confidently, and in more detail, that Jack "Legs" Diamond was involved in the attempted takeover of the Saratoga territory. Several stories detailed Diamond's expansion into the Adirondacks as he was chased out of New York City by Dutch Schultz and the Coll brothers.

That he would come to Saratoga Springs would not be unreasonable if he was looking to expand his empire and certainly, he would not have been too concerned with the Farone outfit, as he had hijacked and muscled in on more powerful rum runners than Doc.

Although Farone alcohol was carried by almost all the clubs in Saratoga, Diamond beer was supplied to at least one Spa City watering hole, as reported on in the local paper.[5] He was known to be staying in Lake George and Glens Falls and it was even reported that Legs had started brewing his own stuff at a plant in Hudson Falls.

We turn now to the possibility that the gun play may be attributed to members of the Mad Dog Coll gang. Some context is in order for this little section of the narrative.

In the early 1930's Dutch Schultz was the undisputed beer baron of New York. On his payroll were two brothers, Vincent and Peter Coll.[6] They worked as armed guards for the Schultz delivery trucks. Some say the Coll brothers, realizing that Dutch was making millions, wanted a larger share of the business's income, which, of course, the Dutchman denied.

The Coll brothers, along with a few other men, decided to break off from Dutch Schultz and started hijacking Schultz beer. Soon a war was on and Peter Coll was one of the first victims. This sent Vincent into a killing rage that eventually earned him the nickname of "Mad Dog."

Mad Dog Coll struck hard and put several of Dutch's top men in the grave in short order. Schultz and company fought back, and the violence escalated until Coll's men attempted a drive-by shooting of a Shultz associate in Harlem. They missed the gangster completely and instead hit five children, killing one.

The baby killing happened at just about the same time that the violence erupted in Saratoga Springs and within days of both events the New York Times was reporting that NYPD detectives had been dispatched to watch the trains headed for Saratoga in order to cut off the Coll gang from escaping the city.[7]

Other papers reported that a team of six plainclothes detectives had been sent to the Spa City in order to hunt down the Coll gang.[8] Of all places, why would the trains to Saratoga be watched for hoodlums looking to escape from New York City? The answer should be obvious.

At the same time Mad Dog Coll was gunning for him, Dutch Shultz was not getting along with Legs Diamond either, and the bad blood between them occasionally spilled over into violence as well.

Now, all wars are expensive. For nations, and for Mafia Dons, funding a war is often the most important factor that determines the outcome. Is it unreasonable to assume that while authorities pressured them on one end and their bitter feuds drew down their reserves of both money and manpower, that men such as Dutch Schultz, Mad Dog Coll, and Legs Diamond would view Saratoga as a source of new income? We have already seen, and will see again, big time organized crime figures taking an interest in the Saratoga market, so why would Dutch, Mad Dog, and Legs be any different in their desire to draw the vice dollar from the Spa City, especially when they were in need of money to fight off their rivals?

It seems to this author that the most likely explanation for the violence that broke out in Saratoga Springs in the summer of 1931 was the theory that one or more of the three above mentioned gangsters did, in fact, try to muscle in on Doc Farone's territory.

In Saratoga, the locals needed their share of the vice profits and the police and politicians could look the other way, so long as everyone played their parts. The major players were welcome in Saratoga, provided they respected the locals' positions, made their graft payments on time, and violence remained at minimum levels. Arnold Rothstein understood that, and so did Joe Adonis, Frank Costello, Lucky Luciano, and Meyer Lansky.

But Legs, Dutch, and Mad Dog Coll were a few of the more volatile gangsters of the era. Embroiled in their New York City war, it is likely that they looked to expand into Saratoga using the same brutal methods they had used to expand in the past. They found the Saratoga system to be stronger than they had found in the usual local thugs they encountered elsewhere.

From their turning the streets of New York City blood red, to the shooting of the children in Harlem, to the shootouts and bombings in the quiet residential streets of Saratoga, the thuggery of Legs, Dutch, and Mad Dog was just too much for the Spa. After the brief spasm of violence subsided, Saratoga quietly went back to the old ways. Doc Farone had survived, no doubt supported by the local constabulary, while Legs Diamond, Dutch Shultz, and Mad Dog Coll were kept at arms' length, all of them meeting a violent end.

For the curious reader: Jack "Legs" Diamond was shot and killed in a boarding house in Albany on December 18, 1931. Dutch Schultz was murdered at the Palace Chop House in Newark, NJ, on October 23, 1935. Vincent "Mad Dog" Coll was machine gunned to death in a phone booth in Manhattan on February 8, 1932.

Saratoga Springs was clearly not immune from the gangland violence that plagued the major cities and smuggling routes of America during the 1930's. The hey-day of the bootleggers and rum runners brought on the rise of organized crime in the United States and where organized crime took hold, it seemed local authorities had little choice in the matter. Indeed, to the casual observer, Saratoga Springs may have seemed to have truly become a gangster's paradise.

Endnotes

Chapter 5

[1] "City, Stirred by New Battle, Acts to End Liquor War Here; Farone Asserts He is Through." *The Saratogian.* July 29, 1931.

[2] "Purse Snatchers Fired at in Lake Avenue by Police." *The Saratogian.* July 31, 1931.

[3] "Discredit Report Gunmen Are on Way to Saratoga." *The Saratogian.* July 31, 1931.

[4] "Gang Wars Break Out in Saratoga Springs." *The Salem Press.* July 31, 1931.

[5] "'Legs' Diamond Beer Being Sold in Saratoga; is Report." *The Saratogian.* April 16, 1931.

[6] Downey, Patrick. *Gangster City: The History of the New York Underworld 1900-1935.* Barricade Books. 2004.

[7] "Wide Aid Offered in Gangster Hunt." *The New York Times.* July 31, 1931.

[8] "New York Police Saratoga Bound." *The Amsterdam Evening Recorder.* August 1, 1931.

Chapter 6

Trouble at the Track

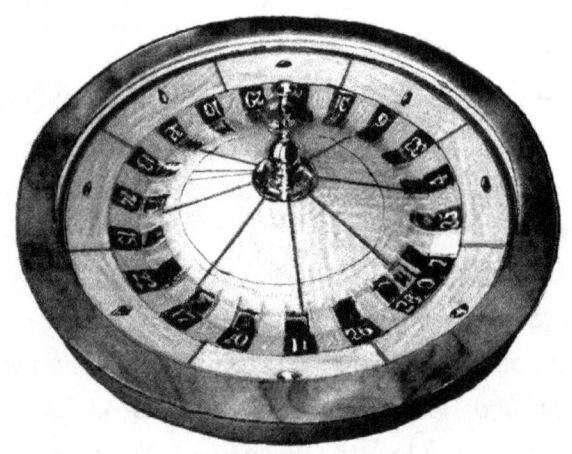

In 1942, New York State Senator John L. Dunnigan, who was known as the "father of the Pari-mutuel law in New York State," said this about horse racing: "In the twenties, racing belonged to the aristocracy. In the thirties, racing belonged to the bookmakers. In the forties, racing belongs to the public."[1]

His comments were related to the implementation of the pari-mutuel system of betting at New York racetracks that began in 1940. Before then, betting at the track was conducted by bookmakers who would take oral bets at set odds that they themselves established prior to a race being run. Ever since John Morrissey opened the racetrack at Saratoga in 1863, the bookmakers had controlled the betting system at Saratoga. The racetrack operators made money by charging admission.

Since oral betting was legal, as long as it was done according to the law, the bookmakers made money on the betting, not the tracks or the state. The public benefited only to the extent that the state could collect property taxes on the grounds and on any self-reported income from winning bettors.

Savvy and experienced bookmakers often made tremendous profits, as they could determine the odds and adjust them according to their "bank." By adjusting the odds, they could attract more (or less) betting on a particular horse and consequently they might be influenced by individuals who had an interest in a race, if we assume that evildoers will look to take advantage of any situation that they can profit from.

The pari-mutuel system, using a mechanical totalizer, collected bets from the public and automatically calculated the odds based on all of the monies bet on a particular race. Each individual bettor was betting against all the other bettors of a given race, rather than against the bookmaker, with whom the bet is placed and who set the odds for any payout himself.

The pari-mutuel system allowed both the track and the state to retain a percentage of the total pool off the top (a more polite term might be "tax" here), thereby increasing their revenue streams while freezing out the individual bookmakers at the track.

The system of bookmaking at racetracks had apparently worked well enough since 1863, at least in Saratoga Springs. The popularity of horse racing remained strong throughout the decades, so why would anyone want or need to change the betting system? The answer lies in the statement made by Senator Dunnigan above, "In the thirties, racing belonged to the bookmakers…" and by extension, one might assume he meant the gangsters as well.

With their riches gained from prohibition and other forms of vice, the sport of horse racing seemed to attract the gangsters. The betting on horse racing was just another way that men like Arnold Rothstein, Lucky Luciano, "Little Augie" Pisano, and any number of lesser known organized criminals could make money. Manipulating horsemen, jockeys, and bookmakers was a relatively easy thing for criminal gangs to get involved with and their activities at Saratoga and elsewhere might lead an observer to think that the "Sport of Kings" may not have always been conducted on the up and up.

In the closing years of prohibition and on through the nineteen thirties, racetracks seemed to be inundated with gangsters. Some were well-known, others just hangers-on, but what was indisputable was that racing had a problem. Organized crime had taken hold at tracks across the country and their activities were revealed only when someone was caught engaging in misconduct, which was not infrequent in those years.

The risk of a jockey being bribed was always on the minds of those responsible for ensuring the integrity of the racing industry. Jockeys were cautioned to stay away from gamblers and the casinos, lest they give the appearance of impropriety or be tempted by a lucrative offer to throw a race. If jockeys and gangsters were pals, it just wouldn't look good and if the public lost confidence that the races were run fairly, soon the thoroughbreds would be running in front of empty grandstands.

A lack of integrity had once cost Saratoga dearly when, just prior to the turn of the 20th century, Gottfried Walbaum ran the track in such a sloppy manner that the leading trainers refused to bring their stallions and mares to Saratoga. The racing, and probably the village, was saved by William C. Whitney, who headed a syndicate that purchased the track from Walbaum.

Bribery was such a concern that track officials sometimes did not even wait for evidence to discipline a jockey. This was the case when, in the mid 1920's, one of the leading jockeys of the day, Clarence Kummer, was seen visiting Arnold Rothstein's Brook resort out Church Street during the Saratoga meet. Racing officials warned Kummer to stay away from the Brook, as it was well known that gambling was carried on there, although the place was never raided. When Kummer failed to heed the warning and visited a second time, he was suspended from riding for a year.[2]

Sometimes, jockeys who had been bribed went to extreme lengths to ensure that the result came out the way their paymasters wanted it. One of the most blatant examples of this was reported by the *Saratogian* on August 16, 1933.

During a steeplechase race the day before, a horse named Cito was entered and the odds makers had him as the clear favorite on the morning line. As post time for the race neared, bookmakers like Tom Shaw noticed irregularities in the betting and immediately thought something was amiss. Someone, he thought, must be trying to push Cito's odds up. He stopped taking bets on the race to protect himself.

If the hidden plan was to have Cito win the race at longer odds, it worked. Cito did, in fact, win the race, but what the crowd, the bookmakers, and the stewards at the track witnessed convinced all observers that there was indeed something amiss.

Cito was clearly the slowest horse in the race that day. Even his owner acknowledged after the race had been run that Cito had no business winning the contest. That he did was the result of the other jockeys riding so poorly that the outcome had clearly been determined in advance of the race.

One horse was described as taking a turn so wide that it appeared as though the horse and rider were headed for Yaddo. Another jockey drew his mount so far outside that he dragged another horse with him, almost into the grandstand. And while one jockey did appear to make a last-ditch effort to catch Cito in the home stretch, it was obvious to all, including the turf writers watching the race, that the jockeys had done "everything but get off and wrestle with their steeds."

The actions of the jockeys confirmed the rumors that the race had been fixed. The stewards immediately voided the results of the race and jockeys Edward Hall and D. Hunt were suspended from further riding at the track. [3]

Another story of jockeys being involved in fixing a race was passed down to the author from a relative of one of the riders. This horse race took place on the last day of the meet one year that could not be recalled precisely, likely in the late 1920's or early 1930's. During a claiming race in the middle of the card, the jockeys had gotten together and determined that one of the long shots would win. Through a third party, the jockeys would place a heavy bet on the predetermined winner and all share in the profits. As it was the last day of the meet, during an unimportant race, the jockeys felt they could complete the scam, skip town, and split the money, with no one the wiser.

By the time anyone suspected the result smelled funny, the jockeys figured, they would all be downstate at Belmont and the race long forgotten.

Unfortunately, at the top of the stretch, the horse that had been designated as the winner suffered a fatal heart attack and dropped dead in the middle of the race. The dead horse's jockey got so mad after he was thrown that he started kicking the downed horse right in the middle of the track, in front of the entire crowd!

Needless to say, all the jockeys in the race had to eat their investment in the "sure thing" and keep quiet. Perhaps they should have sought the advice of an Arnold Rothstein before engaging in such gangster-like behavior.

Fixing a horse race is not easy. Bribing a jockey or trainer might be the most straightforward method for a nefarious character looking to tamper with a race, but the horses will have a say in the outcome and no amount of money will sway them. So, the more despicable of the criminal underworld often turned to tampering with the horses directly. During the gangster era there were typically three ways in which racehorses were meddled with by gamblers or gangsters looking to influence the outcome of a particular race: sponging, doping, and painting (substituting) horses.

The dastardly technique of sponging horses is employed by the most heartless of fiends and involves the placing of a small piece of cloth, sponge, or silk into one or both of the nostrils of a racehorse. The obstruction is pushed far enough up the nose of the animal that it remains unseen and the horse is not outwardly affected by the blockage until the race begins. Once the beast begins running and breathing more heavily, it becomes more difficult for the horse to get air and the runner is slowed. Unless the criminal botches the operation and the sponge can be seen, or the animal is outwardly injured by being cut or some other obvious injury, the sponging will go undetected until after the race.

Sponging horses was a scourge that racetrack officials, Pinkerton detectives, and police tried to stamp out whenever they could. Interfering with racehorses had become such a problem around the tracks that by 1932 Governor Franklin D. Roosevelt signed into law a bill that made tampering with a racehorse a felony.

In 1933, thirteen veteran detectives from New York City were assigned under the direct command of Saratoga Springs Police Chief Patrick Rox to ferret out ne'er-do-wells in and around the track and the Broadway District. Two of those detectives, Charles Meuchner and William Asip, both of Brooklyn, specialized in horse sponging and doping cases.[4] On the track, Captain Clovis E. Duhain used his thirty years of experience as the Pinkerton Superintendent of the Department of Racing to help the police in fighting the gamblers, criminals, and racetrack touts hanging about the race courses.[5]

Two examples of sponging of horses should suffice to illustrate the practice.

In 1930, during the last week of July, Elijah Johnson, a stable hand who followed the racing circuit, arrived in Saratoga. He took employment at the barn where Dr. Irving Jacobs' horse, Sun Mission, was stabled in anticipation of entering the first race on July 31.

Shortly before the horses were brought out for the parade to the post, two witnesses saw Johnson coming out of Sun Mission's stall, a place where he had no business being in that moment. They ran over and confronted Johnson, demanding to know what he was doing.

Before long a tiny string was noticed protruding from Sun Mission's nostril. When pulled, the string was found to be attached to a sponge that had been stuffed up the horse's nose.

After a quick investigation, Johnson was brought to police headquarters while Sun Mission, the sponge removed and cleared to run, finished the race in third place.

Later that evening Judge F. Andrew Hall opened Johnson's trial and, upon examination, declared that he believed Johnson was simply a tool for a "gang of highwaymen" who were operating in the city. He offered to go easy on Johnson if he would only help the authorities track down the men behind the conspiracy, but Johnson remained insistent that he was innocent of the charge and therefore could not help the police.

Since tampering with a racehorse was not yet a felony, Elijah Johnson was sentenced to ninety days in jail on a charge of animal cruelty.[6] None of his alleged confederates were ever caught and the sponging of Sun Mission prompted those responsible for more famous, and more valuable, horses to increase security around their steeds.

To demonstrate the concern that horse owners and trainers had with the menace of gangsters tampering with horses, one needs only to look at the example of the security around Triple Crown Winner Gallant Fox at Saratoga during the summer of 1930.

Gallant Fox was set to run in the Travers Stakes about two weeks after Sun Mission was sponged. While "Sunny Jim" Fitzsimmons, the horse's trainer, was as friendly as could be and did not ban visitors from his barn, he did erect a five-foot-high fence around the entrance of Gallant Fox's stall to prevent anyone, including the horse's fans, from coming within eight feet of the champion. If that was not enough security, round the clock protection was provided in the form of special guards or detectives who were assigned to watch the horse, one during the day and two at night.[7] Despite the added security, Gallant Fox lost the Travers that year to 100-1 longshot Jim Dandy, but not because he was tampered with. Jim Dandy was just one of the longshots to win major races at the Spa, helping to earn Saratoga Race Course the name "The Graveyard of Champions."

Just two years after Sun Mission was tinkered with, another sensational case of horse sponging was heard in the City Court of Saratoga Springs. This time, a horse named Panetian was the victim.

On the morning of August 22, 1932, George Arvin, owner and trainer of Panetian arrived at his barn and discovered that the lock on his horse's stall had been broken overnight. It seemed that the offender had tried to replace the lock but botched the job. In addition, the vile intruder had left blood splattered throughout the stall. Arvin, of course, suspected foul play was afoot but could not detect any sign of Panetian having been touched.

Even though Panetian was the favored horse in the Burgomeister Handicap scheduled for later that day, Arvin jogged his horse around the Oklahoma training track and quickly discovered that the horse was breathing through only one nostril and soon started to bleed from the stopped-up side of his nose. The track veterinarian was summoned and was unable to initially remove the obstruction until, unfortunately, he was forced to push to object down through the nose and into the throat where it could be retrieved through the poor animal's mouth.

Panetian was scratched from the race, so the conspirators would have to earn their money that day on the level. But with no witnesses or leads, it seemed that the people responsible for the attack on poor Panetian might go unpunished.

All that changed a few days later when the track veterinarian, Dr. Clarence H. Richards, was approached on Lake Ave by Belmont Conn, an African- American stable hand employed by Arvin and one of only two people who had the combination to the lock on Panetian's stall. Conn told Dr. Richards he had kept quiet about the sponging out of fear that Arvin would fire him if he, Arvin, learned he had not spent the night at the stable as ordered. Dr. Richards convinced Conn to come clean and report what he knew. So, Belmont Conn told the following story to Pinkerton detectives.

The day before Panetian was to race, Conn was approached by a man that he knew only as "Jimmy," a white man who was a bookmaker at the track. Conn said that Jimmy had visited him several times in the week leading up to the race and that Jimmy had asked Conn to leave the stall door open an hour before the race so that the "boss man" could watch and that he (Conn) would be given a capsule to feed to Panetian that would not harm the horse but slow him enough to affect the outcome of the race. For his part in the plot, Conn was to be paid $500.

Conn told Jimmy to come back to the barn at eleven o'clock on the morning of the race. At that time, according to Conn, he would have Arvin with him and when the capsule was passed into the stall, Arvin could surprise the evildoers and capture them red-handed.

Unfortunately for Conn, he mentioned nothing about Jimmy when he was first questioned by Pinkerton men shortly after the crime. At the time he did tell the detectives about "Frenchy," another stable hand who also ran a handbook at the track and who had been seen looking for some mosquito netting on the night Panetian was sponged. The police and Pinkertons looked for "Frenchy" but were unable to locate any trace of him. He was last seen on the morning of the race Panetian was supposed to have run.

Conn was arrested. His changing story, along with his access to the horse, made him a prime suspect and perhaps some time in custody might help clarify the situation. On August 30, Belmont Conn went on trial in Saratoga Springs City Court and the case became less, not more, clear.

In the middle of his testimony about "Frenchy," a man walked into the courtroom. Conn glanced at him, stopped what he was saying and declared, "There's Frenchy now."

At that, the new arrival slipped quickly out the door, pursued hotly by Garrett Howard, an investigator with the American Society for the Prevention of Cruelty to Animals. Howard soon captured his prey and brought him back to the court. He was identified as Charles Sheridan, a racetrack follower who was, until then, unknown to track officials.

Because of the drama in the courtroom, Judge Hall ordered an adjournment of the case while "Frenchy" could be examined, and the authorities could continue the investigation in light of Frenchy's identification.[8]

While Sheridan, or Frenchy, never did help investigators get any closer to the truth, the original man who approached Conn was identified shortly after Sheridan's arrest. Perhaps Sheridan turned informer, or maybe not, but with some good detective work, "Jimmy" was identified as James Manning, alias Joseph Davis. He was located and held in New York City pending his delivery to Saratoga Springs to face charges.[9] In October, he was indicted, along with Belmont Conn, by the Saratoga County Grand Jury for the new felony of tampering with a racehorse.

That Panetian had been sponged was not in doubt. What was in doubt was the strength of the evidence against any of the three men linked to the crime. Frenchy had already been dismissed from the case by the time the case was ready for trial in February 1933, indicating he might have struck a deal to inform on his confederates. It was in that month that District Attorney John B. Smith was forced to abandon the case when he was unable to locate any of the prosecution's witnesses. Since no one had seen the crime (except for the perpetrator) and without any evidence to make a circumstantial case against the two defendants, the case had to be dropped.[10] Belmont Conn and James Manning walked free. Justice for Panetian was not to be had.

Sun Mission and Panetian were certainly not the only horses that were sponged either at Saratoga or at racetracks in other areas of the country but every once in a while, authorities were successful in stopping an attack before it was carried out. Such was the case when four no-account, would-be horse spongers were stopped by Saratoga Springs Police in 1935.

During the month of August 1935, the Pinkerton men were conducting a confidential investigation around the racetrack and notified the police to be on the look-out for four suspected gunmen. They were reported to be in town, driving a car with a license plate number of 1T-97-94 that was registered to a woman in Brooklyn.

On the night of August 29, around 2:00 a.m., Officer George "Moon" Smith was walking his beat along Congress Street when he spotted the car. Moon was a heavyweight wrestler and veteran law man and, although certainly brave, he must have had in his mind the warning from the Pinkertons that the men might be armed.

Furthermore, Officer Smith was surely aware of reports that the FBI's Public Enemy Number One, Alvin Karpis, had been in town only a few days prior. Karpis was suspected of leading a kidnapping ring in Minnesota and of mailing threatening letters to FBI

Director J. Edgar Hoover and, at the time, had been a fugitive for over a year. He later would join the infamous Ma Barker gang and has the distinction of serving the longest prison term in the notorious Alcatraz prison.

According to reports, Karpis had been hiding out at a farmhouse near Loughberry Lake and taking in the gambling scene at the track and nightclubs of Saratoga.[11] He had only just slipped a trap set for him by federal agents when Officer Smith approached the car on Congress Street.

So, presumably with gun drawn, "Moon" Smith warily approached the car full of men while a bystander went to call for assistance. Soon reinforcements rushed to Officer Smith's location and the suspected gunmen, George Negri, John Tafuri, Carmen Franzese, and Michael Napoletano were taken into custody.[12]

Assuming the men were armed, a thorough search of the automobile was undertaken. No guns were found; however, two small silk sponges and "Chinese Chopsticks" were recovered by the police. It seemed that the men in the car were not gunmen, but rather, horse spongers.

The men had a connection to a house at 39 Ash Street and their direction of travel at two o'clock in the morning certainly indicated that the men might have been stopped from sponging a horse.

They fit the profile of spongers who operated in teams at the behest of bookmakers or gangsters who often hired the thugs as a group. The men were often given large sums of money to infiltrate the stable area of the track with an eye towards bribery. If the offer of a few hundred dollars could not entice a barn worker to cooperate with fixing a race, the men would need to be prepared to do the dirty work themselves. In this case, as in the case of Panetian's sponging, the gang would take the further precaution of operating under the cover of darkness.

The case certainly was circumstantial. Negri had been under surveillance for a few weeks prior to the night in question and the others were known to the Pinkerton men as suspicious characters who tended to hang around the tracks. It was not, and is not, illegal to possess silk sponges and chopsticks while driving toward a racetrack in the middle of the night in a notorious area of town with the apparent intent to shove an obstruction up the breathing passage of a thoroughbred racehorse. Yet that is where the investigation stood.

So, after several hours of intense questioning without anyone admitting to actual intent, the four suspects were released by Chief of Police Rox with the assurance from the Pinkerton men that the hoodlums would not be allowed at any track where they were responsible for security. [13]

In addition to sponging, tampering with a racehorse may also take the form of doping. Doping, as the name suggests, is simply drugging a horse with the intent of affecting the performance of the animal. Sometimes a pill is slipped into the horse's feed, other times a needle placed into a vein will work, and on rare occasions, smoke or vapor will be the method of ingestion. No matter which method is chosen, the horse is helpless and will either run slower or faster than expected, depending upon which type of drug is administered. Anyone who knows that a horse has been drugged will obviously have an advantage when it comes time to place or accept a wager.

Probably the most famous doping of a horse at Saratoga occurred in 1931. A filly named Ladana was entered in the Burnt Hills Handicap on August 13. She had run very well earlier in the meet with a second-place finish in the Test Stakes and was sure to be one of the top finishers in the Burnt Hills Handicap, but another horse, Happy Scot, received a large amount of the betting despite her long odds.

As the horses were being saddled, Ladana's trainer, Frank Taylor, of the top shelf Rancocas Stable, noticed something wrong with his horse. She was frothing at the mouth, her jaw was swelling, and she had blisters around her lips. The track veterinarian gave a report to the stewards, who immediately scratched Ladana from the race. It was determined that Ladana had been given a dose of chloral approximately forty-five minutes before the race with the obvious intention of slowing her down.

Upon learning that Ladana was being scratched by the stewards, and the circumstances of what led to her disqualification, the bookmakers realized that a betting cleanup was planned and the unusual betting on Happy Scot was understood. Without Ladana in the race, Happy Scot had one less competitor. Ladana kept the odds for Happy Scot in favor of the player who knew Ladana would not run a good race that day. With Ladana pulled from the card, the bookmakers dropped Happy Scot's odds to even money and protected themselves from an obvious scam.[14] Happy Scot did indeed win the race, but the bettors who were looking for an advantage never did get the long odds they were hoping for before the plot was discovered.

No one was ever arrested for the poisoning of Ladana but trainer Taylor suspected one of his workers was involved in some way and fired him soon after the race. Taylor himself proved that he thought Ladana had a good chance of winning by showing that he had bet on his own horse to win the race. This was not good enough for track officials, however, and they suspended Taylor and the Rancocas Stable from entering any more horses in overnight races for the duration of the meet on the theory that stables are ultimately responsible for preventing such abuses as occurred with Ladana.[15] (An overnight race is a race in which entries are permitted up until a certain time before a race, for example 24 or 48 hours prior to post as opposed to stakes races where possible runners are named to the race well in advance.)

When another story about horse doping came to light in 1931, it captured the attention of racing fans and Saratogians alike. It was not so much because of the criminal activity that was alleged, but more because of the person whom the allegations were made against, namely, James "Jimmy" Meehan, not to be confused with "Jimmy" Manning, who doped Panetian.

Jimmy Meehan was an associate of Arnold Rothstein who, of course, was the legendary "grandfather" of modern organized crime. All the top gangsters of the day got their start working for Rothstein, otherwise known as "The Brain" or simply "A.R."

In *All the Law in the World Won't Stop Them*, this author documents Rothstein's escapades at the Spa. As far as gambling goes at Saratoga, Rothstein had a stake in the Arrowhead Inn and owned the Brook resort from 1919-1925. Rothstein associates ran a gambling joint at 210 South Broadway that was raided by the police in 1919, just a couple of months before the gamblers at that address went about fixing the 1919 World Series. When not conducting illegal gambling operations and paying off public officials for the pleasure of doing so, Rothstein did have a stable of horses at Saratoga and even won the 1921 Travers Stakes with his horse Sporting Blood.

Jimmy Meehan met The Brain in 1921 and soon was employed as Rothstein's "payoff man" around the racetracks, meaning that Meehan would square up accounts regarding Rothstein's bookmaking operations.[16] Not only was Meehan an employee of A.R., he was also a gangster in his own right and, at Saratoga, he was not unwilling to pull a robbery if he saw an opportunity.

One night in August, 1922, Jimmy Meehan was hanging around one of the gambling places near the lake. Being a Rothstein associate, he might have been at the Arrowhead. Soon enough, Meehan and a partner, John "Boob" Walker, spotted a man named Joseph Josephson, whom they felt provided a perfect target. Walker and Meehan might have seen Josephson winning big at the tables, or Josephson might not have been careful enough in concealing how much money he had in his possession. Either way, Walker and Meehan left the place about an hour before Josephson and set a trap.

When Josephson returned to his summer lodging at 125 George Street and stepped out of his car, he was confronted in the dark by a gunman who pointed a pistol at him and ordered Josephson to "stick them up."

Josephson did just that and, while one of the thugs covered him with the firearm, the other set about searching him, ultimately relieving Josephson of his wallet, which contained $650.[17] Walker and Meehan were released on bail the following day and nothing more was ever heard of the case, which was likely settled quietly, like so many cases were when real gangsters were involved, with or without the consent of the victim. Poor Joseph Josephson.

Although Meehan managed to stay out of the public eye for several years after his arrest in Saratoga, he burst back onto the scene in a big way when he was named as being involved with the murder of Arnold Rothstein in 1928.

During the night of November 4, 1928, a bellhop at the Park Central Hotel in New York City found Arnold Rothstein stumbling toward the service entrance holding his belly. Rothstein had been shot, and soon an ambulance was summoned. Rothstein survived until November 6 but never named his assassin before passing away.

The police soon picked up many men who were suspected of somehow being involved with the killing, which was typical of police action after a major crime in those days. They also gathered some pretty strong evidence against a man named George McManus, whose coat was left in the room where Rothstein had been shot.

The working theory of the police, supported by some good evidence, was that Rothstein was killed because he had welched on a large gambling debt that he incurred during a marathon card game with some pretty big spenders about a week before he was shot down. The location of the game where Rothstein ran up his debt was at the apartment of none other than Jimmy Meehan, the same Jimmy Meehan who robbed Joseph Josephson on George Street back in 1922.

Many gangsters tend to lay low after being involved in some sort of high profile event, like the murder of someone as prominent as Arnold Rothstein, but Meehan continued his gangster ways and in 1931 his name was splashed across the pages of the newspapers in New York City and Saratoga Springs once again when he was arrested as the leader of a gang that was accused of sponging and doping horses at New York racetracks.

Down in Nassau County two suspicious characters were arrested hanging about one of the racetracks, probably Belmont. When detained, the men, James Hartwell and Drummond Jackson, started talking. They told the police that they were part of a conspiracy to drug horses and had been doing so at the behest of Jimmy Meehan for the past two years.[18]

The duo claimed that they were paid $1500 by Meehan for each successful operation. Typically, Hartwell and Jackson would bribe a stable hand to allow them access to the targeted horse at precisely the right time before a race so the drugs could be administered and take effect during the race. If they were unable to bribe a stable hand, the duo would be forced to use the more difficult procedure of sponging, which they did on occasion, usually under the cover of night.

Hartwell and Jackson admitted to doping several horses, some of them at Saratoga. They adamantly denied doping Ladana at the Spa, however, and explained that it was such an amateur job that it made their work more difficult since trainers became more vigilant after the botched Ladana caper, whomever was responsible for that one.

As the case wound through the courts during the fall of 1931, Hartwell and Jackson were both convicted and sentenced to six months in jail. When it came time to deal with Jimmy Meehan though, the prosecution was unable to produce enough evidence to continue the case and the judge dismissed the charges against Meehan on a technicality.[19]

It seemed a miscarriage of justice at the time, but it might have been just as well. Authorities could not find Jimmy Meehan, who was out on bail, and he was never heard from again. Where he ended up, whether retired under an assumed name in Florida or at the bottom of a river wearing cement slippers, we may never know. But two things we might be able to say for certain: one, gangsters were definitely doping and sponging horses at Saratoga and two, if you meet a suspicious guy named "Jimmy" near the racetrack, don't go into business with him!

Any gangster looking to fix a horse race who does not want to take the chance of being seen doping or sponging a horse might simply decide to "paint" a horse. Painting a horse works like this: a fast runner is taken to a secluded area and its hair is dyed (painted) to match the color of a slow runner. The slow runner is entered into a race at long odds but is replaced by the fast runner. Of course, no one knowingly bets on a slow horse and when the slow runner suddenly wins the race, only the people who bet on the long shot make off with any money. Call the better if you know that the real horse is a ringer!

To the casual observer, one brown horse looks the same as any other brown horse. But to the people who work with horses every day and the stewards who are responsible for the integrity of the sport, it isn't easy to substitute a horse. Painting horses and substituting them into a race requires great skill and artistic talent, not the usual characteristics of a gun toting thug, but certainly the specialty of a man named .

Born in Scotland, Peter Christian Barrie first became known to racing authorities in England in 1920 when he and a group of confederates managed to win six races during the fall racing meeting at Stockton, England. He and six others purchased a three-year-old horse named Jazz and painted it to match a two-year-old colt named Coat of Mail.

With Jazz running against two-year-old horses as "Coat of Mail," they managed to win six races. When the jockey, who was not part of the conspiracy, at first found out he was riding a "ringer," Barrie reassured him, "It's all right; it's easy to do this."[20]

Unfortunately for Barrie and friends, the authorities figured out the scam and they were sentenced to seven years of hard labor. Upon his release from an English prison, Barrie made his way to Canada and painted horses all over that country. Needing to stay one step ahead of discovery, Barrie frequently changed his name and location. He went by Pat Wesley and Peter Christie and he was known to have run painted horses in Canada, Chicago, Miami, Baltimore, and Cuba. All the while, Peter Barrie associated with many of the top gamblers of the underworld and eventually he wound up in Saratoga Springs.

On August 15, 1934, the morning edition of the *Saratogian* newspaper boasted the following headline, "BARRIE HELD HERE AS RACE 'RINGER.'" Barrie and three co-conspirators were caught leading a horse named Easy Sailing from her stall in broad daylight, acting as if they had legitimately bought the horse. Pinkerton men, recognizing Barrie as being wanted on an immigration violation, quickly made an arrest and turned Barrie over to the Saratoga Springs Police.

Barrie had once painted two horses to match each other with such precision that he even filed down the teeth of each animal to ensure no detail was forgotten. The switch fooled race authorities and both horses were cleared to run as the other. This all happened at the Fort Erie Racetrack in Niagara Falls, Canada, just days before the Pinkertons caught up with him at Saratoga. Is it any wonder that Barrie was called the "cleverest track swindler" by the newspapers of the day?

In any event, at a hearing in Saratoga Springs City Court, Barrie was discharged on the grand larceny count. Since he did not actually purchase the horse and merely was taking possession of it, and since he had not had a chance to "paint" it yet, there simply was not enough evidence to hold him on any charge. Some interesting facts did come out of his court hearing, however.

Barrie made admissions that he had been hounded by the track authorities for a long time, telling Judge Labelle, "The Pinks were hard after me and if I stayed long in one place they might catch up. By changing my name I could go on again." He admitted to being involved in running a ringer at the Havre de Grace racecourse and to painting many horses in his day claiming, "If a man says to me 'I'll pay you $1,000 to paint my horse,' I'll take the thousand and I don't care where he runs the horse." He also told Judge Labelle that he was in the country illegally and had entered the United States four or five times without following the proper procedures.[21]

Glad to have captured the "cleverest track swindler," the Saratoga police were only too happy to allow Barrie to be photographed leaving his cell and to hold him for Immigration officials who were also quite gratified to end their years-long search for Peter Christian Barrie. He was deported to England[22] and lived the remainder of his life there in relative obscurity.

Doping, sponging, and painting horses were not the only types of trouble at the racetrack. Over the years there were a number of instances of crime and disorder that bear mention here, if only to serve as a reminder that criminal activity at the track was not limited to tampering with horses.

As early as 1875 it was recorded that John Morrissey, founder of the great racing venue, was seen roughly removing a drunk and disorderly patron from the hallowed grounds. Later Arnold Rothstein, although never proven, probably manipulated the odds of the 1921 Travers Stakes, won by his excellent colt, Sporting Blood.[23]

Sneak thieves, pickpockets, and scammers seemed to be attracted to Saratoga Springs and the historic track during the summer. The pickpockets were such a problem that a team of experienced detectives from the New York City Police Department were employed every year by the City of Saratoga Springs and assigned to the track to help deter, detect, and apprehend the sneak thieves.[24] Their presence was certainly a welcome addition to the local police force who had their hands full with the crowds and those who preyed on the unsuspecting during the tourist season.

Long time Saratoga Springs Police Chief Patrick Rox and a couple of Pinkerton men once discovered a couple of hustlers running a three-card-monte game at the back entrance to the track. When confronted, the men offered a short-lived resistance before being overpowered and charged with, "hanging around Wright St., having records, considered undesirables, and being three-card monte men."

The local newspaper described the activity this way, "Three-card monte is an illegal game in which its operators collect from 'suckers' who attempt to bet against them on cards the operators have turned down on small table or folding chair, or newspaper in front of them. The cards are so arranged as to make it impossible for the 'sucker' to win."

Both would-be con artists skipped bail and were never seen again by the Saratoga authorities.[25]

Imagine a man says to you, "If you give me a dollar, I will tell you the name of a horse that is sure to win the sixth race at Saratoga. I can assure you the horse will win because I have fixed the race." And if you gave that man a dollar in exchange for that tip, what would people say? Perhaps, "buyer beware!" or, "there's a sucker born every minute."

However, if you knew that gangsters tended to hang around the racetracks and you had heard of races being "fixed" in the past, it might not sound so far-fetched to believe someone could fix a race. One enterprising group of folks decided to take advantage of that belief and offered fake tips in a publication called the Daily Racing Tab. [26]

The group offered racing tips and insinuated that they could fix races, specifically the sixth race at Saratoga on August 23, 1935.[27] Using the fake name of Theodore Hayes as a front, the scammers claimed that they controlled several stables and jockeys and that they could fix any claiming race they desired. If you mailed a dollar to Mr. Hayes at a Saratoga Springs post office box, he would let you know the name of the "sure thing" and what race he would be running.

Over two thousand people decided it was worth the risk and sent Theodore Hayes a dollar. In return the unsuspecting victims got the name of Skipit who was scheduled to run in the sixth race on August 23. Of course, Skipit, who went off at odds of 6 to 1, finished fifth in the six-horse race, [28] the scam was uncovered, and since the alleged fixers had used the mail in furtherance of their scam, they found themselves on the wrong side of the law.

The fake tip sheet was just a small part of a massive racket that resulted in the indictment of 86 people across the state. The head of the state bureau charged with investigating monopolies and rackets called the scam "the biggest and most vicious being operated in the state" and involved racetracks in Saratoga, Nassau, Westchester, and Erie Counties.[29]

Although state officials, as well as racing representatives and fans, welcomed the effort to keep racing clean, no one ever spent any time in jail as a result of the fake racing tip racket. The most authorities ever obtained from the defendants were small fines. After all, "buyer beware."

Another scam discovered at the Saratoga Race Course involved people obtaining entry to the grounds without paying. The practice probably started as a courtesy to police and other public officials some time before the procedure was stopped in 1929.

Anyone who showed an official badge from the city or county would be granted entry without having to pay admission. However, in 1929, racetrack officials were estimating that up to 1500 persons were entering daily without paying and decided that they had had enough. After all, over one thousand people in the stands without paying admission was serious money. But over the years, not only had local officials been gaining entry to the track without paying, they started lending their badges to relatives and friends so that they too might enjoy the privilege.

So, on August 14, the Pinkertons were directed to turn away anyone found presenting a badge that did not belong to them with further instructions to seize the badges in question. At the end of the day the Pinkertons held over one hundred special officer badges issued by local officials. Those who had their badges seized were offered the opportunity to pay or leave, but no one was ever arrested, and the practice continued, only with much more discretion.[30]

One can give the racing industry the benefit of the doubt and assume that the vast majority of races over the course of history have been run on the level. It also goes without saying, supported by the facts, that Saratoga and the other racetracks attracted schemers and scammers of all types. They would make Saratoga their summer home, just as high society did each year. Police, no doubt, had their hands full and made an honorable effort to keep the track and the surroundings environs as crime free as they could, but clearly, both horses and trouble came to the track every year and Saratoga was all the more colorful for it.

Endnotes

Chapter 6

[1] "Horse Racing Revenue to State $10,397,000 for Biggest Year Yet." *The Saratogian.* November 16, 1942.

[2] Veitch, Greg. *All the Law in the World Won't Stop Them.* Shires Press, VT. 2017.

[3] "They Stand Out." *The Saratogian.* August 21, 1933.

[4] "Men Experienced in N.Y. Crime on Duty in Saratoga." *The Saratogian.* August 7, 1933.

[5] "Captain Duhain, Noted Detective, Dies in New York." *The Saratogian.* January 14, 1936.

[6] "'Sponger' of Racehorse Here Gets 90-Day Jail Term." *The Saratogian.* August 1, 1930.

[7] "Gallant Fox is Well Guarded in Saratoga Stall." *The Saratogian.* August 4, 1930.

[8] "Missing Sponging Witness Makes Stage Entrance." *The Saratogian.* August 30, 1932.

[9] "New Arrest in Sponging Case." *The Saratogian.* September 20, 1932.

[10] "Dunn Trial." *The Saratogian.* February 20, 1933.

[11] "Saratoga County Gangster Inquiry Asked of Lehman." *The Saratogian.* August 29, 1935.

[12] "Arrest of Four May Have Averted Horse Sponging." *The Saratogian.* August 29, 1935.

[13] "Horse Sponging Suspects are Allowed to Go." *The Saratogian.* August 30, 1935.

[14] "Down the Stretch." *The Saratogian*. August 14, 1931.

[15] "Down the Stretch." *The Saratogian*. August 17, 1931.

[16] "Rothstein Friend Held as Race Fixer." *The New York Times*. October 11, 1931.

[17] "Hold-Up Men Get $650 From Roomer in George Street." *The Saratogian*. August 15, 1922.

[18] "Rothstein Friend Held as Race Fixer." *The New York Times*. October 11, 1931.

[19] "Meehan Freed of Conspiracy to Dope Horses." *Long Island Daily Press*. December 23, 1931.

[20] "Scandal on Turf Shocks the British." *The Brooklyn Daily Eagle*. October 10, 1920.

[21] "Has Painted Many Horses for $1000 Each, Says Barrie." *The Saratogian*. August 18, 1934.

[22] "Barrie Ordered Deported" The New York Times. October 24, 1934.

[23] Veitch, Greg...

[24] "Detectives Recalled Early from Saratoga Track." *The New York Times*. August 27, 1925.

[25] "Police Chief Raids 3-Card Monte Game." *The Saratogian*. August 4, 1941.

[26] "Nab 3 More in Tipster Racket." *The Saratogian*. December 4, 1935.

[27] "Indictment of 'Tipster' Sought." *The Saratogian*. October 30, 1935.

[28] "'One Born Every Minute.'" *The Saratogian*. October 7, 1935.

[29] "Indict 86 and Arrest Two in The Race Tip Investigation." *The Saratogian*. December 3, 1935.

[30] "Special Officer Badges Seized at Racetrack." *The Saratogian*. August 14, 1929.

Chapter 7

A Gangster's Paradise

Saratoga Springs had always been an open town. Gambling was a part of the fabric of the village long before John Morrissey arrived and built the race track in 1863. Corruption ran deep in Saratoga Springs. The police and politicians had an inexhaustible appetite for graft and their blatant cooperation with the gamblers and gangsters over the years would shock the conscience of any law-abiding citizen today.

Without the financial influx during the summer months, though, Saratoga Springs might well have disappeared from the map. The residents of Saratoga Springs certainly understood that, and if the very existence of the town meant holding their collective noses while the more unseemly elements of the underworld went about their rotten business at the Spa, then so be it.

While there was by no means unanimous support for the likes of Rothstein, Lasky, Luciano, Adonis, Costello, etc., by and large the citizens of Saratoga Springs elected and supported men like Doc Leonard, Doc Farone, and Jim Leary, knowing full well what they were getting. And while the local authorities got what they wanted, namely power and money, all manner of hoodlums also got what they wanted at Saratoga, namely, a wide-open town. A "Gangsters Paradise," if you will.

We turn our attention now to the various tales of the gangsters at Saratoga that do not merit a stand-alone chapter in this book. We'll try to move through this period chronologically, but the time lines may not always line up cleanly. Sometimes the story is merely a recounting of a specific crime. Sometimes there is a violent encounter between gangsters. Others are merely curious footnotes to the overall theme of Saratoga being a haven for criminals and ne'er-do-wells.

Students of organized crime will recognize many of the names, and Saratogians may recognize some of the places. All should recognize that these stories, while not condoned, help add to the fabric of Saratoga's incredible history.

As we have seen, after the Heffernan investigation, Saratoga Springs Public Safety Commissioner John Sweeney and Chief of Police John Armstrong made an honest attempt to keep the rising tide of crime in check. One of their more impressive successes was the discovery and prevention of one of the most elaborate gambling scams ever devised in Saratoga.

On August 14, 1930, Chief Armstrong and five New York City detectives on loan from the New York City Police Department raided a hotel room and arrested three conmen with national reputations for elaborate schemes.[1]

Herbert Cokes, Earnest Woods (a.k.a. N.K. Pumphrey), and Frederick Callahan were busted in a raid at one of the prominent hotels on Broadway after a lengthy surveillance. The trio had run the same scam on unsuspecting wealthy victims in at least 23 cities across the country. That they were brought to justice in Saratoga Springs was certainly a feather in Chief Armstrong's cap. The scheme was executed in the following manner.

Coke's newlywed wife, said to be exceptionally beautiful, charming, and capable of penetrating any social circle, would lure a wealthy mark into the company of the three con artists. They would then bring the victim back to a hotel that had been prepared in advance for the ruse.

Adjoining rooms were obtained. In one room, a card table was set up. The spot for the unsuspecting player was arranged so that the player's back was toward the wall of the adjacent room. A hole was drilled between the two rooms, placed behind and above the 'sucker.' This peep hole was expertly blended into the wallpaper in such a manner that it was almost undetectable. From this vantage point the spotter could look down onto the cards held by the prey.

Next to the dealer, a cardboard box was placed with the side of the box facing the dealer cut out and a series of fifty-two lights arranged so that only the dealer could see them when lit. The lights indicated which cards were held by the prey and were activated by the spotter through a wire run between the rooms under the rugs. Once the dealer was aware of the cards held by the mark, it was relatively easy to manipulate the outcome of each hand.

Each of the men arrested were bona-fide criminals. Cokes and his wife were the typical scam artists. He, exuding confidence, but with a pleasing demeanor, and she, the beautiful temptress.

Together they were successful in enticing risk-taking wealthy young men into a little card game.

Despite his ability to schmooze his marks, Cokes was once charged, and then acquitted by reason of self-defense, of killing the police chief in Hot Springs, Arkansas, his hometown and, like Saratoga Springs, New York, a notoriously corrupt city where all kinds of felons and Mafia associates liked to hang-out.[2]

Woods, based in Chicago, admitted to City Court Judge Hall that he had been arrested all over the country for gambling and once was charged with possession of a gun down south. It was he who was considered by the police as the mastermind of the plot and he claimed that the scam had been pulled throughout the United States.

Callahan was known by authorities as a master con man who plied his trade for many years on the steamships that crisscrossed the Atlantic. It was said that Callahan lost $1,700 in a card game a few nights prior to the raid. It was a loss, the police believed, that helped to "set up" the mark for another game with even bigger stakes.

The raid was big news. It is always interesting when new and brilliant criminal activity is uncovered by authorities. In Saratoga Springs, not only did the highest levels of American society come for the summer, but so too did the highest levels of the criminal element. Adding to the interest of this particular scheme, however, was that a local man, well known for his gambling and liquor interests in Saratoga and upstate New York, posted bail for two of the con men.

Louis J. "Doc" Farone posted $3,000 cash bail for Cokes and Woods while James Fennell (another Saratoga based gambler) posted bail for Callahan. [3] The posting of bail was not so unusual but the fact that "Doc" Farone was posting bail for an out-of-towner would certainly have raised the eyebrows of anyone paying attention. While posting bail for Cokes did not indicate that Farone was involved in or approved of the scam, it did indicate a certain connection to and, ominously, cooperation between local and national criminal interests.

As prohibition neared an end, it seemed that gangsters had the run of the place in Saratoga. Despite the best efforts of Chief Armstrong and Commissioner Sweeney, there were just too many criminals running around Saratoga Springs. Not only did the local police have to deal with significant organized crime figures, they also had the run-of-the-mill police work that needed to get done.

For example, on a single day in August, 1930, police arrested a man wanted in Atlantic City for running a fake gem scheme, two taxi drivers who got into a fist fight over a fare at Fasig Tipton, and two women on Jefferson Street who were arrested for disturbing the peace. Police raided a shanty, demolished it, and arrested seven men who were found inside it, and finally, as if all that wasn't enough police work, they hauled in twenty vagrants on various charges.[4] All in a single day!

In that same month a motorcycle officer found an abandoned car on South Broadway. He checked the license plate number and received no information that the auto was wanted for anything, so he left it there overnight, figuring the day shift officers could have it towed if the owner didn't come back for it.

The day shift did have the car removed and that same morning they took a report that a car was stolen on Congress Street. At first the two incidents did not seem to be linked but within a couple of days the car that was dumped on South Broadway was linked to an Albany murder that had occurred the evening before the motorcycle officer discovered the car on South Broadway.

A man named Carlo Baggatta had been gunned down on an Albany street in a drive-by gangland shooting.

Putting two and two together, police surmised that the mafia gunmen responsible for the Baggatta killing had traveled to Saratoga looking for a safe haven. They apparently found it on Congress Street or somewhere in the nearby Italian neighborhood, spending the night and stealing the car the following morning.

The Baggatta slaying was never solved and the stolen Saratoga car was never recovered.

Saratogians were getting used to headlines referring to gang wars and violence. On August 11, 1930, the good citizens of Saratoga awoke to a headline in their local paper that read, "Dominick, Taken for a Ride, He Says, Has Knife Wound." The article starts with this: "Gang war, said to involve some of the more prominent of the racketeers in the city, blazed last night in Beekman Street, and as a result, Joseph (Crazy Joe) Dominick, 42 Beekman Street, is in a serious condition at his home today with a stiletto wound..."

Dominick told police that he had been the victim of the "revenue racket." The revenue racket was the general term used for the various scams and robberies pulled by fake prohibition agents. Using fake badges and sometimes fake warrants, hoodlums would "raid" speakeasies or other liquor joints and either rob the owner or demand a payoff.

If the fake agents thought that the victim would believe they were legitimate law enforcement, there would be no need for violence. Since so many prohibition agents and law enforcement officers were, in fact, corrupt at this time in American jurisprudence history, it was not all that difficult to convince the owner of a speakeasy that a payoff was in order.

On the other hand, the more hardened criminals would look to use their fake badges to gain a momentary advantage while making the "raid," planning to overcome any resistance before the victim realized what was happening.

Crazy Joe explained to the authorities that he had been the victim of some fake revenue agents and had been "taken for a ride." Dominick reported that his place was approached by a couple of men who ordered him out of his Beekman Street speakeasy at gunpoint. He said that he thought about making a run for it but was told by his abductors that there were two more men, positioned at either end of the block, holding tommy guns and blocking any escape route.

Dominick was hustled into a waiting car and driven out Washington Street past West Avenue where he was ordered out of the car and robbed of $280. Once relieved of his money, Dominick said the men took up positions, one in front and one behind him. Dominick, inferring that he knew his assailants, thought they were going to give him a knife and fight it out. Instead, the man in front lunged at him and slashed his forehead. As he grappled with thug number one, thug number two stabbed him from behind.

Just then, one of the gang yelled to his friends to not hit Dominick with the knife again as there was a car approaching. The men then jumped back into their car and drove off. Dominick staggered back towards town, was picked up by a passing motorist and brought to the hospital. Crazy Joe ignored doctor's orders to stay in the hospital to rest, and instead went home.

Now all this was according to Joseph (Crazy Joe) Dominick, and police fanned out through the City's west side looking for the men Dominick described. The assumption of the police and the newspapers was that Dominick was the victim of a budding gang war between rival factions in Saratoga. But soon enough, the story changed.

The day after the story ran in the papers, a man named Norman Ellis, a racetrack hand, presented himself at police headquarters and admitted that it was he who had stabbed Crazy Joe Dominick the night before. Only in Ellis' tale, he was the one taken for a ride by Dominick and some of his pals.

According to Ellis, he was walking along a street that he could not recall the name of (he was after all, from Georgia) when a sedan pulled up next to him and he was forced into the automobile by several men.

Ellis claimed that he was driven out Washington Street to a dark place beyond West Ave where he was ordered out of the car. When Dominick pulled a gun and attempted to rob him, Ellis knocked the gun from Dominick's hand, pulled a knife and hit Dominick twice, once in the head and then in his side. Ellis then bolted for the woods nearby and made his escape. [5]

Ellis was even able to identify Dominick's four pals who he claimed were in the car Garage: Natale (17), George Martino (17), and Angelo Martino (25), were all charged with attempted robbery.

When the West Side friends appeared in court the next day, the courtroom was packed with supporters. Derossi's case was moved from the adult to the juvenile court but the remaining defendants, who all lived within a few blocks of each other (Dominick on Beekman St., Natale on Elm St., and the Martino brothers on Walnut St.), faced judge Andrew Hall.

But rather than hearing a charge of attempted robbery read in court, the charges had been downgraded overnight to "annoying and interfering" with Ellis and using vile language and threats against him.[6]

It appears that the charges were later dropped as no record of conviction could be found by this author. It very well may have been that Ellis, as a track worker, left town before the case was prepared for court and therefore prosecutors were unable to produce any witnesses or other evidence against Dominick and company. Or, it could have been a case of everyone just dropping the matter because things like this just seemed to happen from time to time. Or, this was Saratoga, and justice had an apparently different definition here than it did elsewhere.

Crazy Joe Dominick and his crew were local toughs. The west side of Saratoga Springs in those days was a tough place. Congress Street, Beekman Street, and Searing's Alley were notorious for vice, crime, violence, and disorder. But Saratoga Springs attracted big-time mob bosses as well. They didn't always make headlines or ply their trade while in Saratoga, sometimes they just visited.

Take Waxey Gordon and his associates as an example. His real name was Irving Wexler and he rose to become one of the most prominent gangsters of his era.

Waxey began his criminal career as a pickpocket in New York City, partnering with Monk Eastman. He spent time in and out of jail for various crimes like robbery, theft, extortion, and involvement in the labor rackets in New York, Philadelphia, and Boston.[7]

As Prohibition approached, Waxey made his move to the upper levels of the gangland hierarchy when he teamed up with a St. Louis gangster named Max "Big Maxey" Greenberg. With Arnold Rothstein backing their operation, Waxey Gordon and Big Maxey Greenberg imported liquor from England and made a fortune.

Not only did they smuggle liquor into the country as fast as they could, they started taking over territory outside of New York. Waxey Gordon set his sights on the New Jersey beer trade and soon had control of most of the state's liquor business, not because he had better beer or out worked the New Jersey folks, he just started killing them off until his monopoly was secure.

Like Rothstein, Waxey soon transitioned to drug smuggling in addition to all his other criminal endeavors.[8] His smuggling empire was making him more money than he knew what to do with.

Unfortunately, he made so much money that Waxey found himself in the sights of the crusading District Attorney Thomas Dewey, who recognized that Waxey Gordon was the New York version of Al Capone. An exceptionally wealthy gangster who didn't pay taxes.

While Dewey set to work trying to put Waxey Gordon in jail for evading the tax statute, Meyer Lansky and Bugsy Seigel decided that they wanted a larger piece of Waxey's empire. Perhaps they saw weakness in Gordon, or they were anticipating a time when Waxey would be sent off to jail, but in any event, the gangsters were soon shooting and killing each other in what was called the "Jew War" by the newspapers of the day.[9]

The streets of New York were running red with the blood of organized crime soldiers in 1933. Gordon men, fighting off the uprising by Lansky and Seigel, needed a place to find a little rest and relaxation.

Now, a question for you, where does a gang of organized criminals go if it is looking for a vacation? The answer is: the same place everyone else goes, Saratoga Springs, NY.

During the summer of 1933, Gordon's men rented a house on Union Ave and stayed for the summer while the lower level Mafiosi were left to shoot it out in the heat down in the metro New York area. Chief of Police Rox confirmed that the police were aware of the presence of the gang and added that men from the

State Police and Department of Justice were also aware of the vacationers and that law enforcement had been keeping tabs on them while they were in Saratoga.

And just what were these vacationing hoodlums doing at the Spa? Why, according to Chief Rox, "They laid low, didn't attempt to pull anything, played golf a little, and generally conducted themselves as anyone would."[10]

The gang stayed a while past the close of the racing season and left town just a few days before reporters started asking questions about their presence in the Spa City. Two of Waxey Gordon's lieutenants were confirmed to have been in town during the summer and their names were certainly known to the general citizenry at that time.

Chief Rox and the newspaper reporters both acknowledged that Irving Bitz and Salvatore Spitale were in Saratoga during the summer of 1933. Bitz and Spitale were perhaps the most well-known gangsters in the country in 1933, not because of their criminal exploits, or because they had been named by authorities as the top men of any one gang, but rather because they had been appointed by Charles Lindbergh as his go between for anyone in the underworld who had information on the kidnapping of his son the previous year.

Bitz and Spitale were chosen because of their reputation for being "straight shooters" despite their criminal histories.[11]

Beginning with their work for Arnold Rothstein (doesn't it seem that all these gangsters started out working for the Brain?), Irving Bitz and Salvy Spitale partnered up and had a relatively successful criminal career. Spitale became a pretty sizeable drug runner and it was said that Bitz took a pinch for Spitale on a drug charge and was promoted to partner upon his release from prison.[12]

Salvy Spitale once shot a cop and probably fingered Charles "Vannie" Higgins for underworld assassins. He and Bitz were also the two men whom Legs Diamond fingered as the men who had beaten and shot him in the Monticello Hotel in 1931. (Diamond had told this to a reporter who swore to keep the secret until after Legs was dead.)

Legs Diamond was killed in a boarding house in Albany in December 1931, a crime that Spitale and Bitz were also rumored to have carried out. The rubout of Diamond may have been the result of his failure to return $250,000 that Bitz and Spitale had given to him to complete a narcotics deal in Europe that failed to materialize.

When little Charles Lindbergh Jr. was kidnapped on March 1, 1932, the entire nation and the world became enthralled with the investigation. While the facts of the kidnapping, investigation, mysterious ransom drops, and the eventual discovery of the boy's deceased body is beyond the scope of this work, it is mentioned here because Bitz and Spitale were just two of the long line of hoodlums that made Saratoga their summer homes.

Another gangland duo that used to "take the cure" at Saratoga, Louis "Lepke" Buchalter and Jacob "Gurrah" Shapiro, started in the Monk Eastman gang in New York City and eventually became charter members of Murder, Inc.

Lepke and Gurrah took over the "Little Augie" Oren gang after he was assassinated and his bodyguard (Legs Diamond) was wounded. Together they became masters of the labor rackets, not only through extortion, but through infiltrating and taking over the unions from the inside. Expert bootleggers, drug traffickers, extortionists, and murderers, Lepke and Gurrah were the most dangerous gangsters in the United States between 1927 and 1936, as both District Attorney Thomas Dewey and FBI Director J. Edgar Hoover agreed.[13]

The partners had multiple arrests between them but few convictions until their estimated five-million-dollars-per-year empire attracted the attention of the aforementioned lawmen, Dewey and Hoover. Soon Lepke and Gurrah found themselves indicted for drug trafficking and violating antitrust laws.

Jacob Gurrah Shapiro was sentenced to life in prison. Louis Lepke Buchalter, on the other hand, escaped conviction for any murders committed by mob hit squad he headed in the early 1930's), but was instead convicted for gunning down a candy store owner during a gang shooting in New York City and was executed by "Old Sparky" at Sing Sing Prison on March 4, 1944.[14]

Lepke and Gurrah were no doubt dangerous men who vacationed in Saratoga, but they never were formally named "Public Enemy Number 1" by the FBI. That distinction belongs to just four men.

The first man to earn the title of the FBI's Public Enemy Number 1 was John Dillinger. When Dillinger was gunned down by FBI agents in Chicago, Pretty Boy Floyd became the next man to assume the crown. When he was shot and killed by law enforcement, (it is not clear if it was local police or FBI men who did the shooting), Baby Face Nelson became the FBI's top target. Eventually Baby Face Nelson also succumbed to FBI bullets near Chicago but not before he took out two FBI agents in the process. Next up on the Public Enemy Number 1 docket was Alvin Karpis.

Born Alvin Francis Karpavicius in Montreal of Lithuanian parents, Alvin "Creepy" Karpis escaped the fate of the previous three Public Enemy Number Ones as he was captured by the FBI in New Orleans. He holds the record for the most days spent inside Alcatraz Prison.

According to the FBI, Karpis was a leader of the Barker/Karpis gang that robbed banks and trains and completed two kidnappings for ransom in the Midwest in the early 1930's. In the age of the bank robber/gangster, the FBI chased down and killed many of the famous criminals, as we have seen.

After the Barker/Karpis gang kidnapped two wealthy businessmen in St. Paul, MN, the FBI moved the gang to the top of their list. Eventually they captured one of the Barker brothers, then traced a second Barker (Fred) to Florida where agents surrounded the hideout where Fred was staying with his mother, Ma Barker. After some tear gas and gunshots on both sides, Ma and Fred were found dead inside the house. Karpis was the lone member of the gang who remained at large from 1934 through 1936, when he was captured in New Orleans.

While he was on the run, Karpis apparently spent some time in Saratoga Springs. The reader would be forgiven if the first thought upon reading that sentence was, "well of course he did." The record of gangland visitors to the Spa leads to no other assumption.

As reported in the August 29, 1935, edition of the *Saratogian*, yet another good government group was calling for a state investigation into conditions at the summer resort. This time, the National Crime Prevention League called upon Governor Lehman to investigate whether or not underworld figures had been allowed to operate "without fear or interference" in Saratoga during the racing meet.

The request of the National Crime Prevention League, it was noted, came close on the heels of rumors floating through the village that Alvin Karpis had spent three days in Saratoga, visiting the racetrack and carrying on as if he had not a care in the world. In fact, he managed to lose a good amount of money with the bookies during his stay in upstate New York, according to reports.

Of course, there was no official acknowledgement from law enforcement as it was noted by the *Saratogian* reporters that, "Karpis had been traced to a farmhouse on nearby Loughberry Lake, but disappeared six hours before a federal raid..."[15]

Lending credence to the rumors swirling around the nightclubs at the time was the fact that one of Karpis' associates, a man named William Elmer Meade, who had been with Karpis during one of the St. Paul kidnappings, had slipped through the fingers of Northampton, MA, police just a few days earlier and that after Karpis left Saratoga he had been tracked to Boston and Providence. Clearly it was plausible that Karpis was in the northeast United States and, since he had come this far, can we doubt that he paid a visit to the Spa like his peers?

While the location of the Karpis refuge near Loughberry Lake was never identified, he can be added to the list of fugitives and hooligans who made Saratoga their summer home.

Charles "Lucky" Luciano deserves special mention here. He probably came to Saratoga Springs for the first time when he was a young thug working for Arnold Rothstein at the Brook. By the time he was convicted of prostitution related crimes in 1936 and later deported, Luciano had risen to become head of the so-called Genovese Crime Family in New York.

A killer, bootlegger, hijacker, and peddler of all manner of vice, Luciano was a true gangster. He had been arrested over thirty times during his criminal career but was only convicted of one drug offense when he was young, and the aforementioned prostitution conviction in 1936.

During his trial on the prostitution charge, it was brought out that Luciano had a hand in the Chicago Club in Saratoga and that his partner and front man for the upstate operation was none other than James Leary, (although Leary was never charged). Luciano was sentenced to 30-50 years for the prostitution charge, deported to Italy, and years later, when asked what he planned to do if he ever got out, Luciano said, "I'll follow the horses from Saratoga to Belmont to Florida to California."[16]

At Saratoga, Luciano's Chicago Club contained one craps table, two roulette wheels, a bird cage, and a horse room where a staff of three men took bets on the races. Once the horses left town, so did Luciano, and the Chicago Club was left in the capable hands of locals Gus DeMatteo and Matty Byrnes.

Although some have questioned the validity of the book, *The Last Testament of Lucky Luciano*, the authors, Martin Gosch and Richard Hammer, quote Lucky as saying, "It was kind of a joke. There we was in

Saratoga, the tables goin' full steam, the money right out in the open, and nobody doin' nothin' to stop it." And, "In the daytime, Governor Lehman's whole crime staff was screamin' about gamblin,' the underworld, and how we all ought to be closed down. But at night, those same crime-busters was in Saratoga, gamblin' like everybody else."

While Luciano seemed to keep the more unsavory and violent of his tendencies under control at Saratoga, he nevertheless adds his name to the roster of gangsters who have taken a piece of the pie at Saratoga over the years. He collapsed and died at the Naples Airport in 1962.[17] The Chicago Club was razed during an Urban Renewal project and now a Bank of America stands on the site of Luciano's gambling den.

Before we allow ourselves to believe that only the men of the underworld found Saratoga a desirable locale, let us turn our attention to a couple of ladies who were involved with the criminal element during the gangsterism era, Vivian Gordon and Polly Adler.

As a "woman of many acquaintances," Vivian Gordon was well known in gangland circles. She ran gambling dens, scams, and brothels and often lent money to gangland figures. She was murdered in New York City in 1931 and one theory of her murder was that she had financed some shady underworld ventures and threatened to turn in her associates if they didn't pay her back.[18] The investigation into her death was followed closely by Governor Rockefeller and ultimately led to the downfall of New York City Mayor Jimmy Walker. Mrs. Gordon was a regular visitor to Saratoga during the summers and was often, "seen about the streets of Saratoga Springs in an attractive riding habit."[19] The location of the place she kept in Saratoga is unknown to the author. After all, her profession did call for secrecy.

Polly Adler, a friend of Ms. Gordon's and another frequent visitor to the Spa, once had her brothel on Union Ave closed down by the local police.[20] She was Dutch Shultz' favorite madame and we can assume the two would associate both in New York City and the City of Saratoga Springs.

One final gangster story is of note here. At about 5:30 a.m. on January 19, 1932, a car sped up to the front of the Saratoga Hospital and deposited a young man on the lawn before driving off at a high rate of speed.

The young man, Courtney Deitz of Albany, had four bullet holes in his legs but managed to crawl himself up to the front door of the hospital and get the attention of the duty nurse manning the front entrance.

While Doctors George Comstock and Robert Harrington began patching up the holes in Deitz, police were notified and soon Police Chief Patrick Rox and Detective Sergeant Hugh Dorsey arrived to begin the investigation.[21]

According to Dietz, he was a taxi driver from Albany. Around midnight, he was approached by two men who engaged him to bring them to Schenectady.

Upon arriving in Schenectady, the men told Dietz to continue on to Ballston Spa where, according to Dietz, the men asked him to stop the car just north of the village, on Route 50.

The men alighted from the car and walked up a driveway. Dietz waited and when the men returned at a run, he claimed they jumped back in the car and put a gun to his side while ordering the taximan to "Drive like hell!"

Dietz obliged and drove away rapidly. As he tore off towards Saratoga, he noticed a large dark sedan following him, gaining all the while. Before he knew it, Dietz's fares were firing their pistols at their pursuers and their enemies were returning fire. The running gun battle continued as Deitz turned left onto West Ave from Ballston Ave, fleeing the armed men chasing him and his two customers.

Deitz explained to the police that, as the gun battle raged along West Ave., he felt his legs going numb and he eventually ditched the car at the side of the road after turning west onto Washington Street. Deitz said his passengers escaped by fleeing on hands and knees into the scrub brush adjacent to the road.

Just then, two men drove up, took Deitz's coat and wrapped his legs (surely to keep his blood from dripping into their car), bundled him into the back seat and, apparently being familiar with the streets of Saratoga Springs, drove him directly to the hospital where they laid him on the front lawn and sped off.

Deitz never did reveal the identity of his fares and, once he was done telling his tale of the night's events, the police immediately cast doubt on his story.

To begin with, the car was recovered and the many bullet holes on all sides of the car did not match up with the wounds suffered by Deitz. Only one bullet that penetrated the car might have struck the driver's lower legs. Second, both doctors were of the opinion that Deitz had bled for a considerable amount of time, perhaps for as many as three hours before he arrived at the hospital, casting doubt on his timeline of events.

Third, police searched the area where Deitz claimed his fares had fled into the brush. There was a barbed wire fence along the road at that spot and there was no blood trail into the woods, even though there were clearly blood drops around Deitz's car that indicated others, in addition to Deitz, had been shot and jumped from the car where it was ditched.

Fourth, a patch of fur from a woman's coat had been found on the car and the rear seat cushion had been removed. Deitz never mentioned a woman being in the car and the removal of the backseat cushion was typical of rum runners moving liquor in passenger cars. The whole Deitz story was dubbed a "cock-and-bull" affair by police [22] and soon some rather coincidental facts were learned that cast further doubt on Deitz's account of the entire incident.

The simple explanation for the shooting might be that Deitz was a rum runner who had been hijacked.

The missing rear seat cushion might indicate this and as we have already seen, the Church Street - Washington Street - West Ave corridor was used as an alternative route by bootleggers to avoid the traditional Bootleg Trail along Route 9. Maybe Deitz was simply held up, shot, and decided he did not want to involve the police in the matter. But why then did Deitz try to give such a wild cover story to police? Was the shooting a more complex gangland episode?

Courtney Deitz was an employee of the Albany taxi company used by Jack "Legs" Diamond on the night of the gangster's own murder in Albany one month prior to Deitz being shot near Saratoga. On the night that Legs Diamond was shot in a rooming house in Albany (December 18, 1931) the company that Deitz worked for brought Diamond to meet his mistress, Marion "Kiki" Roberts. It was that taxi company that drove Diamond from his secret rendezvous with Kiki back to the boarding house where he was shot and killed.

About a week or two before Deitz was shot, two suspicious men, passing themselves off as Pinkerton Detectives, were stopped by the Ballston Spa Police Chief in that village with a rifle and machine gun in the rear of their vehicle. They were looking for Kiki Roberts, who was reported to hiding out in Ballston Spa after the murder of her lover.

The Pinkerton men said that it wasn't safe for Kiki Roberts to return to New York City and she had taken refuge in the Ballston Spa area at the home of a man named Scott Morris, who lived just outside Ballston Spa in Factory Village. The men claimed they were in town to find Ms. Roberts and ensure her safety.[23]

That enemies of Legs Diamond would be looking for Kiki Roberts is not outside the realm of possibility. Perhaps they would have liked to get information from her about Diamond's operations or any secret stash of weapons, booze, or cash he might have had. Or, Diamond allies might have been looking to kill Kiki Roberts in order to make sure she kept quiet about what she might have learned from her paramour, like they killed Diamond's wife, presumably for talking too much about things better left unspoken. Either way, being Legs Diamond's girlfriend would certainly have put Kiki in a tenuous position after his death. Could it have been a portion of Kiki Robert's coat that was found in Deitz's car?

One more bit of information came out in the press that indicated there might have been more to the story than Deitz told. At 11:30 P.M. on the night before Deitz was dumped at the hospital, residents of Ballston Spa reported hearing a running gun battle throughout the streets of their village. Two cars had apparently engaged in a shootout along South Street, Maple Ave, and through Factory Village. Police speculated that the supposed Pinkerton men were involved and that, if they could be identified, Deitz would finger them for the gunmen who shot him.

But alas, Deitz never gave up any names. Kiki Roberts disappeared, and the shooting remained unsolved. Was the Deitz shooting a simple robbery gone wrong? Who were the people who brought him to the steps of the Saratoga Hospital? Were Diamond associates involved in the affair? Was Kiki Roberts nearly rubbed out that night? All are questions that have never been answered.

While Deitz's story is certainly interesting, at best, it is a minor footnote in the story of organized crime in the United States. Even the press and public in Saratoga didn't seem too interested in the story, as it quickly faded from the pages of the newspapers and Courtney Deitz faded back to the streets of Albany. Perhaps, as prohibition was coming to a close, people thought of the Deitz shooting as just another case of gangsters shooting other gangsters and were used to the almost casual violence of the era.

Whatever the case, Saratoga Springs had almost certainly become a gangster's paradise and, four years later, another man would be shot and dumped at the steps of the Saratoga Hospital. This time though, the man would die, and the papers would not soon forget this shooting episode.

Endnotes

Chapter 7

[1] "Elaborate Layout in Hotel Room for Fleecing 'Suckers.'" *The Saratogian*. August 14, 1930.

[2] "Charged with Confidence Game Here." *The Saratogian*. August 26, 1930.

[3] Bail Furnished for Two Alleged Confidence Men." *The Saratogian*. August 16, 1930.

[4] "Arrest Here in Atlantic City Fake Gem Case." *The Saratogian*. August 11, 1930.

[5] "New Picture of Dominick's 'Ride' Given to Police." *The Saratogian*. August 12, 1930.

[6] "Must Sue on Bad Check According to Court Ruling." *The Saratogian*. August 13, 1930.

[7] Downey, Patrick. *Gangster City: The History of the New York Underworld 1900-1935*. Barricade Books.

[8] Abadinsky, Howard. *Organized Crime*.

[9] Downey, Patrick....

[10] "'Waxey Gordon Gang had Hideout on Union Ave.'" *The Saratogian*. October 6, 1933.

[11] "Lindbergh's Appeals for Baby Fail." *The Saratogian*. March 7, 1932.

[12] Downey, Patrick...

[13] "Lepke a Gang Leader who liked his privacy." *The New York Times*. August 31, 1939.

[14] Downey, Patrick....

[15] "Saratoga Gangster Inquiry Asked of Lehman." *The Saratogian*. August 29, 1932.

[16] Newark, Tim. *Lucky Luciano: The Real and the Fake Gangster*. Thomas Dunne Books, New York. 2010.

[17] Ibid.

[18] "Vivian Gordon Left Only $200 Estate." *The New York Times*. August 11, 1931.

[19] "Vivian Gordon and Polly Adler Both Known Here." *The Saratogian*. March 9, 1931.

[20] Ibid.

[21] "Gunmen Battle on Saratoga Outskirts." *The Saratogian*. January 19, 1932.

[22] Ibid.

[23] "Try to Connect Strangers with Dietz Shooting." *The Saratogian*. January 21, 1932.

In the early days of Prohibition, A.J. "Charlie Blues" Patneaud was the top rum runner in Saratoga Springs. Near this spot, on Church Street where the railroad tracks crossed the street, Patneaud was hijacked while delivering a load of liquor and soon enough, Louis "Doc" Farone became "King of the Bootleggers" in Saratoga and beyond.

Photo Courtesy of the Collection of the Saratoga Springs City Historian.

In 1930, Police arrested three men for running an elaborate scam at one of the fashionable hotels along Broadway. The victim had been lured to a fixed card game where the con men had cut a small hole in the wall behind the unsuspecting gambler and signaled the dealer what cards he held through a system of lights concealed on the dealer's side of the table. Police took this photo of the evidence on the pool table that was kept in the police station for the entertainment of the officers during down time.

Photo Courtesy of the George S. Bolster Collection of the Saratoga Springs History Museum.

During Prohibition liquor flowed south from Montreal along today's State Route 9. Called the "Bootleg Trail" or "Rum Trail," the route was plagued by gunplay and hijackings. The trail ran right through Saratoga Springs along this road, today's Maple Ave near the police station. At center is the American Hotel, where the City Center stands today. All the buildings on the right are gone. At top left the top corner of the Algonquin Building can be seen.

Photo courtesy of the Collection of the Saratoga Springs City Historian.

In 1936, Adam Parillo was shot and dumped at the Saratoga Hospital, shown above. Parillo had only recently been released from a Canadian prison when he was killed on the streets of Saratoga Springs. Was he murdered by a local gunman, or did the Canadian mafia wait fourteen years to get revenge on Parillo, a squealer?

Photo courtesy of the Collection of the Saratoga Springs City Historian.

In 1934 notorious horse painter, Peter Narrie was captured in Saratoga Springs. Internationally known as a man who could doctor the appearance of any horse down to the smallest detail, Narrie was used by the mafia to substitute horses and clean up at the betting windows. He is seen here being led out of his cell at the Saratoga Springs Police Station by Chief Patrick Rox.

Photo courtesy of the George S. Bolster Collection of the Saratoga Springs History Museum.

The New York City Police Department sent the Saratoga Springs Police a photo album of criminals to be on the lookout for during the summer months. Among the rouge's gallery was this photo of Joseph Doto (alias Joe Adonis) who had a piece of the Piping Rock Club and was seen nightly dining at the famous nightclub. He never seemed to pay a bill for his meals.

Photo courtesy of National Archives.

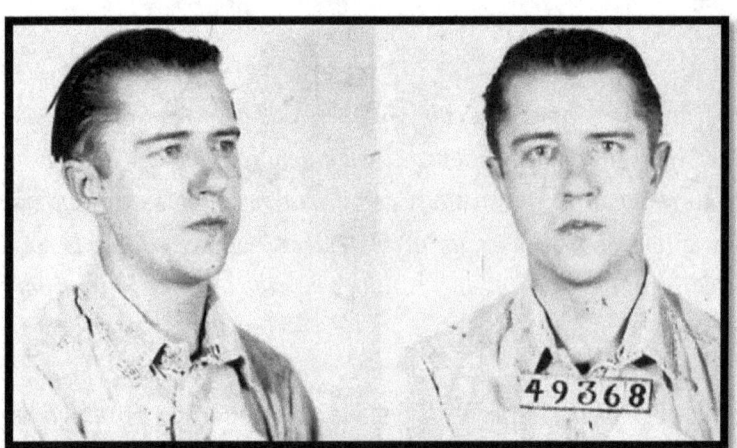

Alvin Karpis, once the FBI's Public Enemy No. 1, visited Saratoga while he was on the run from Hoover's G-Men. He hid out at a farmhouse near Loughberry Lake and slipped a trap set for him by federal agents.

Photo courtesy of the National Archives.

Over the years the Arrowhead Inn played host to such national entertainers such as Sophie Tucker, Bing Crosby and Sammy Davis Jr. National gangsters connected to the Arrowhead at one time or another were: Arnold Rothstein, Joe Adonis, Meyer Lansky, and Lefty Clark of Detroit's infamous Purple Gang.

Photo courtesy of the George S. Bolster Collection of the Saratoga Springs History Museum.

Riley's was a well known casino and nightclub overlooking Lake Lonely. In 1926 it was the scene of a shootout between a night watchman and a young thug named Anthony "Little Augie Pisano" Carfano. An associate of Lucky Luciano, Joe Adonis and Al Capone, Carfano had a stable of horses at Saratoga and was gunned down near Laguardia Airport in 1959.

Photo credit: Saratoga Springs History Museum.

Located on Union Avenue near Gilbert Road, the Piping Rock Club was the crown jewel for the mafia in Saratoga Springs. Joe Adonis, Frank Costello and Meyer Lansky all took a cut of the gambling profits at the Piping Rock. The building burned to the ground in 1954.

Photo Credit: Saratoga Springs History Museum.

Chapter 8

Gang Guns Slay Parillo

On December 9, 1936, Mrs. Marjorie Gunn was working the night shift as the assistant night supervisor at the Saratoga Hospital. Just before 5:20 a.m., she heard two cars blowing their horns outside the main door of the hospital before they sped away, out Myrtle Street. All was quiet again until Mrs. Gunn heard a pounding at the door. Startled, because she was usually able to hear people approaching the door,

Mrs. Gunn looked out and saw a man standing at the door pleading, "Help me, help me."

Thinking it was "just another drunk," the nurse called for an orderly and soon Asa Stewart arrived to help out with the "drunk."[1]

But when they opened the door, it was discovered that the man had slumped to the ground and needed to be helped up. Upon doing so, the hospital employees quickly realized the man was in dire straits. He had left a trail of blood droplets on the steps leading to the door and had been shot a handful of times.

As they carried the victim through the hallway, no doubt frantically calling for a doctor, they probably did not know that they were trying to save the life of a notorious criminal who had recently been released from a Canadian prison. They surely would not have known that they were in the opening act of a drama that was to capture the attention of the entire city and become the most famous unsolved crime in the history of Saratoga Springs, the murder of Adam Parillo.

As Dr. G. Scott Towne began treatment of Parillo, the police were notified, and Sergeant Burt Wakeman ordered Officers Theodore Winship and William Lucas to go to the hospital and begin the investigation. When the two officers entered the operating room, they immediately attempted to get any statement they could. Parillo was dying and they needed to know from him where to start looking for the shooter or shooters.

Winship leaned in and asked, "Who shot you Eff?"

"Effie" or "Eff," as Parillo was known around Saratoga, muttered something that couldn't quite be made out. Officer Winship moved even closer and asked again, "Who shot you Eff?

Parillo responded, just a little more clearly this time, "S-o-n-n-y P-o-m-p-a-y."

The two officers knew that finding Parillo full of lead would be a big deal and it can be assumed that they would have known that Chief of Police Rox would be headed their way any minute to take personal charge of the investigation. But in the meantime, the two officers dutifully tried to get more information and asked Effie where he was shot and if he was shot in a house. The questioning was in vain, as Parillo died of his wounds before he answered the additional questions, roughly thirty minutes after he had been half-dragged into the hospital by Mrs. Gunn and Orderly Stewart. He made no other recorded statements regarding the person, or persons, who shot him.

By now Chief Rox had arrived at the hospital and he sent Officer Winship to the police station where he filled in Sergeant Wakeman, before heading over to Jackson Street where he was to pick up Anthony "Sonny" Pompay.

When Officer Winship first arrived at 69 Jackson Street, he found the home dark. He had a few other duties to take care of, namely, to turn on the traffic lights along Broadway, and when he was done with that task, he returned to Pompay's home and found Pompay's car backed into the driveway. The lights of the car were still on, so the officer reached in and turned them off. He then looked up and saw Pompay, silhouetted in a second-floor window, wearing a coat as if he had just arrived home.

The time was about 7:30 in the morning, roughly two hours after Parillo had died of "lead poisoning." Officer Winship managed to bring Pompay back to headquarters without any trouble, where the two men met Chief Rox.

Chief Rox knew who Anthony "Sonny" Pompay was. Since it was well known that the Chief and Louis "Doc" Farone had a close relationship, there was no doubt that Chief Rox would have known that "Sonny" was a high-ranking member of the Farone outfit and that he had certainly been involved in the liquor business during prohibition, among other questionable activities. The reader should also be familiar with "Sonny" Pompay from the gun play back in 1931 as detailed in a previous chapter.

In the interrogation room Chief Rox got right to the point:

Pompay: "What do you want?"

Chief Rox: "I want you."

Pompay: "What for?"

Chief Rox: "For shooting Adam Parillo."

Pompay: "Is he dead? Who shot him?"

Chief Rox: "He says you did."

Pompay: "He's full of shit."[2]

The interrogation produced nothing more of any value.

Before we get too far along in the story of the murder of Adam Parillo, perhaps we should take a moment to examine the life of the man who was gunned down that cold December morning in 1936.

Adam Parillo was born in Saratoga Springs, NY, on November 27, 1896. His parents, Joseph and Ornella Parillo, were Italian immigrants, both having been born in Italy around 1860. The Parillos (Adam had two sisters) lived most of their lives around the West Side of Saratoga Springs. 66 Beekman Street, 66 South Franklin Street, and 21 ½ Marvin Street were all family homes at one time or another.

Adam was at one time married to a woman named Mary, but she is rarely mentioned in the newspaper accounts of his life, mostly because Adam only ever made news by either being arrested or because he was serving as a pallbearer for one unfortunate soul or another. He never really had a profession other than crime, and to say he was a bad egg from the very start is probably not an exaggeration.

Adam Parillo first came to the attention of the Saratoga Springs police when, as a lad of only ten or twelve, he was snatched up by the beat officer for intoxication.[3] He was adjudicated a truant in his teen years and sent to a reformatory in the western part of New York State. It was at this time that it is likely that Parillo started hanging around with more serious criminals and where he probably met a man named Stone, Harry, an international drug smuggler from the Buffalo area who will figure prominently further along in this story.

In 1918, Parillo had his first serious brush with the law. Now twenty-five years old, Parillo was hanging around Buffalo, NY, with a man named Thomas Siff. In June of that year, the two friends were riding in a car along Main Street in Buffalo when they were stopped by police. Whether they were stopped for some minor traffic offense, or they had been ratted on by an informant, the police soon discovered Parillo and Siff were transporting a significant load of drugs. All told, the two traffickers had in their possession heroin, morphine, codeine, and other drugs valued at $1,500.[4] For comparison, the value of drugs Parillo had at that time would be worth about $25,000 in the year 2018.

Parillo was sentenced to two years at Clinton Prison in Dannemora, NY. He served about a year before being released on parole, at which time Parillo returned home to Saratoga Springs. Having apparently not learned his lesson, Parillo managed to make himself a nuisance and get himself labeled a gangster by the local authorities and press.

He was so grateful to be home that he decided to heap so much verbal abuse upon his father (his mother had died in 1918) that poor Joseph eventually had him arrested for using vile and abusive language at the family home on Beekman Street.[5] Only a few months later, Parillo was picked up again by the police, this time for fighting with Thomas Smaldone and Tony LaCoppa in the middle of Beekman Street.[6]

Those offenses were child's-play, though, and on one Monday evening in late September 1919, Adam Parillo teamed up with Paul Farone and burst into 102 Congress Street, the residence of one James Paletto, and robbed him of seventy-five dollars.

Now, Paletto was no choirboy himself. A proprietor of several eateries on Congress Street, including the Turf Inn, Paletto's criminal history included violating the alcohol laws, carrying a weapon, assault, and compounding a felony. On more than one occasion he was found beaten and robbed and he was once stabbed.

In 1918, the Troy police found Paletto staggering toward one of their precinct houses, sliced from his ear to his chin, the so-called "Squealer's Gash," because of the propensity of the Italian mafia in those days to inflict such a wound on informants. Paletto though, never did squeal on his assailants in Troy, NY, and asked only to be returned to Saratoga.[7]

Detective George Mason was assigned to investigate the robbery at 102 Congress Street and made the arrests of Parillo and Farone. But when it came time for court, Mason was unable to produce Paletto to testify. It seems that between the date of the crime and the arraignments of Parillo and Farone, Paletto had agreed with the accused to drop all charges in exchange for the return of his seventy-five dollars.[8]

Without the cooperation of the victim and the only witness, the case was doomed. Detective Mason, and probably everyone else who knew about the case, understood from the beginning that this was how it would go. Paletto might have gotten his money back (unlikely) or he might have just gotten scared by the reputation of the two thugs (more likely). But either way, Parillo and Farone escaped this charge.

As a curious historical footnote, while they escaped criminal responsibility for the robbery, both Farone and Parillo shared the same ultimate fate.

On New Year's Eve, 1928, Paul Farone was found dead. He had been shot fourteen times and dumped from a car near Bargaintown, NJ. At the time, police blamed gang warfare for the death and theorized that Farone had been shot somewhere else before being dumped on the side of the road in South New Jersey. His body went unidentified for four days until his fingerprints were matched through his criminal record.[9]

Parillo had his parole revoked as a result of his involvement in the robbery, and he was sent back to Dannemora Prison. Eventually Parillo was transferred to Comstock Prison where he finished out his stint on the parole violation (he still owed time for the original drug charges) before he was released in the early part of 1921, back to Saratoga Springs where he was reunited with his wife, Mary.

As they say, a leopard doesn't change his spots, and Adam Parillo proved the old adage true.

On April 11, 1921, Adam Parillo, Frank "Funny" Dominick, and Gus "Gasoline" DeMatteo, along with two others, broke into the home of Paul Tabbano at 43 Mulberry Street in Mechanicville, NY. The gang robbed Tabbano at gunpoint of $600 that Tabbano had recently withdrawn from the bank.[10]

Poor Tabbano had withdrawn the money so that he could fund his journey back to his Italian homeland. Instead, Adam Parillo and friends made off with his money. Later, when Tabbano failed to identify Parillo or Dominick in court, the two friends escaped a prison sentence.[11] Gus DeMatteo and the others received relatively light sentences.

Next up on Adam Parillo's criminal schedule was a break-in at 35 Caroline Street, the general store of one Frank Garant. On the night of July 14, 1921, Adam Parillo teamed up once again with his nefarious friends, Gus DeMatteo and Frank Dominick, for a little criminal fun. This time they were joined by Gus' brother Louis "Dynamite" DeMatteo.

Well after Frank Garant had closed his store for the night, the four men paid a visit to the building and quickly broke in. They stole 9 X 12 rugs worth about $2500 and brought them to Schenectady, where they sold them to a couple of fences, Ralph Caputo and William Perris. Before long, however, Detective Mason managed to track down the rugs and arrested the Schenectady men, who in turn provided information about the Saratoga gangsters.

The Saratoga boys had been involved in many crimes in and around Saratoga Springs and as far away as Burlington, VT. In addition to the Garant burglary and the Mechanicville robbery mentioned already, the DeMatteo brothers and Dominick had been indicted around the same time in Warren County for highway robbery. [12] Dominick and Louis "Doc" Farone partnered in a robbery behind the railroad depot in Saratoga shortly after the Garant theft, where they were accused of beating and robbing Mr. Herbert Kilberry.[13] And within a year Louis DeMatteo, with fellow Saratogians Ceylon Delorenze and Miss Winifred McNeary, were arrested for burglarizing the Central Vermont Railroad freight station in Burlington.[14]

As the group of Caroline Street burglars was being rounded up, police recovered much evidence. Several stolen winter coats, stolen phonographs, a quantity of opium along with a smoking pipe, ten gallons of alcohol, and stolen government seals used to certify alcohol and other regulated products were seized from the men.

Witnesses who lived at 15 South Center Street and at the Naples Restaurant in Schenectady were able to identify a couple of the Saratoga men, but the case was falling apart and what looked like solid evidence against the entire group soon turned into a solid case, only against the men from Schenectady and Gus DeMatteo. Parillo, Dominick, and Louis DeMatteo were released from custody (Parillo on $20,000 bail) while the court case was being heard.

Gus DeMatteo eventually received a sentence of two to six years in prison for his part in the Garant Store burglary and at his sentencing the judge told him, "You have been mixed up in almost everything under the sun. You have been known as one of a gang that exists in Saratoga Springs and which must be cleaned up."[15]

The sentencing of Gus DeMatteo certainly did not clean up the gang, though. In fact, Parillo escaped any penalty for the Garant Store affair and he was free to continue his criminal career. But before we get back to recounting Parillo's exploits, one bit of information about the Garant burglary needs to be mentioned, if only to reassure the reader that the "Saratoga Way" permeated nearly everything in those days.

The police officer on whose beat the Garant Store was located on the night of July 14, 1921, was Genaro Pompay. Pompay had checked the business at midnight and found it all secure, later reporting the break in at 2:00 a.m. From the author's previous work, *All the Law in the World Won't Stop Them,* one might recognize the name Genora Pompay as having been arrested by the Saratoga Springs Police in 1919 for gambling, along with Paul Smaldone and the DeMatteo brothers, the same DeMatteo brothers suspected of the Garant burglary. The gambling charge had not yet been resolved at the time Officer Pompay was walking his beat on the night in question in 1921. And, yes, if you recognized that Officer Pompay has the same last name as "Sonny," the man accused of murdering Adam Parillo (also one of the Garant accused) and wondered if they were related, the answer is yes, they were brothers.

Let's try to put that more succinctly. In 1919, Genora Pompay was arrested for gambling. While the gambling charge was still pending, Genora Pompay was appointed to the police force. On his beat, a store was broken into by two of his co-defendants on the gambling charge. Years later, his brother was accused of killing yet another of the co-defendants in the burglary on his beat. You can be assured that this is a true story because this writer is admittedly not creative enough to come up with that series of coincidences on his own.

For those interested in the history of fires in Saratoga Springs, 35 Caroline Street was part of the Kearney Block between Pavilion Row and Henry Street. As reported in the April 12, 1955, edition of the *Saratogian,* the building burned to the ground, killing all seven members of the Abeel family that lived on the top floor of the three-story structure, and a ten-year old visitor of one of the Abeel children. Today the location is the Union Coachworks auto body shop.

Since Parillo managed to escape any serious consequences for either the Mechanicville robbery or the Garant burglary, he was free to continue his rough and tumble ways. He did not disappoint. A few months after the Garant store crime, Parillo celebrated Christmas by getting thoroughly drunk at five o'clock in the morning and pulling a pistol on Officer James Donohue, who had moved to arrest Parillo for his drunk and disorderly condition on Broadway. While there were several witnesses to the altercation, none of them agreed to testify and the authorities had to settle for charging Parillo with the minor charge of public intoxication.[16]

By now though, Parillo's parole officer must have had just about enough of Adam Parillo and his antics. He might beat criminal charges when witnesses failed to testify against him, but pulling a gun on a law enforcement officer was probably the straw that broke the camel's back and Parillo still had almost two years left on his sentence for trafficking drugs out in Buffalo back in 1919. So Parillo was sent back to prison, as evidenced by a lack of reported criminal arrests in 1922 and 1923.

Now, Parillo's drug sentence would only hold him so long, and eventually he was released. A rough estimate of the original sentence would put his release date sometime in late 1923 or very early in 1924. He was certainly out of prison by February 6, 1924, because we have yet another example of Adam Parillo's ability to find trouble.

On that night, Parillo was at a craps game in the basement of the New Commercial Garage, at a place called the Dugout. The New Commercial Garage was at the corner of Church Street and Woodlawn Ave (today it is a Stewart's Shop). The garage and Dugout were operated by a man named Thomas Leonard and, if the name Leonard sounds familiar, he was the brother of Public Safety Commissioner Dr. Arthur Leonard. No commentary is necessary regarding that last bit of information.

Around midnight, Parillo was one of the players in the game. After one roll of the dice, a dispute arose about the result. A heated Parillo pulled a gun (hopefully not the same gun he pulled on Officer Donohue in 1921) and pointed it at another participant. Men started diving for cover, but one brave soul knocked the gun down as Parillo pulled the trigger. A single shot was discharged, and one can imagine the bedlam that ensued.

The altercation moved from the basement, up the spiral staircase, and spilled out into the street. By now, Parillo had either been disarmed or had put the gun back in his pocket, but he was getting the worst of the fight until Officer Stevens arrived on the scene. The presence of just one officer was not enough to stop the brawl over the tossing of dice, and the disorder continued until Officer Stone arrived to assist his fellow officer.

By the time the two lawmen managed to get Parillo under control, the other participants in the brawl had dispersed, although witnesses did see Officer Stevens place Parillo under arrest and walk him down to police headquarters where, it was assumed, Parillo would be charged with firing the shot and fighting with both the patrons of the Dugout and the police.

But alas, according to the local newspaper, while Parillo was being held in the police station, a call was received from the "commish" and Parillo was soon a free man again. The fact that Parillo was a political supporter of Dr. Leonard or that the altercation started in the place of business of the Public Safety Commissioner's brother, may or may not, have played any role in his release…

The headline of the story of the event in the *Saratogian* on February 4, 1924, said it all, "Fight Started in Leonard's Place by Paroled Convict, Bystanders Say, No Arrests."

After the dust-up at the Dugout, Parillo's crime record in Saratoga Springs dried up. He did manage to stay out of trouble for about two months and during that time he traveled to Montreal, where he hooked up with some high-level mafia figures and committed what was considered at the time the "crime of the century" in Canada.

The crime was so daring and exceptional that it is still recognized as one of the great Canadian crime stories and is included in the Canadian crime anthology, *The Desperate Ones: Forgotten Canadian Outlaws* by Edward Butts, and was covered extensively by the *Montreal Gazette*, the *New York Times*, and the *Saratogian*, all of which are relied upon here to give a general overview of the incident.

On Friday, April 1, 1924, employees of the Banque d'Hochelaga were finishing up collecting deposits from the various bank branches in the eastern sections of Montreal, Canada. In all, the bank messengers had collected over $200,000 and were making their way back to the central bank when they approached a railroad underpass on Ontario Street East, just west of Moreau Street.

Unbeknownst to the bank employees, a vicious group of bandits, including Adam Parillo, had positioned themselves for an ambush in the tunnel under the railroad tracks. They had staged two stolen cars in the tunnel under the railroad tracks, one to appear as if it had a flat tire, and the other used to block the path of the bank machines. They also cut the electrical trolley car wires above so that no unexpected streetcars would interfere with their plan, and once the bank car entered the tunnel, members of the gang pulled a long heavy chain across the road so that no other cars could enter the ambush zone and their prey could not escape by reversing direction.

As the bank messengers entered the tunnel, the trap was sprung. The gangsters blocked the road with one of the stolen cars, set the heavy chain across the road, and opened fire on the bank employees as soon as the money laden vehicle came to a stop.

Henri Cleroux, the driver of the bank car, recognized immediately that they were in serious trouble. Four to eight masked men were closing in, firing as they approached. Three other bank employees were with Cleroux, who attempted to speed away, but the bank car stalled, and the money men were sitting ducks. Cleroux leapt from the driver's seat and tried to run for help while his fellow workers pulled their revolvers and returned fire.

Cleroux was struck by a bullet almost as soon as he exited the car and his ill-fated dash to get assistance ended after about ten feet where he fell, dead, in the middle of Ontario Street East. With shotguns, rifles, and semi-automatic pistols, the gang fired dozens of rounds at the bank men, who continued firing back until they were out of ammunition and were forced to surrender.

Holding Cleroux's friends at gunpoint, the gang started grabbing the money from the banker's bullet riddled car. While transferring the money bags from the bank car to their stolen getaway vehicle, the bandits suddenly came under fire from above. A Canadian Pacific Railroad constable, A. Chaput, was checking the tracks over Ontario Street East when he heard the commotion below.

Chaput's firing drew the attention of the gangsters, who returned fire. That gunfire drew the attention of nearby officers of the Montreal Police Department, one of whom was motorcycle officer Israel Pelletier. Dropping his motorcycle near the fallen Cleroux, Officer Pelletier joined in the shooting. He managed to hit one of the gangsters, who was dragged (or crawled) into the escape car.

Along with Pelletier and Chaput, the gang was now under fire from a second Montreal PD officer who arrived at about the same time as Pelletier, and with police reinforcements now swarming to the scene, the hijacking team made a hasty dash for freedom, pursued by Pelletier and another motor officer. In their haste, they had left behind several of the money bags and made off with only about half of what was being transported, $142,000.

As they fled, the gangsters continued to shoot at the pursuing MPD officers and eventually the police lost them on the congested streets of Montreal's Villeray neighborhood.

About twenty minutes after the tunnel shootout, police found the getaway car overturned at the intersection of Everett Street and Christopher Columbus Avenue. It had struck a telephone pole and overturned. Underneath the vehicle, the police found the man Officer Pelletier had shot, one Harry Stone.

The discovery of Stone's body was the first sign that this robbery was no run-of-the-mill local stick-up. Stone was an internationally known drug smuggler with over a dozen aliases, who once had the tip of his finger shot off during a shootout with police.

In 1921 he had been arrested, attempting to smuggle nearly half a million dollars into the United States at Massena, NY, and had escaped from both the Port Arthur Prison in Ontario and the Federal Penitentiary in Atlanta. While on the run after his escape from the Atlanta prison, he fled to England where Scotland Yard put so much pressure on him he slipped back into Canada and was still wanted by police, basically in every region of the United States and Canada, when he was shot by Officer Pelletier.[17]

A phone number was located in Stone's pocket which led police to the home of Giuseppe Serafini and his wife Mary. When police arrived at the Serafini home, they found the Serafinis along with an Italian national, Ciro Nieri, a low-level soldier in Frank Gambino's crime family. All three were taken into custody and interrogated.

Nieri quickly decided that cooperation with the Montreal authorities was in his best interest and he told the police everything he knew about the crime. He struck an immunity deal and sang like a bird.

In addition to Adam Parillo, the deceased Stone, himself, and the Serafinis, Nieri named each of the other conspirators. The group raised eyebrows in the law enforcement communities in two countries and captured the attention of the public throughout America and Canada.

The group included the top figures in the Montreal Mafia: Tony "The King" Frank and Frank Gambino. Tony Frank had contacts and influence with the Montreal police and elected officials. He was known as a political fixer and often bribed his way out of criminal charges and secured the release of many of his associates through extra-legal means.

Frank Gambino had a long criminal history in Canada that included charges of kidnapping and murder. Gambino's organization provided manpower and weapons to the robbery conspiracy.

Louis Morel, said to be the mastermind of the robbery plot, was a champion amateur athlete and former Montreal Police Detective who was thrown off the force when he tried to start a union. He turned to dealing drugs and was suspected of the killing of a Canadian baseball player over a drug debt. Butts indicates that Morel's motivation was to dig himself out of a financial hole he was in due to his drinking and gambling.

Mike Valentino, another member of the gang and high-level Mafia member, had a long criminal history and, at the time of the Montreal hold-up, was wanted in Detroit, MI, on two counts of armed robbery.

Two men, Salvatore Arena and Joseph Carreri, were hired muscle belonging to the Frank Gambino organization, while the final member of the group was Leo Davis, a small man from New Jersey whose specialty was stealing cars.

The day after the robbery, only Nieri and the Serafinis were in custody. Mary Serafini's part in the robbery was that she and another female accomplice (possibly Nieri's girlfriend) were strategically placed blocks from the scene where they waited for the passing getaway car to hand off the money and weapons in the event that the men were stopped before they reached the safe house. The other members of the group were placed under surveillance and the police planned to sweep them all up once the whereabouts of each of the principals was known.

Nieri placed Parillo inside the tunnel and told authorities that the Saratogian was one of the shooters, maybe even the one who fired the fatal shot at Cleroux with a .45 handgun provided by Mike Valentino. This claim was backed up by Louis Morel.

Unlike the Canadian gangsters who were relying on Tony Frank's connections to get them off, Parillo did not stick around Montreal. He fled back to America, but was tracked to Bridgeport, CT, where he was arrested for the Montreal robbery on May 6, 1924.

The Bridgeport cops had been looking for Parillo since a letter to his wife, Mary, was found in one of the stolen cars associated with the robbery. Mary's brother lived in Bridgeport and she might have been staying with him while Parillo made his trip to Canada. By carelessly leaving the letter in one of the cars used in the conspiracy, the robbers gave the Bridgeport police a location to watch and soon they had established a twenty-four-hour surveillance of Parillo's brother-in-law's house.

Parillo was not caught at the Bridgeport home of his wife's brother, rather he purchased a new car with the proceeds of the robbery and was tracked through the license plate to the business district in Bridgeport where Bridgeport PD officers stopped and arrested him. When they took Parillo into custody, he was found with nearly $9,000 in Canadian cash and a couple thousand dollars of jewelry.[18]

Adam Parillo was soon extradited to Montreal where he followed Nieri's lead and testified against his confederates for the Crown. Salvatore Arena also struck a deal and testified for the prosecution.

Justice in 1924 Montreal moved swiftly. The defendants were all tried together and, by June, they had all been found guilty. Death sentences were handed down against Morel, Gambino, Frank,

Valentino, Serafini, and Davis. Valentino and Davis later had their sentences commuted to life in prison.

Parillo pled guilty to manslaughter and received a life sentence. At his sentencing, Judge Wilson had this to say:

"I do not know what words will touch your heart or your soul. You have apparently been a participant in all manner of crime, and the Crown has been placed in the unenviable position and under the hard necessity of compromising the deal in order to convict your accomplices. You turned King's evidence, or in the parlance of your world, you "squealed." You sacrificed the liberty and even the lives of your confreres to save your own skin. The very least that can be said about you is that you were an active participant in this abominable crime. You knew and understood all that was done, and all that was going to be done. Four of your accomplices have paid their debt to society with their lives, and very largely by your hand... I will now pronounce sentence upon you. You will pass the rest of your life in the penitentiary."[19]

Of the other informers in the case, Ciro Nieri was deported to Italy after giving his testimony, while Salvatore Arena skipped bail and soon disappeared, later turning up in New York City.

Joe Carreri skipped bail and fled to San Francisco. He was identified many years later, returned to Montreal, and was eventually tried but acquitted of all charges. Likewise, Mary Serafini was also acquitted.

Parillo was sent to the St. Vincent de Paul prison, just north of Montreal in Laval, Quebec, where he remained for the next twelve years while Morel, Gambino, Frank, and Serafini kept their date with the hangman and were executed on October 24, 1924, at the Bordeaux Prison in Quebec.

How Adam Parillo from Saratoga Springs got mixed up with the top men in the Canadian Mafia is not known. Perhaps he met one or two of the men while in prison for the drug trafficking charge back in 1919. Harry Stone might be the connection, the theory being that he and Parillo knew each other through the drug trade while both were operating in western New York at about the same time.

It is interesting to note that while Parillo was never considered to be anything other than a street level gangster in Saratoga Springs, while researching the crime, this author found a few references in Canadian based sources that considered Parillo as a major Mafia figure from New York who was thought to be part of the "Board of Directors" of the Montreal underworld.

The robbery was in 1924, certainly during the wild days of prohibition, and there is the possibility that Parillo's Saratoga underworld contacts might have put him in the same circles with international criminals such as Arnold Rothstein and therefore expanded his criminal horizons. Maybe he hooked up with Lucky Luciano or Meyer Lansky in the early 1920's while they were just starting to come into their own as international gangsters. In any event, Adam Parillo, Saratoga native and notorious criminal, found himself in a Canadian prison for all of his thirties.

Parillo was released from prison in late August 1936 and returned to Saratoga Springs. He did not attract too much attention, although rumors throughout the City were that Parillo might have been attempting to muscle in on some local racket and that he had been involved in a hold up of some local men shortly before he was shot and dumped at the hospital. Parillo also reportedly flashed a .45 caliber pistol (could it have been the same gun given to him by Valentino in Montreal?) but was never charged and police never found the weapon.[20] By December 9 he was dead and "Sonny" Pompay was being held in connection with the murder.

Here we return to Police Headquarters where Sonny is being interviewed by Chief Rox and Assistant District Attorney John F. Doyle:

Pompay: "He's full of ----." (One printed curse word per chapter is the limit)

The Chief and Assistant District Attorney got no further. By 1:00 p.m. the Assistant District Attorney and the Police Chief announced that they had no clues in the case, but Pompay would continue to be held as a material witness.

In all, Sonny Pompay was held for thirty-six hours. He never made a confession. While in the Saratoga Springs lock-up, Pompay was allowed visitors. His lawyer and family members visited him and provided him with blankets and a pillow. He was finally released on $10,000 bail as a material witness when Assistant District Attorney Doyle admitted that the state was not prepared to file a charge of murder against anyone after two days of investigation.

Doyle did state on the record that Parillo had named Pompay as his assailant and the possibility existed that charges against Pompay could still be brought. Pompay's lawyer did not object to the bail and stated that his client was eager to clear away any suspicion that he was involved in gunning down Parillo.[21]

Police truly were not getting anywhere. Reports of gunshots on Broadway and in the area of Jackson Street were deemed to be unfounded after being looked into by Detective Charles Ballou.[22] Chief Rox called in the new forensics unit of the New York State Police to help with the physical examination of the bullets recovered from Parillo's body as well as the tablecloth Parillo was clutching when found. The presence of the tablecloth was the reason that Officer Winship had asked Parillo if he had been shot in a house as Parillo lay dying in the hospital.

Detective Ballou also was unable to track down anyone who could verify a rumor around town that Parillo had been walking along Circular Street near Caroline Street when a car approached and shot him down in front of the Presbyterian Church, about an hour before he showed up at the hospital. [23]

What police were able to trace, though, were Parillo's movements in the hours before his death, and they only added to the mystery of the situation.

George Smaldone, a friend of both Adam Parillo and Anthony Pompay was with both men on the night of the murder. Smaldone met up with Parillo at the Lake Ave Armory around 10:30 p.m. on December 8. They later visited a couple other places in Saratoga, including Smith Tolmie's home at 25 Lake Ave and Jock's Lunch on Church Street, before ending up at the Adelphi Grill on Broadway.

While Smaldone and Parillo were at Jock's Lunch shortly after midnight, two State Troopers arrived and asked Parillo to step outside to have a private conversation. Parillo did so and returned after a while, not bothering to mention to Smaldone what they had talked about. The Troopers never gave a public accounting of the encounter.

If we allow our imaginations to run free, perhaps the Troopers were using Parillo as an informant. Maybe they were warning Parillo to watch his step around the vicinity, letting him know they had their eyes on him. A more sinister thought might occur to us that the Troopers might have been imposters, verifying for the assassins that Parillo was in fact in Saratoga Springs.

Shortly after Smaldone and Parillo arrived at the Adelphi Grill, Sonny Pompay came in with Joe Dominick and Jess Lemmons. There were several witnesses at the bar that night who all told of Parillo and Pompay conversing without argument. They even moved off to a side room to have a private conversation where they stayed for some time and were served drinks. Testimony of witnesses, and Pompay himself, admitted that Parillo had asked him for one hundred dollars to pay his rent and that Pompay gave him twenty-five, promising to give him the balance the following day.[24]

At 3:00 a.m. the Adelphi Grill closed for the night. Smaldone walked out with Pompay and Parillo. Smaldone offered to drive them both home and Pompay took up the offer while Parillo insisted that he wanted to walk up to an all-night lunch counter on Railroad Place and was last seen by Smaldone headed in that direction. Smaldone later learned of Parillo's murder and voluntarily went to the police and offered his testimony.

Smaldone's story about dropping off Pompay at home seemed to present a problem for Sonny. Recall that when Officer Winship initially arrived at Pompay's house, there was no car in the driveway and no answer at the door. The house was dark.

Pompay had told Chief Rox that he didn't answer upon Winship's first visit because he had been drinking pretty heavily and had fallen asleep. When

Officer Winship returned about 7:30 a.m. and found the automobile still warm and Pompay with his coat on, it seemed to not fit with his story about being dropped off and falling asleep. This, of course, was not sufficient to convict a man of murder and the police investigation came to a standstill.

Adding to the intrigue of the case, the hospital intern who treated Adam Parillo on his deathbed, Dr. Robert Anderson, left for China and Mongolia for missionary medical work just a couple of months (February 1937) after he conversed with the dying Parillo on the operating table. The court ordered Dr. Anderson to post a $2500 bond to ensure his return and appearance in court if needed.[25]

Dr. Anderson's trip, of course, started rumors around Saratoga that he had been pressured to leave town to avoid testifying against Pompay. When looked at objectively, it is unlikely that Dr. Anderson planned a wedding (he married just prior to leaving) and a lengthy, overseas trip all within two months of attending to Parillo, and just to avoid testifying in court.

Within a couple of days of the murder, Pompay was released, all leads and rumors were tracked down and debunked, and the "Scotland Yard" of the State Police had been called in, but police were no closer to solving the murder than they were on the morning Parillo was shot. Reports of shots being fired in various neighborhoods had been investigated and led to nothing. The State Police forensics team could only determine that Parillo had been felled by .32 caliber bullets, but could offer nothing to link the defendant to the crime by means of physical evidence.

While there was good reason to believe that Parillo had named Anthony "Sonny" Pompay on his deathbed, a dying declaration may only be admitted into evidence in court if a judge determines that certain conditions are met and with Dr. Anderson in China, no prosecution seemed likely.

The case stood stagnant for years until April, 1942, when District Attorney John F. Doyle announced the arrest of Anthony "Sonny" Pompay on a charge of second-degree murder in the death of Adam Parillo on December 9, 1936. Sonny had been in the federal prison in Atlanta and was brought back to Saratoga County to stand trial at the expiration of his term for operating illegal alcohol stills, an investigation detailed in another chapter of this book.

There was never a public explanation as to why Pompay was indicted in the spring of 1942, almost six years after Parillo named him as his killer. Dr. Anderson had returned from his missionary work in China, but he had been back for some time and there had been no public movement on the case. During the years between the murder and the indictment of Pompay, occasionally rumors would flow through Saratoga County that the grand jury was looking into the matter, but at the end of each term, no indictment was ever announced.

The answer to the question of why there had been no movement on the case as well as why there was an arrest at this time, might be found in a petition filed by Adam Parillo's sister, Christine Manilla, with Governor of New York Herbert Lehman, asking that a special prosecutor be appointed for the trial.

Mrs. Manilla's quest for justice for her brother might have been the reason why charges were finally filed in the case. She had hired a private attorney to advocate on her behalf and maybe this, rather than any new evidence, was the reason the prosecution was pursued in 1942.

In her letter, Parillo's sister held nothing back and made several unsubstantiated allegations. Her petition to the governor included the following accusations:

- That District Attorney (then Assistant District Attorney) Doyle had declined to press the case because Parillo had accused "a Pompay" when he had in fact named "Sonny Pompay" as the shooter.
- That no coroner's inquest had been conducted as required by the Criminal Procedure Law and that henceforth all criminal proceedings were not legal.
- That no public statements about the murder had been made by authorities for over four years.

- That then District Attorney John Smith had requested the involvement of the New York State Police because he was not satisfied with the performance of the Saratoga Springs Police.
- That Mr. Doyle had given her and her attorney the distinct impression that he was not interested in pursuing criminal charges against Pompay and only did so when they threatened to petition the governor to have a special prosecutor appointed.
- That Anthony "Sonny" Pompay was a lieutenant in the well-known Louis J. "Doc" Farone criminal organization and had been convicted in federal court as a co-defendant with Farone.
- That Doyle had referred to a $10,000 payment around the time of the murder to Public Safety Commissioner Arthur "Doc" Leonard that may have been related to the case.
- That "Doc" Leonard and "Doc" Farone were close associates in politics and business.
- That Daniel Prior, Pompay's defense attorney, was "Doc" Leonard's personal attorney.
- That attorney Prior had been allowed into the jail cell where Pompay was being held by Chief Rox despite orders from the District Attorney's office that no one was to speak to Pompay until further advised by the prosecution.[26]

It should be noted that there was never any charge filed or evidence presented that "Doc" Leonard had received a $10,000 payment related to the Parillo murder. However, the remainder of her accusations were accurate or could reasonably be inferred from other actions and events.

Whether the accusations were accurate or not, Governor Lehman let District Attorney Smith know that he should, perhaps, request a special prosecutor rather than having the Governor simply appoint one. Doyle conceded, and August 20, 1942, Rensselaer County District Attorney Charles F. Ranney took the oath of office as Special Prosecutor in the case of the People vs. Anthony Pompay. [27]

The first day of testimony was December 15, 1942. The presiding judge Andrew W. Ryan, and everyone else, knew that there was only one issue that needed to be addressed. Would the deathbed statement, made by Parillo, that Sonny Pompay had shot him be admitted into evidence? If not, there was no other evidence pointing to Pompay as the killer.

The question centered on a relatively simple legal issue, that of a dying declaration. Typically, hearsay evidence is not admissible in court since everyone has a right to cross examine their accusers and, if hearsay evidence were allowed in court, the defendant's rights would be violated. Hearsay is simply an out of court statement used to prove a fact. In this case, Parillo's statement that Sonny shot him would be an example of hearsay evidence, since the statement was being introduced into court not by Parillo who made the statement, but by people who heard him say it.

Now, there are exceptions to the exclusion of hearsay evidence in court and one is called a "dying declaration," which is a situation where, if someone were to know they were dying, without any possibility of recovering, any statement that they make could be repeated in court by those who heard it. The theory behind the exception is that someone who is near death, knowing they will not recover, has no reason to tell a lie and therefore the statement may be considered reliable, even though the person who made the statement cannot be cross examined in court.

Special Prosecutor Ranney made a valiant effort to introduce Parillo's statement, but was not able to overcome the legal hurdle and prove that Adam Parillo knew he was dying when he made the statement. Ranney could not prove, to the satisfaction of Judge Ryan, that the testimony of Officers Winship and Lucas, or the attending nurses or Doctor Anderson, showed that Parillo knew he was dying and therefore his statement that it was "Sonny Pompay" who shot him was inadmissible.[28]

Without any other evidence linking Pompay to the murder, Judge Ryan instructed the jury to deliver a verdict of not guilty. The jurors dutifully retired and returned after five minutes, which worried defense attorney Prior so much that he inquired with the judge if he thought the jurors understood the instructions.

He need not have worried; the jurors followed the judge's instructions perfectly. Anthony "Sonny" Pompay was declared not guilty of the murder of Adam Parillo.[29]

Even though Parillo said he was shot by Pompay, other testimony and circumstances pointed to perhaps a more likely identity of the killer or killers.

Chief Rox claimed that, on the night of the murder, a car with Canadian license plates was seen on Broadway. He added that nearby was a second car in which three mysterious men were seated, wearing caps.[30] In fact, on the morning of the shooting, Chief Rox had told reporters for the Saratogian that, "I have been jittery ever since he came here because I was afraid some of his old associates would catch up with him." [31]

Underworld "squealers" are often murdered. The fact that Parillo had informed on some of the top mafia figures in Canada, with his testimony being largely responsible for the death sentences of his cohorts, certainly justified Chief Rox's concern. But he wasn't the only person concerned about the release of Adam Parillo.

Parillo himself was concerned for his own safety. The day after Parillo was shot to death, the *Montreal Gazette* reported that he had petitioned the St. Vincent de Paul prison authorities to allow him to stay an additional two years in their prison and the *Troy Record* reported that his release in August was done in secret to protect him.

Parillo, like Rox, had reason to be concerned. He undoubtedly knew by then that his fellow snitches in the robbery case had already been killed.

Ciro Nieri, picked up the night of the robbery and the first to make a deal with Montreal Police, was deported immediately after the trial and was reportedly slain in Italy.[32] A report, years later in the *Saskatoon Star-Phoenix* claimed that Nieri had been tortured before being killed.

Salvatore Arena, the third informer, was attending a Nazi rally in New York City in 1932 when he was chased to a subway platform and shot down by a lone assailant. Arena was hailed as a Nazi hero and received an impressive funeral, attended by the Italian Consul General in New York, before being buried with military honors near his hometown in Italy.

Within days though, Montreal Police confirmed the dead Nazi supporter was in fact Salvatore Arena, the same man who had skipped bail back in 1924 after having squealed on his pals. No one seemed to wonder why, among all the thousands of pro-Nazi supports at the rally, Salvatore Arena was singled out, chased down, and murdered on the streets of New York.

The unsolved murder of Adam Parillo lives on in Saratoga lore. In addition to an old family legend in which the author's great grand-father was at the scene of the crime, the author has heard over the years three various locations of the murder, two different names of people who were really the shooter, and that the guns used in the murder are still in the attic of a house on the City's West Side.

The possibility exists that Parillo was actually telling the truth about who shot him, or that someone else known to either Parillo or Pompay had done the shooting. Although, given his criminal history and unreliability, it is also reasonable to assume that Parillo was simply lying about Pompay.

It is also entirely plausible, given the history of corruption among Saratoga authorities at that time, that authorities did not much care who shot Adam Parillo. They may have secretly been glad that they no longer had to deal with him.

But an honest look at the evidence and a much more interesting and reasonable theory is that the Parillo murder was, in fact, as described by Chief Rox, an act of "vengeance, long planned." The Canadian Mafia had finally caught up with Adam Parillo.

Endnotes

Chapter 8

[1] Unless otherwise noted, all information about the Parillo murder comes from the reporting in the Saratogian between 1936 and 1942.

[2] "Jurors Acquit 'Sonny' Pompay in Spa Slaying." *The Glens Falls Post-Star.* December 17, 1942.

[3] "Gang Guns Slay Parillo, Saratoga; Found Dying at Doors of Hospital." *The Saratogian.* December 9, 1936.

[4] "Convicted of Having Drugs: His Companion on Trial." *The Saratogian.* June 26, 1918.

[5] "Adam Parillo Arrested." *The Saratogian.* May 5, 1919.

[6] "Charged with Grand Larceny." *The Saratogian.* September 2, 1919.

[7] "Local Saloon Man Victim of Slasher." *The Saratogian.* June 19, 1918.

[8] "Arrest Complainant in Robbery Case." *The Saratogian.* September 25, 1919.

[9] "Saratoga Man Murdered in New Jersey." *The Saratogian.* January 5, 1929.

[10] "Saratogians Held by Mechanicville Police for Hold Up." *The Saratogian.* August 12, 1921.

[11] "Unable to Fasten Hold Up on Parillo and Dominick." *The Saratogian.* August 17, 1921.

[12] "Arrest Gangsters for Garant Store Theft." *The Saratogian.* July 25, 1921.

[13] "Man Beaten at Trolley Station; Thug Attacks Woman with Blackjack." *The Saratogian.* May 8, 1922.

[14] "Arrest DeMatteo and M'Neary Girl in Pennsylvania." *The Saratogian.* May 9, 1922.

[15] "Gus DeMatteo Gets Two to Six Years in Dannemora Prison." *The Saratogian.* February 9, 1922.

[16] "Adam Parillo Arrested." *The Saratogian.* December 27, 1921.

[17] "Stone, Drug Ring Head, is Killed." *The Watertown Daily Times.* April 2, 1924.

[18] "Claim Adam Parillo, Held for Montreal Murder and Robbery, is Director of Organized Band." *The Saratogian.* May 7, 1924.

[19] "Will Attempt to Reduce Parillo's Life Sentence." *The Saratogian.* December 3, 1924.

[20] "Gang Guns Slay Parillo…"

[21] "Pompay Named by Parillo, Says Doyle in Court." *The Saratogian.* December 11, 1936.

[22] "Gang Guns Slay…"

[23] "To Make Charge Against Pompay in Gang Murder." *The Saratogian.* December 10, 1936.

[24] "Pompay Jury Ordered to Free Defendant." *The Saratogian.* December 16, 1942.

[25] "Dr. Anderson Dead at 47; Witness in Murder Trial." *The Saratogian.* August 9, 1948.

[26] "What Petition in Parillo Case Charges." *The Saratogian.* April 18, 1942.

[27] "Ranney Tales Oath in Pompay Case." *The Saratogian.* August 20, 1942.

[28] "Hospital Nurse Found Parillo Dying." *The Saratogian.* December 15, 1942.

[29] "Pompay Jury Ordered to Free Defendant." *The Saratogian.* December 16, 1942.

[30] "To Make Charge Against Pompay in Gang Murder." *The Saratogian.* December 10, 1936.

[31] "Gang Guns Slay Parillo…"

[32] "Second Gang Witness is Dead After a Ride." *The New York Times.* December 10, 1932.

Chapter 9

Dutch and Doc go to Malone

A little more than ten miles from the Canadian border in upstate New York lies the village of Malone, the county seat of Franklin County, where the picturesque Salmon River runs through the middle of town. Today the area near Malone is dotted with correctional facilities, but in the heyday of the gangsters, the village's roughly 12,000 souls were treated to two federal criminal trials that drew the attention of the entire state and beyond.

In 1935 the Federal Court in Malone played host to the tax evasion trial of "Public Enemy Number One," Arthur Flegenheimer, whom you might know as Dutch Schultz. Later, in 1940, the Federal Court welcomed Saratogian Louis "Doc" Farone as he answered a charge of illegally manufacturing alcohol in Schenectady, Saratoga, and Essex Counties.

Both men sat before the same judge, five years apart, in the same courtroom, in the same small upstate village. And, as both are of interest to the seemingly never-ending story of gangsterism in Saratoga Springs, their adventures to the North Country will be recounted here.

We will tell the tale of Dutch Schultz first, if only for chronological consistency. The Dutchman, as he was sometimes called, was, for a time, the preeminent gangster in the Northeast United States. Hailing from the Bronx, his criminal organization brought in an estimated twenty million dollars per year. Dutch was involved in all manner of criminal enterprise including, but not limited to, bootlegging, extortion, and union and policy rackets, not to mention murder and assault. But, according to his own declarations, never did he make a dime off either prostitution or drugs.[1]

Early in his criminal career Schultz drove trucks for Arnold Rothstein and worked for Jack "Legs" Diamond. It was Rothstein who likely introduced Schultz to Saratoga and Legs who probably introduced the Dutchman to the rest of upstate New York, likely through the beer smuggling routes he perfected during prohibition. That Dutch Schultz had criminal interests and connections throughout New York's Capital Region, including Saratoga, was indisputable.

After all, Dutch did kill his bookkeeper, Jules Martin, in Cohoes when he discovered discrepancies in his ledger, his favorite prostitute kept a place on Union Avenue in Saratoga Springs, and, when he was on the run from the law, it was said that Dutch kept a hideout between Saratoga and Lake George with an airplane on standby, just in case he needed to make a quick getaway.

Dutch Schultz was cozy enough with upstate law enforcement that he was appointed Deputy Sheriff in Hamilton County towards the end of the prohibition years. The appointment by Sheriff Peter Wilson allowed Dutch to carry a concealed firearm legally. But in the Sheriff's defense, he was under the impression that Shultz had purchased a camp in the rural county and wanted to protect it. When public pressure became too much to bear, Sheriff Wilson revoked the appointment. [2]

As noted in a previous chapter, there were rumors that the spasm of violence in 1931 might have been an attempt by members of the Schultz faction to muscle in on the lucrative Saratoga summer market. In any event, his connections to Saratoga Springs aren't important to this part of the tale, but his history and his trial in Malone are.

Dutch Schultz, by the time he had gained national attention for his liquor and policy empires, had already been involved with some of the worst of the worst gangsters of the era. When he worked for Legs Diamond, they both operated under the umbrella of Arnold Rothstein. Soon, however, Legs followed Rothstein into the drug trafficking business, something that Schultz (as a gangster with some standards) was not too keen on participating in. Rothstein managed to keep peace between the two up-and-coming gangsters, for a time.

In 1928, after Rothstein was gunned down at the Park Central Hotel (over a supposed gambling debt) Dutch Shultz and Legs Diamond, who never did like each other, went to war.

Legs was able to kill Joey Noe, a partner of Dutch Schultz, during their battle for supremacy, which led to speculation that Dutch had a hand in the murder of Legs Diamond at a boarding house in Albany in December, 1931.[3]

We will pause here, to be fair to the Dutchman, and mention that a number of others were also suspected in the shooting death of Legs Diamond, including the Oley brothers, who were Albany area gangsters, along with members of the Albany Police Department,[4] Anthony "Little Augie" Carfano, Salvatore "Salvy" Spitale, and Irving Bitz. A case could be made for any one of them, and the final three on that list appear elsewhere in this account of the gangsters of Saratoga.

Legs Diamond was not the only gangster to shoot it out with Dutch Schultz. In 1931, Chink Sherman, carrying a Saratoga County Deputy Sheriff's badge that allowed him to possess a concealed handgun, got into a shootout at the Club Abbey in Harlem with the Dutchman. Schultz was shot and injured; Sherman was killed during the affair.[5]

Just like Schultz had a violent break with his former employer Rothstein, soon two Schultz employees decided they would like a bigger piece of the profits of the Schultz empire, and when they were told no, they too broke from their employer in a violent manner.

When Vincent "Mad Dog" Coll and his brother Peter split with the Schultz group, the consequent war resulted in at least fifteen gangland deaths on the streets of metro New York. Schultz associates managed to gun down Peter Coll early in the war and his brother, Mad Dog, replied with guns-a-blazin'. He started hijacking Schultz trucks, shooting at Schultz men wherever they could be found, kidnapping gamblers for ransom, and generally creating havoc wherever he went. Coll gunmen even got into a shootout with police near Albany.[6]

The Coll group was after Schultz so desperately that the Dutchman put a bounty of $50,000 on the head of Mad Dog Coll. According to biographer, Paul Sann, in his book *Kill the Dutchman*, Schultz was so desperate for relief from the constant attacks by Coll that he walked into a police station and offered to buy a home in Westchester County for any officer who managed to kill his rival.

The Coll-Schultz war had some unintended consequences. The well-known shooting of five children on the streets of New York, mentioned elsewhere in this book, was just one instance. Another unfortunate incident occurred in June, 1931, at the height of the battles between the two hoodlums, when two detectives set up surveillance of Schultz in New York City.

Seated on a park bench across from a Shultz hideout, the officers kept watch, but Schultz and his men mistook the detectives for Coll assassins and confronted the men. Dutch and a friend approached the two officers. Words were exchanged, guns were drawn, and bullets fired. The Schultz associate was killed, and the Dutchman fled, tossing a gun as he ran. When he was finally chased down, Schultz had on him $18,000 cash and a ledger showing that he had collected $52,000 in just eleven days from his Harlem policy racket.[7]

The Coll-Schultz war dragged on for nearly two years. Both sides suffered many dead and injured. The battles raged until February 8, 1932, when Vincent "Mad Dog" Coll was machine-gunned to death in a telephone booth in New York City. Thankfully, there were no reports of police officers suddenly taking up residence in Westchester County after the murder.

That Dutch Schultz was making a killing in the Harlem policy racket was undeniable, but authorities had trouble getting evidence against the gangster. Nobody would talk and honest cops, like one vice squad that almost brought down the entire racket, along with Dutch and his friends, soon found themselves transferred to Staten Island or another outpost where their zeal for the enforcement of the law could more easily be controlled.

With so many bodies littering the streets, though, authorities were eventually going to make a move, and Paul Sann tells us that the end for Dutch Shultz was put in motion when an agreement was struck between New York City Mayor Fiorello La Guardia, Secretary of the Treasury Henry Morgenthau, (who had been U.S. Ambassador to the Ottoman Empire during World War I), and FBI Director J. Edgar Hoover, that Dutch Schultz needed to be dealt with. The Dutchman was subsequently dubbed, "Public Enemy Number One."

Soon thereafter, federal, state, and local resources were brought to bear on the Dutchman and he found himself, like Al Capone before him, facing tax evasion charges, based in part on the money and ledger recovered that fateful night when he and his buddy confronted the two detectives near Central Park.

Schultz was indicted in January 1933. Teams of law men sent out to bring him in never could seem to get ahold of him. Agents tracked him throughout the state, including to Newburgh, where the authorities learned of the Saratoga hideout and plane mentioned earlier. They looked for Dutch throughout the Hudson and Mohawk valleys, but only found him when he turned himself in at Albany in November, 1934.

With twenty-two months of undeserved freedom behind him, Dutch Schultz went to face trial at the Federal Building in Syracuse, NY. It was to be a short visit. One of the witnesses against Schultz, Dan "Deafy" McCarthy walked out of the courtroom, telling folks he was going to get a haircut. He never returned and was never heard from again. A mistrial was declared, and the case was rescheduled for the summer of 1935 in Malone, NY.

The Franklin County Historical and Museum Society in Malone has an excellent collection of local newspaper articles, photographs, and other items dedicated to the trial of Dutch Schultz. The remainder of the Schultz story in Malone recounted here is based on their resources.

Charged with avoiding $92,000 in taxes on $481,000 income from 1929-1931, Dutch Schultz stood before Federal District Court Judge Frederick H. Bryant, who also happened to be a native of the village of Malone.

His defense was simple, Dutch claimed that he had asked a lawyer if he needed to pay income tax on ill-gotten gains. The lawyer had told him no, bootleg income and the like was exempt from taxes. According to his defense team, when he learned that his former lawyer was mistaken, Dutch Schultz went to the US Department of the Treasury and offered to settle the entire bill for $100,00, rather than the $92,000 that he owed. The offer was rejected and so the wheels of justice spun on over to Malone, NY.

His defense was easily understood, but just in case, Dutch and his friends arrived for the trial a little early and started lavishing the townsfolk with cash. They took a whole floor of rooms at the finest hotel in town, the Flanagan Hotel. Strangers in town left money at local restaurants with the instructions that any meal ordered by anyone of importance in the village was on the generous Dutch Schultz. Locals remembered Dutch as a generous and charming man who bought toys for the children of the town and sought his exercise by horseback riding around the local farms and countryside. The Dutchman was practically the guest of honor at a baseball game against a team from Plattsburgh, sitting in the press box with his lawyers and other prominent locals.

Being a product of Malone, Judge Bryant didn't take too kindly to the unseemly behavior of the Dutch team. He promptly revoked the Dutchman's bail and threw him into the Franklin County Jail, where he spent the duration of the trial sharing his lodging with three counterfeiters and two Canadians charged with illegal entry. If Judge Bryant could help it, Dutch and his crew would not give the villagers a bad name by essentially buying off the town.

Despite the fact that, back in 1933, the office of the prosecutor in the case had been broken into and the files on Dutch Schultz had been stolen, the court case proceeded with overwhelming evidence presented against the Dutchman. Prosecutors detailed his operations for the jury, and two of his associates were jailed during the trial for failing to cooperate on the witness stand. After all, the ledger and the money (along with all the other evidence the prosecution had) couldn't lie or disappear like human witnesses tended to do in gangster cases of the day. Recall poor "Deafy" Dan here.

With both sides resting their respective cases, Judge Bryant charged the jury, and the men retired to deliberate. Local newspaper accounts mentioned that Dutch looked very nervous during the time the jury was deliberating. They took twenty-eight hours and twenty minutes to decide the fate of Arthur Flegenheimer and when they came back into the courtroom, the jury foreman declared the then "Public Enemy Number One," NOT GUILTY!

Celebration broke out immediately. Both inside and outside the courtroom, the good citizens of Malone, NY, burst into applause and offered congratulations to the beer baron of the Bronx. It was not unlike the good citizens of Saratoga, who were known to celebrate the acquittal of various public officials charged with bribery, neglect of duty, and such. There is a rather famous picture of Dutch leaving the courthouse surrounded by Malone townsfolk wearing expressions of apparently unmitigated glee.

Nevertheless, one Malone man was unimpressed. Judge Bryant told the jurors, "You have labored long, and no doubt have given this case careful consideration. But your verdict shakes the confidence of law-abiding people in the reliability of juries. You have rendered a blow to law enforcement."[8]

The stinging rebuke was taken as an insult by the jurors, all of whom refused to shake hands with the newly freed gangster. Perhaps the jurors had simply weighed the evidence and decided the case was not as strong as it appeared. Perhaps they were influenced by their fellow townsfolk's good feelings towards the defendant. Perhaps there was some other reason (nefarious or not) as to why they acquitted the Dutchman. Whatever the reason, Dutch Schultz was a free man. He had beaten the rap and celebrated by throwing a grand bash at the Malone Elks Club, buying drinks for everyone who came to revel in his good fortune with him.

Dutch Schultz was acquitted in August 1935 and, as summer faded to fall that year, Malone went back to its relatively quiet existence and the Dutchman went back to New York City.

It is unlikely that Dutch ever forgot the people of Malone, not because he had any particular affection for them, or because they had made an unforgettable impression upon him, but rather because he never had time for his fond memories of Malone to fade. He lived only a couple of more months after his acquittal.

On October 23, 1935, Charley "The Bug" Workman and Mendy Weiss walked into the Palace Chop House in Newark, NJ, and shot Dutch Schultz, along with two of his associates. Dutch Schultz died the following day.

The story of Dutch Schultz and his federal court trial in Malone might seem out of place in this narrative about the gangsters of Saratoga. But the trouble was taken to detail the Dutchman's case because in 1940, Malone, NY, played host to another federal criminal trial, this time involving Saratoga's own king of the bootleggers, Louis "Doc" Farone.

Prohibition had ended in 1933 but that did not mean that purveyors of the forbidden drink stopped production altogether. Anyone in the beer production business could go legal, if they chose. And Doc Farone's brother, Alfred did. Some former rum-runners however, did not.

First, some gangsters might not have wanted to deal with the regulations and taxes that came with legitimate enterprise. Second, perhaps their consumers had developed a taste for their particular brand of alcohol and therefore the law of supply and demand continued to favor the illegal bootleggers after prohibition ended. Third, in Canada, liquor had become so heavily taxed that producers in the United States found a new market in Canada for their cheap spirits and soon the bootleg trail of olden days was running in reverse.

Whatever the reasons, illicit alcohol stills dotted the American landscape for many years after prohibition officially ended. Doc Farone and his associates were one group who chose to continue manufacturing the illicit drink.

Doc's operation was complex, and he took pains to ensure both quality and security. His managers were known to visit his various stills and warehouses unannounced and at all hours of the day and night to ensure things were running smoothly. He trained his men in marksmanship, shooting at rats in the basement of the Grand Union Hotel for practice (Sonny Pompay was the top shot.) He employed counter surveillance measures to guard against rivals and the police. Whenever he sensed the law, or a double cross was near, he packed up shop and started over, never hiring the same crew at the new spot, just in case one of the laborers was a turncoat.[9]

By 1939 the Doc Farone group had long since solidified their control of the liquor, and to a lesser extent, the gambling trade from the Mohawk Valley to the Canadian border. Farone had stills in Schenectady, Saratoga, and Essex Counties. His apparently close friendship with Saratoga Springs Police Chief Patrick Rox probably allowed Doc to hold frequent meetings with various underworld figures and criminal associates at several places in the city, specifically at the offices of Farone's own appliance store, the Modern Appliance Store, along with the Chicago Club,[10] and the Commercial Garage at Woodlawn and Church, where a Stewart's Shop stands today.

The reader will recall Doc Farone's takeover of the beer business in Saratoga during Prohibition and his men's shooting affairs in the early 1930's that were recounted previously in this book. His interests in the beer and gambling trades was an open secret and in July, 1939, state and federal law enforcers in upstate New York decided that they had had enough. They began a four-month investigation into the Farone operation that relied heavily on the ancient art of surveillance.

James Donohue, in his book, *Illicit Alcohol*, details the extensive surveillance that was conducted on the Farone group and their activities. Although he uses aliases for the players involved, it is not difficult to match his account with newspaper reporting of the trial in order to figure out who was who in Donohue's story.

Donohue, an investigator with the Federal Alcohol Tax Unit, recounts agents watching the Farone operatives at various locations in Saratoga Springs. In all, thirteen defendants were arrested and charged with being involved with the conspiracy which included seven Saratogians. They were Louis "Doc" Farone, Anthony "Sonny" Pompay, Joseph "The Fox" Volpe, Louis "Dynamite" DeMatteo, Bartholomew Sabino, Clifford Mackey, and Nicholas Caressi. Four others were from Schenectady (including Harry "Harry the Jew" Harrison), and two from Brooklyn.

The details of the surveillance efforts are best left to Mr. Donohue, but we will mention here that the group established stills in Schenectady, at Harry Carter's Pig Farm near Petrified Sea Gardens Road in the town of Milton just beyond the boundary with Saratoga Springs, at the abandoned Ricket's farm in Minerva, Essex County, and at Shady Acres Farm in Wilton. The group used various drops and warehouses, including one at the corner of South Franklin and Ash Streets in Saratoga Springs.

After months of surveillance, the law men were ready to make their move. On November 2, 1939, they raided the Carter Farm and found one of the largest stills ever found in upstate New York.

They discovered a two-thousand-gallon capacity still valued at $10,000 and arrested five men on premises. Officials estimated that the still could produce one thousand five hundred gallons of beer per day when fully operational.

At some point during the investigation they learned that Bart Sabino had been the Saratogian who had approached the owner of the Carter Farm, Harry Dunham, with an offer to lease the property. The farm was in an out-of-the-way place with a good water supply and seemed like a perfect place to operate a distillery. Soon thereafter, Mr. Dunham signed a lease with Harry Harrison for the property, although Harrison signed under the name of Leo White.

Harry "Harry the Jew" Harrison not only signed the lease for the Carter Farm under a fake name, he sold a truck used in the operation using the name Robert Ryan and had on his person, when arrested at the Carter Farm on November 2, a piece of paper with the address of the Schenectady still on it (594 Paige Street), as well as keys that fit the locks at the warehouse at South Franklin and Ash.[11]

Later that evening, Saratogians Joseph "The Fox" Volpe, who lived at 16 Clark Street, and Louis "Dynamite" DeMatteo, who lived at 124 Beekman Street, were arrested at the Chicago Club in connection with the conspiracy. They had previously been observed picking up a bottle of sulfuric acid at the warehouse at Franklin and Ash. Sulfuric acid was used in the production of alcohol as an agent to speed up the fermentation process.

When he was arrested, Dynamite DeMatteo had the keys that opened a padlock on the door to one of the barns at the Carter Farm.[12] Despite trying to duck out of the gambling joint when the federal agents approached, "The Fox" was nabbed and found to possess papers and receipts linking him to the Carter farm. Specifically, "The Fox" had on his person a recipe for distilling alcohol, a $1,000 check from Farone, a detailed expense account for equipment commonly used in alcohol stills and an address book that contained the addresses for Farone, Pompay, and a couple dozen others.[13]

Whether it was their extensive surveillance or cooperation from the defendants, the investigation soon shifted to the warehouse at South Franklin and Ash. On November 9, the warehouse was raided, and Agent Donohue and his men recovered two hundred and seventy-one drums of molasses and more equipment used in the manufacture of alcohol. Regarding the warehouse, the owner of the building said that Anthony "Sonny" Pompay had paid the rent for the previous four years.

On the same day that the warehouse on the city's west side was visited by the federal men, another group of lawmen traveled over to Farone's Shady Acres Farm on Route 9 in the town of Wilton about three miles north of Saratoga Springs. The Wilton branch of the operation was not nearly as extensive as the Carter Farm, but agents and troopers did find molasses, vat staves, and various other equipment used in the production of alcohol.

The conspirators were all indicted by the federal government and would soon be tried on various charges related to the illegal production of alcohol. With the trial scheduled for the middle of July in Malone, most of the conspirators decided to plead guilty to the charges and avoid the potentially life-altering trip to Malone. In fact, ten of the thirteen defendants plead guilty before the trial. Only Doc Farone, Sonny Pompay, and one of the Schenectady men, Emil Vores, decided to face the Malone farmers and businessmen who would sit in judgement of them.

So, on July 17, 1940, almost exactly five years to the day since he opened the trial of Dutch Shultz, Judge Bryant once again opened a trial of considerable public interest in the sleepy village. This time however, the people of Malone were not treated to a lavishly spending federal defendant. Doc and his associates simply went about their business and apparently tried to avoid any undue attention.

Farone chose Dean Taylor of Troy as his primary attorney, with W. H. Main assisting. Main was a prominent attorney in Malone who also served as the local legal advice for the Dutchman. Pompay and Vores had their own attorneys, but all three would stand trial together.

The prosecution opened with witnesses describing trucks coming and going from the stills at all hours of the day and night. [14] Prosecutors brought out that "Harry the Jew" Harrison had purchased a farm in

Minerva and, similar to the Carter Farm in Milton, had dammed up a nearby creek to use as a water supply.

Prosecutors called a truck driver from New Jersey to Malone who testified that he had delivered molasses to a warehouse in Saratoga Springs that was near a set of railroad tracks.[15] It was a description that matched the location of Ash and South Franklin in Saratoga, although the driver had no idea what the names of the Saratoga streets were.

Almost as soon as the trial got started, Judge Bryant suddenly revoked the bail of all thirteen co-conspirators. Locals recalled a similar move by Judge Bryant during the Dutch Shultz trial, when Dutch and his associates were thrown in jail. Although it seemed at that time that Judge Bryant might have been trying to prevent an entire village from being corrupted, the action in the present case went without public statement by the good judge, but press reports suggested that perhaps there was some funny business involving the jury. After a short delay, though, the trial went ahead under a cloud of mystery.

Another truck driver, Jacob Reichler, from Saratoga, was put on the witness stand by prosecutors. Reichler told of being paid to deliver barrels of molasses from New Jersey to Saratoga Springs at the rate of two dollars per barrel. Although Farone's lawyers tried to make a big deal of the fact that Reichler was at that time himself under indictment for the illegal transport and manufacture of alcohol,

Reichler did testify that he was paid, at various times, by Farone, Pompay, or Volpe. Of course, he didn't have any records to prove the payments.[16]

Slowly building their case, prosecutors patiently called more witnesses and one, a Schenectady County Sheriff, testified that he had seen Farone, Pompay, and Vores all visiting the area of the Schenectady still over the course of time. They also introduced evidence that the Farone group used aliases to register trucks used in the operation.

One truck used by the group was sold to someone named "Frank Kelly" (almost surely an alias of one of the conspirators) and when the vehicle was no longer useful, one of the group sold the truck to a Saratoga garage and told the owner to credit the profit from the sale to Doc Farone's account. When prosecutors introduced the receipt for the sale of the truck into evidence, it was noted that the bottom half of the document was ripped off.

Why, the garage man was asked, was the bottom half of the receipt missing?

"Farone tore off part of it," was the answer. Continuing, he said, "I told him I didn't like to have him do it, that we didn't want our records mutilated."

"What did he say?" The prosecutor asked.

"He said nothing, just tore it to pieces," was the reply.[17] Of course the section of the paper that was torn off was where Farone's name was probably located.

The remainder of the prosecution's case was more mundane. It included testimony from a federal agent who had taken up residence across from the Modern Appliance office on Putnam Street for three months and recorded the comings and goings of the people and vehicles from the place that was alleged to be the headquarters of the conspirators. Furthermore, chemists were put on the stand to testify to the various chemicals that were recovered and what they were used for which, coincidentally, happened to be the same chemicals needed to manufacture alcohol.[18]

With their case complete, the prosecution turned the proceedings over to the defense. Farone and Pompay's lawyers moved quickly. They presented thirteen witnesses, most of whom testified that they conducted legitimate business at the Modern Appliance Company office, purchasing plumbing equipment and the like, instead of engaging in a conspiracy to manufacture illicit alcohol, as the prosecution alleged.

Vores took the stand in his own defense, admitting to operating a still in Schenectady County along with Pompay, Volpe, and others, but claimed to have never had an interest in any stills in Essex or Saratoga Counties. While this should have been good news for the prosecution, Vores' testimony was that his interest in the Schenectady still had ended in 1936, outside of the statute of limitation of three years.

Farone and Pompay declined to take the stand, and since the prosecution had been unable to introduce any solid evidence that Vores had been involved in the conspiracy after 1936, Judge Bryant freed Vores before the summation, citing a lack of evidence against Vores obtained after 1936.[19]

Louis "Dynamite" DeMatteo then took the stand for the defense. Although he had already plead guilty to being involved in the conspiracy, DeMatteo testified that he had never been engaged in manufacturing alcohol with Farone and Pompay and that, while he admitted there was a still at Shady Acres Farm and that Farone owned the property, he, himself, had never seen Farone there.

Furthermore, DeMatteo could explain the $20,000 in cashiers' checks that the government claimed had been paid to him by Farone. They most certainly were not proceeds from illegally selling alcohol; no, according to DeMatteo, the $20,000 were operating funds for the Chicago Club that he, Matthew (Matty) Burns, and Farone ran on Woodlawn Ave in Saratoga.

Finally, DeMatteo claimed that Farone and Pompay had nothing to do with the still in Essex County. Rather, that operation was the joint effort of himself, "Joe the Fox" Volpe, and someone named "Tony." The three had met up in front of one of the prominent hotels along Broadway in Saratoga when the idea had come to them to open the Minerva plant.[20] At least that is what DeMatteo swore to, anyway.

In summation, Farone's Malone lawyer, Main, said that Farone was the victim of an "unfortunate chain of circumstances and friendships," and asked his fellow Malone men, "How would you feel if you were separated from your home on such testimony?"[21]

After being instructed by Judge Bryant, the Malone jurors retired to their chambers to ponder the question posed by attorney Main. It took them all of one hour to consider the case and return a verdict of guilty.

With guilty verdict in hand, Judge Bryant set about sentencing Farone and Pompay. Recall that Vores had been freed, and so the two remaining defendants would bear the brunt of sentencing. "Doc" and "Sonny" both got two years in federal prison. Farone was fined $10,000 and Pompay, $7,500.

They were tough sentences to be sure, but Judge Bryant took the unusual step of making a public comment about an unresolved matter while sentencing the Saratoga duo. Addressing Farone he said, "An attempt to corrupt the court was made and I don't know whether it was made by you or not. But I know strangers are not making attempts to corrupt the court unless prompted by someone interested in the case."[22]

The day after pronouncing sentence on Farone and Pompay, the remaining conspirators learned their fates. Judge Bryant sentenced the remaining defendants to serve jail terms of between ninety days and two years and fined them between $500 and

$1,000 each. The Saratogians involved were sentenced as follows:

Joe "The Fox" Volpe: Eighteen months prison, $1,000 fine.

Bart Sabino: Two years prison suspended, four years probation.

Louis "Dynamite" DeMatteo: Eighteen months prison, $1,000 fine.

Nicholas Carresi: One year and one day prison suspended, three years probation.

While he was not a Saratogian, the sentence of Harry "Harry the Jew" Harrison will be mentioned here, owing to his prominence in the conspiracy. He received an eighteen-month term of confinement with a fine of $500 to be paid.[23]

About two weeks after they had been sentenced, the prisoners were being prepared for transport from the Franklin County Jail to the federal intake prison at Lewisburg, PA. A *Malone Evening-Telegram* reporter managed to speak with the men as they were being loaded into four automobiles by U.S. Marshals. One of the men told the reporter that he would rather sign up to fight in the war raging in Europe at the time than to spend one more day in jail, to which "Doc" Farone added simply, "Me too."[24]

But by then it was too late. Farone and his associates were federal prisoners. They were all done with this chapter in their lives, except for "Doc." He still had the little matter of the supposed "attempt to corrupt the court," as Judge Bryant had termed the irregularity with the jury.

It wouldn't take long to learn what all the fuss was about. On August 29, 1940, Farone and two others were indicted by a federal Grand Jury on charges of jury tampering. Farone's co-defendants were James Kendrick of Albany and Ozias Elderbaum from Churubusco, a small hamlet near the Canadian border in Clinton County, NY. Neither of Farone's co-defendants were mentioned during the previous trial or associated with Farone at any other time when Farone found himself hauled, once again, before the federal court in Malone.

According to the indictment, "The object of said conspiracy was to bribe one Wallace Barnes, Malone, a member of the jury, . . . with a sum of $500 to vote for the acquittal of the defendant."[25]

Although jury tampering is a serious crime and the image of gangsters bribing jurors surely brings to mind one of the worst aspects of organized crime, it seems that, in this particular case, since the potential juror, Barnes, came forward and cooperated, that the matter was not worth the expense of a trial or the effort to make a vigorous defense. All the defendants quickly pled guilty to the charge and, while Kendrick and Elderbaum escaped any serious legal consequences, on June 22, 1941, Farone quietly pled guilty, also, and received a three-year sentence for attempting to bribe Barnes.[26]

It was the same village, the same courtroom, the same judge, the same defense attorney, defendants that were both prominent bootleggers, and nefarious activity that led to the defendants being thrown into the same jail. All made the "Doc" trial seem like a movie sequel to the "Dutch" trial produced nearly five years to the day earlier. That "Dutch" and "Doc" both went to Malone is too coincidental and too interesting to exclude from this account of the gangsters of Saratoga.

One matter needs to be cleared up before we move on, though. While "Dutch" Schultz was murdered shortly after his Malone adventure, Farone and Pompay spent two years in federal custody. Pompay was released on April 10, 1942, just in time to stand trial for the murder of Adam Parillo. Farone was released on July 20, 1942, just in time to enjoy the fabulous profits of the lake house era at the Spa.

Endnotes

Chapter 9

1 Downey, Patrick. *Gangster City: The History of the New York Underworld 1900-1935*. Barricade Books. 2004.

2 Sann, Paul. *Kill the Dutchman*. Arlington House. 1971.

3 Downey.

4 Kennedy, William. *O' Albany!* Penguin Books. 1983.

5 Sann.

6 Downey.

7 Sann.

8 "Schultz, Freed by Jury, Plans Return to New York Home." *Malone Evening Telegram*. August 2, 1935.

9 Donohue, James A. *Illicit Alcohol*. The Chronicle Express. 1965.

10 Ibid.

11 "Federal Man Testifies of Actions in Still Case." *The Saratogian*. July 24, 1940.

12 "DeMatteo Linked to 2 Saratoga Still Raids." *The Saratogian*. November 13, 1939.

13 "Jail Farone with All Defendants in Still Case." *The Saratogian*. July 25, 1940.

14 "'Doc' Farone 2 Others Go on Trial in Still Case." *The Saratogian*. July 19, 1940.

15 "Metal Drums, Pipe on Farm Rented From Farone, Malta Farmer Tells Jury." *The Saratogian*. July 20, 1940.

[16] "Testifies He Hauled Molasses for Farone." *The Saratogian*. July 22, 1940.

[17] "Link Farone with Truck Purchase for Unknown." *The Saratogian*. July 19, 1940.

[18] "Government Rests Still Case Against 'Doc' Farone." *The Saratogian*. July 26, 1940.

[19] "Court Frees Vores, Still Conspiracy Defendant." *The Saratogian*. July 31, 1940.

[20] "DeMatteo Testifies for Still Defendants." *The Saratogian*. July 30, 1940.

[21] "Court Frees Vores..."

[22] "2 Years in Prison for Farone and Pompay I Still Case; Fined $10,000 and $7,500." *The Saratogian*. August 2, 1940.

[23] "Farone's Aides Given Prison and Fines; Volpe and DeMatteo to Serve 18 Months." *The Saratogian*. August 3, 1940.

[24] Farone Taken to Prison to Begin Term." *Malone Evening Telegram*. August 15, 1940.

[25] "'Doc' Farone Indicted for Jury Tampering." *The Saratogian*. August 29, 1940.

[26] "Farone Gets 3 Years, Fine in Bribe Plot." *The Saratogian*. June 23, 1941.

Chapter 10

The Lake Houses

In the August 13, 1927, edition of the *New Yorker* there appeared a cartoon map of Saratoga Springs and vicinity. It had the look of those tourist maps you often find in resort towns across the country. One of the contributors to the aforementioned *New Yorker* map was Clarence Knapp, Mayor of Saratoga Springs from 1924-1927.

The map showed, among other notable local landmarks, the "Route of Izzy and Moe-1925" and the "Canadian Ale Trunk Line," both referring to people and places we have already come across in this story. There was "Frank's Barber Shop," "The Spa's Harlem" and "McGregor Golf Club," along with the grand hotels and summer residences of famous people.

A small airplane is depicted near Lake Lonely with the note, "Airplane Landing Where Dope Sheets Come In." Although this author has heard rumors that one organized crime group did use seaplanes to land liquor shipments on Saratoga Lake and Lake Lonely, the historical record is void of any mention of the use of air transport to bring dope sheets into town.

A "dope sheet" or "dope book," if you are not accustomed to using those terms in your everyday vocabulary, is a circular or listing of entries and past results for horses designed to inform bettors. Mayor Knapp was a friend of noted humorist Frank Sullivan and therefore, the air delivery of dope sheets might simply be a joke, or he could have been referencing the massive amount of gambling that went on at the Lake Houses in the area, which were also shown on Mr. Knapp's map.

The Saratoga Lake Houses were, and are still remembered today, as having some of the finest dining, gambling, and entertainment that you could find anywhere. Richard Canfield's casino in Congress Park might have earned the name the "Monte Carlo of America," but by the golden age of the gangsters (the nineteen twenties, thirties, and forties), the Lake Houses had become the playground of the rich and famous and a significant source of income for the mob. A "Gangster's Paradise," if you will.

You could not beat the dining at Newman's. Sophie Tucker and Joe Lewis performed at the Piping Rock. You might find Bing Crosby or Cary Grant at the Arrowhead. Riley's saw Grace Fields and Cross and Dunn play to the revelers dancing on its octagon shaped dance floor.

Professional gamblers, who cared little or not at all for the entertainment, flocked to Smith's Interlaken.

Any number of civic groups, schools, religious organizations, and political parties held events, awards nights, fundraisers, and dinners at the Lake Houses. These events were frequently attended by various public officials, including local, state, and national politicians, as well as Chief of Police Rox, Commissioner Leonard, Mayor Knapp, Sheriff Austin, Jim Leary, and others.

Now, before we get the wrong idea, in each of the lake houses, the gambling areas were meticulously separated from the dining or entertainment rooms. Any patron would need to pass through a doorway, small hallway, or head out to an unattached building to gamble. So, it was possible to attend an evening's event at one of the places and not have really seen any gambling taking place. It's something to keep in mind when we get to the Kefauver investigation.

The clear distinction between the gambling and the dining and dancing areas was mainly to protect the liquor license of the business. Typically, the lake houses were organized into two parts. They generally had one manager who oversaw the dining room and entertainment; usually this was the official owner. The gambling operation was subcontracted to a third party, a local or national gangster or gambler.

The lake houses were in a perfect spot. They were all still within the city limits and therefore were the responsibility of the city police force, which as we have seen, did not always enforce the gambling laws with anything approaching professional zeal. But they were also some distance from town and therefore did not attract the same level of attention as they would have if they had been located right on Broadway.

Their location allowed for two forms of soft graft to exist. First, all that money needed to be escorted from the outskirts of the city to the banks, which were downtown. Police officers often moonlighted as protection for the money transfers or were hired outright as security for the casinos. Second, each of the lake houses was required, unofficially of course, to hire five or six limo drivers during the summer season at a rate of between twenty and thirty dollars per day, per man, in order to get the green light to open and the assurance that they wouldn't be raided. The clubs would have to hire the men, regardless if they needed the cars or not. [1]

Of course, there were also direct payoffs to public officials, but the do-nothing employment assured that the graft flowed down to the common man, who played a minor part in the gambling drama, but kept men like Leary and Leonard in power and allowed the gangsters to come back, year after year, until Kefauver finally put an end to the party.

We will get to Senator Kefauver and Governor Dewey soon enough, but before we do, let us take a historical look at each of the lake houses in turn. We will start, in no particular order of importance, with Newman's Lake House.

Newman's Lake House sat on Crescent Avenue, basically across from the entrance to the city beach today, overlooking Saratoga Lake. The place got its name from the long-time owner and proprietor, Henry J. Newman, who opened in either 1871 or 1874; there are conflicting accounts.[2]

Newman reportedly had worked at Moon's Lake House prior to taking over at the roadhouse that would come to take his name. He purchased the property from a man named D.P. McQueen and ran the restaurant and entertainment venue with his wife, Katherine, until his death in 1914, at which time Katherine took over until she suddenly passed away in 1921.[3]

Henry Newman's Lake House was a favorite of the wealthy visitors to Saratoga Springs. Lillian Russell and "Diamond" Jim Brady were patrons, along with the Vanderbilts and the Whitneys. The food and service were second to none. The solid mahogany bar was said to have come from the Waldorf Astoria Hotel in New York City and may very well have been the longest bar north of metro New York. The facility could accommodate 500 dinner guests at one time.[4]

The Newmans, originally from Long Island, lived on the property. For many years, Henry Newman hosted trotting races on the ice of Saratoga Lake during the winter. In 1902, Newman put up a prize of a well-made hood and blanket for the winner of one of the feature races. The horse blanket and hood were left on display at C.E. Black's shop window to entice the owners of the trotters to try their luck on the kite shaped track.[5]

During the years that Newman operated the place, he rarely had trouble with the law. Most of the trouble that Newman experienced during his tenure was when fire threatened his property. Several times the building was threatened with fire and, on more than one occasion, the fires had been set deliberately. Thankfully, the only time the building was significantly damaged by fire was in the late 1960's when the place was called the College Inn and long after gambling had left the property.[6] In fact, the wood-frame Newman's Lake House stood in its original spot until the early 1970's when it fell into disrepair and was demolished.

Any run-ins with the law that Henry Newman did have were few and far between until, as with everyone else, prohibition came to Saratoga.

In 1908, Fish and Game Wardens descended on a couple of the lake houses and raided both kitchens, where they found trout possessed out of season. Seventy-three trout were found at Newman's and another one hundred trout were confiscated at the Arrowhead Inn.[7] Fish eaten out of season generally do not taste any different than fish caught in season and so the illicit nature of the fare at Newman's, at least in 1908, could not account for the popularity of the dining options offered there.

It would seem to a casual observer, though, that an establishment that provided illicit alcohol might have an advantage over their competitors. During prohibition, those restaurants that served beer or liquor definitely had an advantage in drawing in customers and, even before prohibition became the law of the land, selling alcohol on Sundays in violation of the law gave the places that did so an extra day of sales and profit compared with those places that played by the rules. Henry Newman's place apparently served alcohol on Sundays.

In 1909, someone nursing a grievance against Mr. Newman reported to the sheriff that Newman was operating in violation of the law. The sheriff sent two deputies over with the intent of trapping Newman on a charge of selling alcohol on Sunday. When they arrived, one of the deputies ordered two drinks of whiskey. He needed two because he had never had whiskey before and needed to have the first shot so he could be sure of what he was drinking for the second serving, which formed the basis of the charge against Mr. Newman. Whatever the quality of the testimony of the deputy, the judge decided there was not enough evidence against Newman and the charge was dropped.[8]

Henry Newman died on January 22, 1914, at his home on Saratoga Lake. He was buried at his hometown of Babylon, Long Island.[9] Upon Henry's death, his widow Katherine operated the resort with the assistance of Matthew (Matty) Dunn, a well-known local restaurateur. Katherine retained control of the business until 1921 when Matty Dunn and John Bleeck of New York City partnered to form Newman's Lake House, Inc. and bought the business and the grounds from Mrs. Newman.[10]

Of course, 1921 was during the advent of Prohibition and a place like Newman's was sure to be involved in the selling of liquor. No respectable resort in Saratoga would deny its patrons the pleasure of illicit drink. That being the case, Newman's would eventually draw the attention of the probies and soon enough, the law was knocking on the door.

In May 1921, Saratoga County Deputy Sheriff Clarence Hovey arrived at the door of Newman's with a search warrant. It just so happened that Deputy Covey had been investigating the theft of a large cache of liquor in the town of Lake Luzerne and had traced a portion of the illegally stolen, illegal liquor, to

Newman's. Unfortunately for Matty Dunn and his partners, Deputy Hovey discovered $8,000 worth of illicit alcohol in the place.[11] It was the largest liquor haul in the district up to that time.

Since neither Dunn nor Bleeck were present at the time of the raid, the caretaker of the place, Leon Kenny, was left to take the charge on behalf of the business. Although later reports were that gambling had been introduced at Newman's in the early 1920's, there was no mention of gambling equipment found during the 1921 raid by Deputy Hovey. Perhaps Matty Dunn had not yet had time to open up the games of chance, and since the raid was conducted in May, they were still a month or two away from the summer season's official start anyway.

Unfortunately for Mr. Kenny, while he was being processed at the city lock-up, someone entered his sleeping quarters on the grounds and stole about $500 worth of jewelry. Kenny reported that a diamond stick pin, a watch fob, and a ring were stolen while he was in the custody of the Sheriff.

A report in the *Saratogian* on May 14, 1921, indicated that the thieves responsible for the Kenny theft had actually been planning to steal the liquor that the Sheriff had seized, and the raid foiled their plans. They then settled on the Kenny jewelry as a consolation prize.

The persons responsible for stealing Leon Kenny's property were never arrested and Kenny had the charges against him dismissed within days for lack of evidence.[12]

In 1925, Newman's was the scene of great excitement in August of that year. On August 12 the headline of the *Saratogian* screamed, "WATCHMAN SHOT IN GUN BATTLE AT NEWMAN'S!"

We will get to that in a minute, but before we do, less than a week after the gunplay just mentioned, Newman's was raided once again by law officers looking for liquor.

On August 17, two undercover agents ordered a couple of whiskey shots at Newman's and, after the drinks were served, the agents promptly arrested bartender Thomas Stanton and manager John Blake.

The lawmen produced a warrant and, searching the premises, the agents found three bottles of creme de menthe, four pints of champagne, three quarts of rye gin, twenty quarts of whiskey, sixty-six quarts of ale, two quarts of champagne, and thirty-one, one-ounce bottles of whiskey.[13] A nice haul for the law men.

Now, as was mentioned briefly already, the gambling at Newman's started sometime in the early to mid-1920's. Like most of the gambling resorts in Saratoga, the gambling was kept separate from the dining and entertainment area and Newman's set-up was no different. The dining room was in the front and the gambling was in the back. In addition, to keep things separate, the leases for the restaurant and the gaming were always held by different people. In the case of Newman's, while Leon Kenny managed the restaurant until the 1940's, a number of people held the gambling interest in the place.

The Grennan brothers out of Schenectady ran the gambling for a while. In later years (the late 1940's) Anthony "Hawk-Eye-Tinny" Lombardo and Tommy O'Brien out of Rochester joined Patty Grennan as the professional house gamblers while Gerard King and Al Pepper owned the property.

The official tally of games of chance that could be found at Newman's in the late 1940's was: seven roulette wheels, one wheel of fortune, two craps tables, and one bird cage.[14]

If one was travelling east on Crescent Avenue and made a right at Newman's Lake House, he or she would travel a short distance through the woods and come to Riley's Lake House overlooking Lake Lonely.

Riley's Lake House was established in the mid 1880's, most likely 1886, by James H. Riley. Jim Riley was born near Lake Lonely in 1847 and became a champion rower in his younger days, once setting the world's record for the distance of two miles at Saratoga Lake.

He built the first "Riley's Lakeside Hotel" on a bluff overlooking Saratoga Lake, basically across Crescent Ave from Newman's Lake House. Riley's hotel was there for about ten years until he moved the location to its final spot overlooking Lake Lonely.[15]

Riley's was well known for its dining room while Jim ran the place. He had a very popular toboggan slide in the winter months and the only real trouble that was ever reported during Jim Riley's tenure was a small scuffle between a millionaire Wall Street man and one of the bookmakers from the track in August 1907.[16]

As he grew older and times changed, Jim Riley seemed unable to hold off the nefarious forces approaching the lake houses. In 1917 Arnold Rothstein became a partner in the Arrowhead Inn gambling and made an enormous profit. By 1919 the other lake houses were starting to follow suit and the men who held the lease for Riley's place added gambling to the dining and entertainment. Riley himself did not appreciate the new arrangements and even complained to the city court judge at the time, Michael McTygue.[17]

Riley was quoted as telling Judge McTygue, "I have spent over thirty years building up my property and heretofore its good name has never been questioned." He went on, referring to a scuffle that had broken out the previous night, "I am afraid murder will be committed before the end of the season."[18]

Judge McTygue told Riley to report the matter to the police, who promptly informed Jim Riley (wrongly) that the lake house was outside their jurisdiction and he would need to call in the state police. Fortunately, no one was killed on the property that summer, but poor Mr. Riley seemed powerless to stop the gambling forces from taking over.

By the time Matty Dunn took over the helm at Riley's in 1923, adding the place to his portfolio, which already included Newman's Lake House, gambling and liquor were both available at Riley's. In 1924, the famed prohibition duo, Izzy and Moe, paid a visit to the place, purchasing a pint of whiskey from one of the waiters.[19]

The following year, three men were arrested at Riley's in violation of the Volstead Act. They were released into the custody of their attorney, Saratoga Springs Mayor Clarence Knapp. Mayor Knapp, himself having been a United States Commissioner handling Volstead Act cases until his resignation from that post in 1923, should have known the proper procedure to have the men arraigned properly.

It had been the custom, at least in Saratoga Springs, that bootleggers were released to their attorneys, who would then produce the defendants to the appropriate commissioner. In this case, Mayor Knapp brought the men before Commissioner Coons at Ballston Spa. Commissioner Coons refused to arraign the men and Federal Judge Cooper in Auburn directed Mayor Knapp to bring his charges to Commissioner Dunham in Corinth. By the time Knapp showed up at Corinth, the men arrested at Riley's had disappeared.

This caused Judge Cooper to berate Mayor Knapp in open court and express his belief that having the Mayor of a city defending people charged with federal crimes in his own jurisdiction conflicted with ordinary principles of good government.[20]

While Mayor Knapp insisted that he did nothing out of the ordinary and that the men had broken their word to him to stay within the city, the *Saratogian* saw fit to point out the problem that Judge Cooper had with Mayor Knapp was in no way linked to a shooting earlier that summer at Riley's. Why would the *Saratogian* see fit to mention a shooting in an article about a few men charged with possessing alcohol?

Well, go back a few pages and recall when it was mentioned that on August 12, 1925, the *Saratogian* had run the headline, "WATCHMAN SHOT IN GUN BATTLE AT NEWMAN'S!"

Only it wasn't Newman's where the shooting took place, it was Riley's. And not only did the police initially conceal the location of the shooting, when one of the defendants was brought into court, he was identified as a gunman from New York who, as we shall see, went on to have a prolific criminal career of his own. The reader was promised that we would get to the story of the shooting, and we will do so now.

According to police, at about 4:00 a.m., Charles Cook, who was then living at 19 Andrews St, was working at Newman's as a night watchman when he encountered two men attempting to force entry to the building.

Cook, of course, confronted the two men. He called out to them that the place was closed and that they couldn't get in. Almost immediately, one of the men fired a shot that nearly struck Cook in the head. The two men then retreated to a waiting vehicle, while firing another shot at the watchman. When the two would-be burglars reached their car, Cook bravely charged towards them, shouting at the driver to turn off the engine. For his trouble, Cook was fired upon once more; this time he was hit in the shoulder.

Still endeavoring to do his duty, Cook drew his own pistol and fired twice at the fleeing felons. He was able to hit the car, but not any of the occupants, and just before he passed out from the searing pain in his shoulder, Cook thought he could hear women's voices coming from the direction of the car as it sped off.

While all this was happening, according to police, a woman placed a call to the police and said only, "shooting at Newman's, car on way to Saratoga."

Naturally, this rallied all available police officers, and Patrolmen McGirr, Cummings, and several others sprinted from the station to their cars and motorcycles and headed off towards the lake. Around the area of Yaddo on Union Avenue, McGirr and Cummings encountered the suspect vehicle racing towards town and took up the chase.

As they followed the fleeing car, Cummings leaned out of the patrol car and fired five shots at the suspects. Another shot, probably from a beat officer, was fired at the fleeing auto on Circular Street, south of Union Ave. None of the occupants were hit by police projectiles, but the vehicle did have several bullet holes in its body when the chase finally came to an end.

When the chase came to Union Ave where it intersects with Circular Street, Detective (soon to be Chief) Patrick Rox fell in behind McGirr and Cummings as they chased the suspects in the shooting. From Circular, the pursuit headed down South Broadway to the bridge over the Kayaderosseras Creek where the pursued men crashed their car into a ditch.

McGirr and Cummings were travelling so fast, they overshot the disabled vehicle of the bad guys while the two male occupants jumped out and tried to run into the woods.

Being in the third position during the chase, Detective Rox saw the crash ahead of him and was able to subdue the two men quickly as McGirr and Cummings came back to assist. One of the men, Thomas O'Neill of New York City, was apparently caught while he was grabbing for a gun he had dropped when the car crashed into the ditch. A .32 caliber revolver was found a few feet from the overturned car. His partner, Anthony "Little Augie Pisano" Carfano, also of New York City, was captured, along with two local women who were riding in the car and were present at the shooting. They were Annette Mayone and Gladys Pullman.

All four of the party were brought to police headquarters and questioned. The young ladies were released after talking to the police and claiming that they had only met the two men from New York earlier that evening and had been drinking and dancing with them. Their story was that they had gone for a joy ride with the men which ended with the shooting, chase, crash, and their arrests.

O'Neill and Carfano were held on bail pending the investigation and the status of watchman Cook whom, it was feared, might not recover from the gunshot wound in his shoulder.

Cook did recover though, after a two-week stay in the hospital. O'Neill and Carfano were both released on bail pending trial. After two delays requested by the defense, O'Neill was the first to go to trial in June of 1926.

From the time of the shooting, the police and District Attorney Andrus attempted to piece together a case and untangle a confusing mess of witness statements. Based upon the press accounts in the *Saratogian* during O'Neill's trial, the basic story of the shooting was this:

On the night of the shooting, O'Neill, Carfano, and the two young women met with a man named Dewey Bentham or Louis Bennet, who was said to be the secretary for the Deputy Fire Commissioner in New York City, at Beefsteak Charlie's on Phila Street. O'Neill had been drinking and, when it was suggested that the group head out to Riley's, Bennett drove O'Neill's car with Little Augie and the ladies in the back seat.

Although one report had the purpose for the visit as Little Augie and O'Neill looking for a welsher on a bet,[21] the story told in court by Bennett and the two women was that O'Neill went out to talk with Matty Dunn and Blake, the two men who were then running the gambling at Riley's.

When he was denied entry, O'Neill, being intoxicated, argued with Cook, the watchman. As other special officers, including a New York Police Detective assigned to work the summer in Saratoga, approached the disturbance, O'Neill was pushed back into the car. With Bennett starting to pull away, a shot was fired from the vicinity of the car. No one could remember exactly from where or by whom.

Bennett leaped out of the driver's seat of the car and made a beeline for the nearby woods as Carfano jumped into the driver's seat and sped off. Bennett was secured by the New York City detective and the story of the rest of the chase was recounted earlier.

During O'Neill's trial it was clear that someone in the party had shot watchman Cook. And while Cook identified O'Neill as his assailant in the hospital on the night of the shooting, he was unable to do so in court.

It was however, established that the revolver found by Detective Rox at the scene of the car crash was the gun used to shoot Cook, but the police never were able to definitively put that particular gun into the particular hand of any one particular person and while O'Neill was indicted for shooting Cook based upon the grand jury testimony of the others in the car, they apparently told different stories at the trial.

An exasperated Judge Lawrence B. McKelvey lamented about Anthony "Little Augie" Carfano that, "I don't know who he is or where he came from, but I have never heard a more ridiculous statement made by a witness in this courtroom than the witnesses' testimony from the beginning to the end. I cannot tell, in my own mind, beyond a reasonable doubt, whether it was he that fired the shot or whether it was O'Neill."

Judge McKelvey figured that he had no choice but to dismiss the charges against O'Neill.

It shall be noted for the reader here, without commentary by the author, that Thomas O'Neill's attorneys were Richard Sherman, Saratoga Springs Commissioner of Finance, and Theodore Knapp, brother of former mayor Clarence Knapp, who we met earlier.

Now, back to Judge McKelvey's comment, "I don't know who he is or where he came from" about Little Augie and about whom District Attorney Andrus added, "We can't indict Carfano for the shooting, and once more 'Little Augie' has escaped, but someday he will not escape."[22]

Why would Carfano, an unindicted co-conspirator, warrant such attention from the judge and district attorney and why was he in Saratoga anyway? Perhaps a short biography of the man will explain it.

At the time of the shooting, Anthony "Little Augie" Carfano was already known for his racketeering and bootlegging in Brooklyn. In earlier times, he was muscle for Al "Scarface" Capone, first in New York and then over in Chicago where he would "persuade" folks to buy Capone liquor in the Windy City and its environs. By the 1930's Carfano and Capone had teamed up in a horse racing stable that Carfano managed at Saratoga.[23]

Carfano would rise to become an underboss in the Genovese Crime Family in New York and worked under Lucky Luciano and Frank Costello.

Starting in 1916, Little Augie was arrested around a dozen times and was often brought in for questioning whenever a gangland murder had taken place. He was suspected of being involved in the murder of racketeer Frank Marlow and the murder of a Union City, NJ, police sergeant. [24] Author Patrick Downey claims that Carfano was the person who placed the call that led Frank Uale (Frankie Yale) to his death. "Little Augie" was also closely associated with major mafia figures Giuseppe "Joe the Boss" Masseria and Albert Anastasia.

In the mid 1920's, when the shooting at Newman's, oops - we mean, Riley's, had occurred, Carfano was in the early stages of his long criminal career. But like so many other gangsters of his era, eventually he would come to an abrupt end.

In September, 1959, Little Augie Carfano was dining with a married woman in New York City. Carfano took a phone call and the two left the restaurant shortly thereafter. Two gunmen, hiding in the back seat of his car, suddenly appeared and assassinated Carfano and his lady friend on a street near LaGuardia Airport.

Now, to answer the question as to why the police would report the location as Newman's and not Riley's? The answer is relatively simple. It appears that the police reported the incident as a case of possible burglars attempting to enter Newman's because Newman's was not yet a gambling destination. Although Matty Dunn was running both Newman's and Riley's, Newman's was still primarily a dining place, not linked to organized criminals yet.

Perhaps the officers felt that public opinion would not look kindly on gunplay at one of the gambling joints and the story they told was more palatable to the general conscience. Violence linked to the gambling dens would surely bring on public and/or political pressure for a law enforcement response.

The shooting at Riley's was not the last time Riley's would attract unwanted attention and scandal for the Saratoga Police. A brief timeline will be important to keep in mind for the next adventure at Riley's.

Patrick Rox, as we have seen, was initially a detective in the early 1920's and his testimony was deemed unbelievable by Judge Heffernan in 1927. Although he probably perjured himself, Rox survived the trial's aftermath and, when Dr. Arthur Leonard won the public safety election in 1927, after he had resigned, rather than face removal by the Governor on Judge Heffernan's recommendation, Rox was appointed Chief of Police. From the late 1920's through the mid 1930's Leonard remained Public Safety Commissioner and Rox, Chief of Police.

The public however, eventually tired of all the gangsters having the run of the place through the 1930's, and who could blame them? With the stories we have already seen, the gunplay on the streets of the city and the rumored mishandling of the Parillo murder by Chief Rox, the citizens of Saratoga Springs voted for change in 1937. Incoming Commissioner of Public Safety, Joseph A. Doherty, demoted Rox to the position Rox formerly held, that of detective.

So, on August 12, 1939, Patrick F. Rox was once again a detective. On that night he received a call at police headquarters from Chief of Police John A'Hearn who instructed Rox to head on out to Riley's Lake House and take charge of some gambling evidence that had been discovered there.

A squad of deputy sheriffs and Saratoga Springs Police officers had been patrolling around the lake when they saw a light coming from a small building on the grounds of Riley's Lake House. There was supposed to have been no gambling out at the lake that summer and the two sheriff's deputies pushed their way past a local man serving as the doorman, followed by the city officers.

Once inside they found the well-dressed clientele gambling the night away. When the lawmen announced their presence, the crowd departed in an orderly, respectful manner.

As the crowd was leaving, Chief A'Hearn was notified of the gambling and he detailed Detective Rox to go to Riley's and take charge of the investigation. The team of officers had gathered up four roulette table tops, one roulette wheel, a wheel of fortune, two craps tables, and several boxes of chips and brought it all to police headquarters.[25] They took special care to places mattresses between the table tops so as not to scratch them on the trip.

Unlike when gambling apparatus was secured at the police station back in 1919, this time the gamblers did not pay a visit to the police station and steal the evidence against them. However, the discerning reader will notice that there were four roulette tabletops discovered at Riley's, but only one roulette wheel made it to the police station. Was this another case of evidence gone missing while in possession of the Saratoga Police?

That is exactly what Chief A'Hearn wanted to know and inquired with Detective Rox, the officer in charge of transporting the stuff from Riley's to the police station. Chief A'Hearn also wanted to know what happened to a bird cage that had also been at Riley's but never made it to headquarters.

Rox explained to Chief A'Hearn that when he arrived at Riley's, employees of that establishment (rumored to be Farone men) were busy dismantling the roulette tables, while the police, about officers in all, stood by and waited for the workers to finish.

According to Rox, he also did not realize he was in charge, despite his being the highest-ranking officer on scene. Perhaps we should at least be grateful that Detective Rox could now recognize gambling equipment when he admitted that he did not know what gambling apparatus looked like a decade or so earlier, during the Heffernan investigation.

Not buying his explanation, Chief A'Hearn gave Rox ten days to produce the missing three roulette wheels and bird cage. When Rox did not, he was suspended.

Now, keep this in mind for the next part of the story. The owners of Riley's Lake House at the time of the raid were Louis "Doc" Farone, Matty Dunn, and Thomas Leonard, brother of former Public Safety Commissioner "Doc" Leonard. Rox and Farone had known each other at this time for about twenty years and it was Farone men who dismantled the roulette wheels on the night of the raid.

The raid at Riley's was on August 12. Rox was suspended by A'Hearn on August 23. He remained on suspension through the fall of 1939. Arthur "Doc" Leonard was nominated by the Democratic Party to try to win his old position back from Commissioner Doherty. Everyone in town knew that if Leonard was returned to the public safety department, he would try to reinstate Patty Rox and open up the town for gambling once again.

Unsurprisingly, on election day, the voters of Saratoga Springs returned "Doc" Leonard to office. Doherty, despite having made a valiant attempt at keeping Saratoga clean, was defeated.

In addition to his election loss, Doherty suffered another defeat. That same fall, the Grand Jury of Saratoga County had failed to indict anyone for the gambling uncovered at Riley's on the night of August 12, 1939. At the time, Chief A'Hearn and District Attorney Smith had decided that the case would be presented to the fall term of the Grand Jury and, therefore, no arrests had been made that night.

Of course, failing to indict gamblers during the fall term of the Grand Jury was as solid a Saratoga tradition as visitors taking the mineral waters, but Doherty blamed Rox. If he hadn't been negligent in securing the evidence at Riley's Lake House, the Grand Jury would have come back with indictments against the operators of the place. So, he decided to fire Detective Patrick Rox.[26]

Rox was terminated on December 6, 1939. On January 1, 1940, when "Doc" Leonard came back into office, he "reviewed" the case against Rox, overturned Doherty's dismissal, and reappointed Patty Rox to the position of Chief of Police. Both Leonard and Rox believed that Rox's firing was politically motivated and that he should not have been fired for the missing roulette wheels and birdcage.

The rest of the City Council was not sure that someone who was fired from the police force could be installed as Chief of Police, while Commissioner Leonard felt the city charter gave him the authority to appoint whomever he wished. He also felt, with some justification, that the results of the 1939 election indicated that the people of Saratoga Springs supported his view. So, the Mayor and the Finance Commissioner, on the advice of the city attorney, decided to let the courts decide the issue and withheld Rox's pay as Chief as his labor lawsuit wound its way through the courts.

After a few months, Rox was reinstated by Supreme Court Justice O. Byron Brewster, who agreed with Rox and Leonard that his dismissal was politically motivated. The decision was upheld by the highest court in New York State, the New York State Court of Appeals. Chief Rox was back, with full pay and the support of Doc Leonard. Another chapter in the sordid saga of the "Saratoga Way" was completed at Riley's Lake House.

We now turn to the famous Arrowhead Inn located at the end of Arrowhead Road off Crescent Avenue. The place was built by Ben Riley, not to be confused with Jim Riley of Riley's Lake House. A Saratoga native, Ben Riley opened the Arrowhead as a roadhouse in either 1897 or 1899. The land had previously been the property of a gentleman farmer named Hull. The name of the house reportedly comes from the fact that workmen for Ben Riley uncovered a Native American burial ground and several arrowheads while building the place.[27]

Riley sold his Arrowhead Inn on Saratoga Lake in 1907 and opened a new resort, also called the Arrowhead Inn, down in Yonkers, just north of New York City on the banks of the Hudson River. Both roadhouses catered to the wealthy and, with his roadhouses and some real estate investments, Ben Riley became a multi-millionaire. At age 73, Ben Riley died in a fire that consumed his Arrowhead Inn at Yonkers in 1944.[28]

After Ben Riley sold his Saratoga holdings to Matty Cahill around 1907, the place continued to be an eating establishment until it burned to the ground. It was sold and rebuilt in 1915 by James Welch, who, along with James Fennell, Charles Manny, and John Coakley, made extensive improvements and renovations to the place, just in time for the gambling scene to burst wide open in Saratoga.

In 1917, Arnold Rothstein was looking to invest in a gambling joint at Saratoga. His story is told in greater detail in this author's previous work, *All the Law in the World Won't Stop Them*. Suffice it to say here, the gambling at the Arrowhead was helped along by the $40,000 donation that Rothstein made to the local political parties and the $150,000 investment in the property that Rothstein's partners made the following year.

After the Bascom raids in 1920, a couple of the partners at the Arrowhead paid small fines after pleading guilty to various gambling charges. By then, Rothstein had moved on to concentrate on his sole ownership of the Brook resort out Church Street, leaving the gambling operations over the years to men like John "O.K." Coakley of New York City, "Lefty" Clark of Detroit's notorious "Purple Gang," and mobsters Joe Adonis, Frank Costello, Joseph "Doc" Stacher, and Meyer Lansky.

According to his informative work, *Chippin' Away...At the Gambling Scene of Saratoga*, Richard Carbin, nephew of Patrick Rox, informs us that the Arrowhead had five roulette tables, five card tables, three craps tables, two Bird Cages, and one Wheel of Fortune.

Until the Kefauver Committee hearings, the Arrowhead avoided any major incidents like the "Little Augie Pisano" shootout and the missing roulette wheels that Riley's Lake House suffered through.

But like all the others, the Arrowhead had a few brushes with the law. The gamblers arrested during the Bascom raids in 1919 have already been mentioned. Back in 1907, one of Ben Riley's employees embezzled a large amount of money from the Arrowhead. When confronted, the suspect agreed to pay back all the stolen money and Ben Riley declined to press charges.[29]

In 1924 and 1925 prohibition agents visited the Arrowhead. Izzy and Moe, called "liquor smelling sleuths" by the *Saratogian,* arrested three men in 1924, with Izzy remarking, "The place was crowded with men and women, dancing, eating, and drinking. You know it is a high-class place, and everybody was in evening clothes." The three men arrested were released into the custody of Mayor Knapp.[30]

The following year, the federals returned. This time they arrested four men for selling and possessing liquor, and again all four men were represented by Mayor Knapp. This time the authorities grabbed Canadian Ale and whiskey, two bags of assorted liquors, three bags of ale, and some champagne. [31] Mayor Knapp was successful in appealing the convictions of the men based on a technicality involving the warrant used during the investigation.

The Arrowhead was one of the most prominent of the illegal casinos at Saratoga. As such, the operators were required to pay an elevated price for the privilege of opening. In the mid nineteen twenties, the going rate for the green light to open was between $10,000 and $50,000 for the season. [32] Arrowhead, Piping Rock, Riley's, and the Brook would be at the higher end of that scale. Each house had to pay, and it was estimated that local authorities pocketed around $150,000 in graft during the summer of 1925, just about 2.1 million dollars today.

In September of 1969, the Arrowhead Inn burned to the ground.

Now we come to the Piping Rock Club. Located at the intersection of Union Avenue and Gilbert Road, the Piping Rock was not technically on any lake, but it was close enough to be considered as one of the Lake Houses. It was most famous as the place connected to Meyer Lansky, Frank Costello, and Joe Adonis during the Kefauver Committee hearings. If the reader will be patient, we will get to that, but right now, an overview of the Piping Rock Club should suffice.

Situated on about 130 acres, the Piping Rock was originally called Mitchell's before opening as the Lido Venice in 1927. The gambling, dining, and entertainment nightclub was counted among the more fashionable places in Saratoga, ranking with the Arrowhead, Riley's, and the Brook.

During the latter half of the 1920's, when the place was the Lido Venice, other than a few raids by the prohibition men, nothing of any major legal consequence was associated with the Lido Venice. There was a brief moment when the gambling and graft connected to the Lido Venice was in jeopardy, however.

In 1931, former Saratoga County Sheriff William Cromie was nominated by President Hoover to the post of United States Marshall for Northern New York. During Cromie's confirmation hearing in the United States Senate, the New York Civic League produced an affidavit from a Ballston Spa resident who claimed,

"…about two years ago (the witness) was at the Lido Venice, so called gambling house at Saratoga Springs and saw Sheriff Cromie call the proprietor of Lido Venice, Mr. Kellerhan outside to his automobile, and saw him peel off five bills from a roll and hand them to Sheriff Cromie through the window of his automobile."[33]

Cromie made a complete denial and the Chairman of the committee would not allow a fishing expedition so Cromie was confirmed by the Senate, much to the disappointment of the New York Civic League.

If the intent of the Civic League was to force testimony into the open about the conditions of Saratoga Springs, it didn't work. The places went right on gambling.

Despite the fact that the Lido Venice was one of the most popular dining and gambling spots in Saratoga, with uniformed valets, top entertainment, and a six-ton safe[34] to guard all the money, the Lido Venice was upgraded and renamed the Piping Rock Club under the ownership of the Flat Rock Holding Company in 1930.

By 1935, one year after the Brook burned to the ground, the Piping Rock had seemingly taken first place on the list of swanky Saratoga nightclubs. With Al Delmonico, famous head chef out of New York City, two twenty-piece orchestras, and one thousand guests per night at the height of the summer season, there was little doubt the Piping Rock was tops in the business.

The press could not praise the new venue enough and one western New York newspaper describing the Piping Rock this way: "The club rates a standing equal to the best casinos in the world and is comparable to those to be found in Montreux, Interlaken, and other Swiss resorts. Like them, the Piping Rock Club house is a large structure standing in the midst of a big garden of great loveliness where flowers, shrubs, fountains, and turf by the direction of eminent landscaping architects, present a charming picture."[35]

The description of the Piping Rock brings to mind the recollection of Richard Canfield's Casino being called the "Monte Carlo of America" at the turn of the twentieth century. It was no wonder the fabulous resort out Union Avenue attracted the attention of the mob.

By the early 1940's a combination of mafia figures had taken over at the Piping Rock, Frank Costello and Joe Adonis primarily, along with Myer Lansky and the typical local front men. The staff of Frank Costello's Copacabana Club in New York City spent the summer working at the Piping Rock.[36]

When they are careful, mafia backers of certain nightclubs generally stay out of the press. Yet, in 1944, both Costello and Adonis were linked to the club by a New York City detective who gave testimony during a hearing related to the cabaret license of the Copacabana Club in New York City.

Detective Joseph Bonanno said that he had been to the Piping Rock in 1943 and the place contained the typical gambling equipment, roulette tables, dice games, chemin-de-fer, bird cages, and other games of chance. The detective claimed that Joe Adonis, already known as a major underworld figure, was in the Piping Rock every night during the summer, playing cards and never seeing a check for his expensive meals.

Bonanno described the Piping Rock as a virtual playground for Miami gangsters and New York Racketeers with Frank "The Prime Minister" Costello running the entire show.[37]

Like the Arrowhead and the Brook, the Piping Rock Club burned to the foundation. The year was 1954.

While Sophie Tucker and Bing Crosby entertained at the Piping Rock, no such big-name entertainment was found at the final "Lake House" we will consider in this book, Smith's Interlaken.

Smith's Interlaken was located through the woods near Riley's Lakehouse, and shared the grounds with the Interlaken trailer park.

As a no-frills operation, Smith's Interlaken did not provide nightly entertainment and dining like the other Lake Houses. One could get drinks, though, and so the prohibition agents naturally called on Smith's in 1931. It is unlikely they celebrated too much as they only managed to arrest one person for possessing about one quart of distilled whiskey.[38]

Smith's managed to operate relatively under the radar and really only made news in its early years when the property was seized by the city for back taxes. It wasn't until William "Scotchy" Morrison from Albany, and "Doc" Farone teamed up to operate the place that is stabilized and became known for the gambling carried on there.

A bus ran hourly from Congress Park to Smith's Interlaken, ferrying players to the games. With a house limit of $300 and bets as little as one dollar accepted, Smith's was a popular destination for locals and visitors alike. All were apparently welcome to play roulette, craps, blackjack, or take a turn at the bird cage or wheel of fortune.

As with the other Lake Houses, Smith's Interlaken succumbed to a fire in 1970 while crews were beginning demolition work. And, as with all the other Lake Houses, Smith's Interlaken would be identified as an open gambling joint in the Kefauver hearings, to which we now turn.

Endnotes

Chapter 10

[1] Memorandum dated February 3, 1951. Saratoga Springs Public Library.

[2] "Remember When?" *The Saratogian*. August 8, 1961.

[3] "Operation Fatal to Mrs. Newman." *The Saratogian*. February 14, 1921.

[4] "Newman's Lake House Put in Seller's Block." *The Saratogian*. August 28, 1963.

[5] "Trotting Meet Saturday on Saratoga Lake." *The Saratogian*. January 14, 1902.

[6] "Fire Department's Action Contains College Inn Blaze." *The Saratogian*. January 30, 1968.

[7] "Lake Hotels Raided." *Hudson Valley Times*. September 10, 1908.

[8] "Mr. Newman Freed; Miss Davidson Sues." *The Daily Saratogian*. August 4, 1909.

[9] "Final Tribute to Henry J. Newman." *The Saratogian*. July 24, 1914.

[10] "'Matty' Dunn New Owner of Newman's." *The Saratogian*. January 21, 1921.

[11] "Sheriff Raids Newman's; Seizes $8,000 in Liquor; Arrests Caretaker Kenny." *The Saratogian*. May 11, 1921.

[12] "Court Frees Kenny, Held in Booze Raid." *The Saratogian*. May 21, 1921.

[13] "Dry Agents Find Liquor Hoard in Newman Garage." *The Saratogian*. August 17, 1925.

[14] Kefauver, Estes. *Organized Crime in America.*

[15] "Riley, Founder of Lake House, Dead; Leading Sculler." *The Saratogian.* August 20, 1927.

[16] "J. Brandt Walker Has a Man Arrested." *The Daily Saratogian.* August 21, 1907.

[17] "Gambling at Lake Lonely, Says Riley." *The Saratogian.* August 27, 1919.

[18] Ibid.

[19] "Bought Whiskey at Riley's, Say Federal Agents." *The Saratogian.* August 25, 1924.

[20] "Cooper Scores Mayor Knapp; Order Police Probe." *The Saratogian.* October 20, 1925.

[21] "Girls in Saratoga Shooting Affair Are Held as Witnesses." *The Schenectady Gazette.* August 14, 1925.

[22] "O'Neil Goes Free in Shooting at Riley's." *The Saratogian.* August 24, 1926.

[23] "All Boroughs Join in War on Crooks." *The New York Times.* August 30, 1930.

[24] "'Little Augie' Free; Held for 13 Hours." *The New York Times.* June 2, 1946.

[25] "Raid Gambling Games at Riley's and Piping Rock." *The Saratogian.* August 14, 1939.

[26] "Detective Rox Dismissed by Doherty For Loss of Seized Gambling Apparatus." *The Saratogian.* December 7, 1939.

[27] "Early Life in Saratoga Pictured by Goldsmith for Historical Society." *The Saratogian.* April 30, 1938.

[28] "Ben Riley, Arrowhead Inn Founder, Dies in Yonkers Fire." *The Saratogian.* February 18, 1944.

[29] "Ben Riley, Robbed, Makes Thief Give Back Spoils." *The Saratogian*. May 22, 1907.

[30] "Arrowhead and Forty-One Raided by Izzy and Moe." *The Saratogian*. August 12, 1924.

[31] "Charge Warrant was Defective in Arrowhead Raid." *The Saratogian*. August 25, 1925.

[32] "Blackmail of Sporting Places Causes Comment." *The Saratogian*. August 15, 1925.

[33] Kavanaugh and Public Office Holders Warned by Leaders of Civic League in Fight on Cromie." *The Saratogian*. February 23, 1931.

[34] "Move Heavy Safe from Broadway." *The Saratogian*. April 23, 1930.

[35] "So They Say." *The Clyde Herald*. August 7, 1935.

[36] "Piping Rock Leased to N.Y. Group." *The Saratogian*. June 5, 1941.

[37] "Gamblers Linked with Copacabana." *The Kingston Daily Freeman*. September 13, 1944.

[38] "Interlake in Prohibition Net." *The Saratogian*. August 22, 1931.

Chapter 11

The End of the Saratoga Way[1]

By the time Senator Estes Kefauver opened the Special Committee to Investigate Organized Crime in Interstate Commerce, the American public had become fascinated with the Mafia. Some twenty million citizens tuned in to watch the televised hearings, and although Kefauver never did establish that there was a national controlling body for the Mob, the hearings did reveal two major criminal syndicates operating throughout the country, links between national figures like Meyer

Lansky, Joe Adonis, and Frank Costello, and far too much local corruption to be left unaddressed.[2]

Perhaps the most important revelation that came out of the Kefauver hearings was the complete lack of effective law enforcement in areas where the Mafia had been able to gain a foothold. Among cities that were exposed by Senator Kefauver were notorious Mafia strongholds like New York, Miami, Chicago, New Orleans, Los Angeles, and Cleveland.

Making its way into the Kefauver inquiry was little old Saratoga Springs, NY, infamous for years for its open defiance of the gambling laws of the state.

Kefauver himself summed up the situation perfectly in his book, *Crime in America*, when he said, "Also we directed our attention upstate to Saratoga Springs. Turning the spotlight of exposure on the flagrant operation of gambling establishments, in which both New York City and out-of-state hoodlums had a hand. The evidence left little doubt that these had the acquiescence of Saratoga police."[3]

The situation at Saratoga might have been a shock to a senator from Tennessee, but Saratogians knew the truth. They knew full well that Saratoga had been a gangster's paradise for as long as they could remember.

Arnold Rothstein bragged publicly about his place out Church Street, the Brook. Owney Madden was photographed in the Grand Union Hotel, apparently with not a care in the world. Joe Adonis was seen nightly at the Piping Rock. Meyer Lansky was no stranger in town. Lucky Luciano was always at the track, the Chicago Club, and the Grand Union Hotel. The list could go on, but it had to come to an end, and it was Kefauver who started the dominoes falling.

When Kefauver and his team went to New York City and started taking testimony, it became clear that there was a strong connection between New York–New Jersey hoodlums and Saratoga Springs. Soon enough, the committee was calling representatives of the New York State Police to explain how they had knowledge of the gambling at Saratoga but never took any action.

In 1947, three years before Kefauver's committee had been established, Superintendent of the State Police John Gaffney ordered a survey of the gambling situation in Saratoga Springs. According to Gaffney, he ordered a survey, but not an investigation, because he believed the State Police were prohibited by law from enforcing the law in cities without an invitation from local officials or a direct order from the governor. He ordered the survey so that the State Police would know where to start if such an order or request ever were received.

The assignment went to Inspector Charles LaForge of the Bureau of Criminal Identification from the Troop C Barracks in Troy, NY. LaForge was directed to complete the survey and submit a report, nothing more.

So, with six or seven other troopers, LaForge set about surveying the gambling situation at Saratoga. He knew Police Chief Patrick Rox and had worked with him before.   LaForge had found Rox completely cooperative in all matters except gambling. Chief Rox refused to talk about the gambling situation at all, which LaForge understood to mean that the police were politically controlled. In fact, Rox believed that he was powerless to stop it, since Commissioner of Public Safety, Arthur "Doc" Leonard, had such control of the department that he knew his job was on the line if he took steps to enforce the gambling laws against the wishes of Leonard.

Of course, the logical question that follows such a statement is, "Why would Commissioner Leonard object to the enforcement of the laws that he was supposedly elected to enforce?" The answer probably lies with the comment recorded in an internal memorandum attributed to the former Saratoga County District Attorney Al Simon, who claimed that annual graft payments in Saratoga County were in the area of $300,000 per year, with $200,000 going to James Leary and the remaining $100,000 to Doc Leonard.

While large payoffs to the two public officials probably is not a shock to the reader, it wasn't the only form of graft that was present in Saratoga at the time.

Doc Leonard's brother, Thomas, although he managed Riley's Lake House,[4] was on the payroll of the police department as a driver. Chief Rox rented his car to the thoroughbred racetrack for $900 for the month of August and was paid $10 per night to escort the money from the harness track to the local bank.

Police officers were paid extra duty pay to do security work at the tracks and Detective Walter A'Hearn and his partner were paid to escort the daily profit from the Arrowhead Inn and Piping Rock to the bank every night.

The arrangement to have the police escort the money from their gambling dens to the banks must have been a relief to the gangsters. They wouldn't need to go to the lengths that were required of the money runners for Newman's Lake House in earlier times when, at the end of each night, the manager would place the nightly deposit into one of three bags. Each bag was placed in one of three cars, escorted by armed men. The three cars then raced to the bank in town, hoping to avoid being hijacked on the way. Upon arrival at the bank, the three bags were opened and only then did the men escorting the bags learn which one contained the money.[5]

Detective A'Hearn had a partner. It was a man identified as John Faets in the newspapers (he was also referred to as Don Peets or Petes) from Montreal, who was an instructor at Sir George Williams College there. He was always teamed with A'Hearn and was assigned to the lake district. He never made an arrest in Saratoga, his name never appears in any reporting in the local papers as being involved in an investigation of any kind, and he is never mentioned by Chief Rox or anyone else publicly. His presence is a mystery and the only mention of him is in a memorandum written by

Stanley Russo of the New York State Police during the survey of the gambling situation ordered by Gaffney.

One is left to wonder what Faets (if that was his true name) was doing in Saratoga, assigned to assist the one detective whose job it was to make a nightly check on the gambling places during the summer and to protect the money runs for at least one of those same casinos.

Was this a link to the Montreal Mafia and did they have some sort of interest in the gambling joints in Saratoga? It is certainly possible. After all, Saratoga native Adam Parillo had been associated with the top echelon of the Montreal underworld back in 1924 when he pulled that robbery job in Montreal.

Everyone else seemed to be dipping their beaks into the vice profits at Saratoga, so why not the Montreal mob as well? Was Faets a Canadian representative of the Montreal mob, keeping an eye on their interests at the Spa? Perhaps we will never know the answer to that question.

Additional "ice" paid by the gambling operators to the local population came in the form of do-nothing employment. The clubs that had gambling were forced to hire five or six local men as limo drivers, even if they had no need for such drivers. Each man was paid between $20 and $30 dollars per day and were typically politically connected men, often members of the local political committees. Everybody, it seemed, got a little taste of the shake in the Spa City.

In typical bureaucratic fashion, the State Police survey contained many facts about the Saratoga Police and the wide-open gambling places running in Saratoga between 1946 and 1950.

It was noted that the police department consisted of 40 patrolmen and two detectives with an additional forty officers and one detective (Faets) hired for the summer season. Chief Rox had no specialized police training, but Detective A'Hearn was a graduate of the FBI National Academy. There was a pool table and a card table in the recreation room in the police department on Lake Ave.

During one visit to the department, a team of State Police Investigators noticed several police officers playing cards in the rec room with a few dollars laid out in front of them. The Detective Bureau door was left unlocked and no gambling files were kept by the local police, as gambling was a misdemeanor and they didn't keep files unless a felony was involved.

As the survey was not testimony in court and they were not concerned with having to prove the allegations contained therein, the memorandums completed by State Police investigators related to the survey named the alleged collectors for Jim Leary and Doc Leonard.

For Leonard, it was recorded that Deputy Commissioner of Public Safety Peter Hofsses was the go-between and Detective A'Hearn and Officer George "Moon" Smith were the collectors, meaning that

THE END OF THE SARATOGA WAY

A'Hearn and Smith picked up the money from the gangsters and gave it to Hofsses, who then passed it on to Leonard.

For Jim Leary, Deputy Sheriffs Wesley DeVoe and Henry Winn were the supposed collectors while additional bagmen for Leary were said to be Vic Urquhart and Scott Crannell, a lookout at the Piping Rock Club.

To be fair, none of the men alleged as collectors for Leary and Leonard, other than Urquhart who was acquitted, were ever charged with being the bag men for the two political powers in Saratoga.

As far as the gambling joints were concerned, the State Police survey was laid out in a just-the-facts manner. The gambling apparatus at each place has been laid out previously in this work and the State Police included a list of the owners of each building along with the names of who held the gambling lease.

For the Arrowhead Inn, Herman and JoAnn Weiner were the owners, while the gamblers involved at various times were listed as: Charles Manning and John "OK" Coakley of New York City; Lefty Clark out of Detroit; and Doc Stacher, Meyer Lansky, and James "Piggy" Lynch of New York City. The percentage of the gambling interest in 1947 was fifty percent to Doc Stacher and twenty-five percent each to Lansky and Lynch.

At the Piping Rock Club, where the weekly expenses in 1948 ran to about $35,000, the Flat Rock

Holding Company was listed as the owner of the property. The gamblers with an interest in the property from 1946-1949 were: John and Edward McEwen of Albany; Arthur Clark, Sam Gold, Pete and Joe Sokol, and Joe Adonis of New York City; Henry Kelleher of Fort Edward; and Arthur Verra of Schenectady.

Riley's Lake House was owned variously by Margaret Farone, Al Delmonico, and Louis "Doc" Farone. The gambling lease was held by Peter Sullivan (Troy), Sam Gold (New York), Eddie Altman (New York), Abe Cohen (Albany), and Al Garfield (New York).

John and Gerard King, along with Allie Pepper, owned Newman's in the late 1940's. The gambling was run by Anthony "Hawk-Eye-Tinny" Lombardo and Tommy O'Brien out of Rochester and Patty Grennon from Schenectady.

Gaming at the Meadowbrook Casino was run by Gilbert Outhwaite from Troy with Joe Kulik out of Albany and Doc Farone of Saratoga. Matty Brown and Steve Tolk from Lodi, NJ, also had a hand in the gambling there.

At Smith's Interlaken, several men had or held the gambling lease over the years. They were William "Scotchy" Morrison of Albany; Abe Baker, Ed Hofmeister, and Patty Grennan from Schenectady; Tommy O'Brien and Tommy O'Connell from Boston; and Hy Samuels from New York City. Doc Farone also had an interest in Smith's.

Finally, the report identified several horse rooms operating openly throughout the town. In addition to the Chicago Club on Woodlawn Ave, the following places were noted:

- **20 Phila Street:** Operated by Allie, George, and James White
- **6 Railroad Place:** Operated by Vic Urquhart
- **The Paddock on Union Ave:** Operated by Scott Crannell
- **29 Caroline Street:** Operated by Jack Brophy
- **24 Caroline Street:** Operated by Allie Pepper

When the State Police survey was completed, it was submitted to Superintendent Gaffney, who promptly placed the report in the file and took no action. He would later explain to the Kefauver Committee that it was his understanding that the State Police did not have jurisdiction in Saratoga Springs and that law enforcement in cities was always left to the local police forces.

Since this had been a longstanding State Police policy, although it may not have been an accurate interpretation of the actual law establishing the State Police, Governor Dewey absolved Superintendent Gaffney of any wrongdoing related to his handling of the survey conducted by Inspector LaForge.

If the State Police were discreet in their information gathering, and unwilling to take independent action to clean up Saratoga Springs, one Saratogian was not discreet in her efforts to clean up the town.

Two years after the state police had quietly made their survey of the gambling joints in Saratoga, Mrs. Phillip Weiss filed a lawsuit seeking an injunction to restrain four gambling places from opening in the summer of 1949.

According to Mrs. Weiss' suit, her husband, Phillip had lost $14,000 gambling at Smith's Interlaken, The Kentucky Club, Pepper's, and at Vic Urquhart's place on Railroad Place. Mrs. Weiss had given her husband the money to buy cars and to start a taxi business. When he gambled the money away, Mrs. Weiss sought to hold the gamblers responsible and to prevent them from opening up again.[6]

Now, Phillip Weiss had been no stranger to the gambling scene, and one of the more unsavory elements of the fraternity at that.

In 1938 Weiss had shot and killed a man named Jack Sylvester, who had gone to a garage off Phila Street to collect money owed to him. When he arrived, he was shot by Phil Weiss. Weiss was arrested on a charge of manslaughter but released when the grand jury failed to indict him for the shooting.

His criminal history in New York City included charges of disorderly conduct and criminal usury (charging excessive interest on a loan). He was once picked up outside a gambling joint in Saratoga and charged with disorderly conduct. Another time Weiss was charged with third degree assault for a beating he administered to a Saratogian, presumably over a gambling debt, and at Mechanicville; while employed at a gambling house, he beat up a young man who refused to pay up on his losses.[7]

Weiss opened a candy store at 39 Phila Street in the 1930's. He didn't sell much, if any, candy, but he did hire an electrician to tap into the wires of a nearby horse room and thereby steal the signal of the race results so he could run his own horse room. This didn't sit well with the local gamblers and he started to be harassed by them and their allies on the police force.

Eventually the police came by and demolished Weiss' set up. In his testimony before Kefauver, Phillip Weiss said that, because he was not paying off any police or politicians, and since he was stealing the signal from another member of the gambling fraternity, the police came in and "broke up the place." After that, Weiss claims, he was blackballed by the gamblers and he could no longer operate his horse room, even though he tried. Nobody wants to be on the wrong side of the police *and* the mob.

Mrs. Weiss' lawsuit was dismissed about a week later and eventually the Weiss family opened the Four Sons Restaurant in place of the horse room on Phila Street. In later years it was the Executive Restaurant, still run by the Weiss family. Today it is Peabody's sports bar.

With the state police sniffing around and Mrs. Weiss publicly going after the gamblers, it must have seemed to the gangsters that the heat would eventually come. But no moves seemed to be forthcoming from the authorities. Leonard still controlled the city police and Leary still had a stranglehold on the county. Things seemed to be under control until that crusading Senator from Tennessee started barnstorming the country, holding hearings at various cities throughout the land.

By the time Kefauver got around to visiting New York City in February 1951, his investigators had already identified several witnesses that would be called to give testimony about the situation in Saratoga. The transcripts of the testimony regarding Saratoga Springs before the Kefauver Committee stretches over hundreds of pages. As is true of much testimony before government committees, a lot of it is boring, evasive, and of minor importance. Keeping in mind the chronology of events (the 1947 State Police Survey, the 1949 Weiss lawsuit, the 1951 Kefauver hearings) the author will attempt now to summarize the relevant testimony before Kefauver that related specifically to Saratoga Springs.

That an underworld syndicate consisting of Meyer Lansky, Joe Adonis, and Frank Costello was operating gambling joints in Saratoga Springs during the summer season was undeniable after the Kefauver hearings.

Inspector LaForge had testified that he had seen Meyer Lansky at the Arrowhead Inn during his survey in 1947 and on another occasion in 1948. In fact, many people had seen him in Saratoga Springs over the years.

Frank Costello, who had taken over the Genovese crime family after Lucky Luciano was deported to Italy, testified himself that he had an interest in the Piping Rock Club dating back to the early 1940's. A document was introduced into the hearings showing that Costello had a thirty percent interest in the "Saratoga Venture" (which was the Piping Rock) along with several other men, one of whom was Meyer Lansky's brother Jake.

Hoping to clear up exactly what his "interest" in the Piping Rock was, Costello tried to insist that he had no actual interest. He testified that a man named Joe Stein had approached him in 1940 or 1941 and wanted Costello to finance a share of the casino at Piping Rock.

According to Costello, "This Joe Stein come to me with the proposition, and I was not interested. So, he practically insisted, because he wanted to make some money, and I said, 'All right, then I will finance you. And whatever you do, we will go 50-50'. So, I personally had no interest in the Piping Rock."

Perhaps because he never physically oversaw the games at the Piping Rock, Frank Costello could justify in his own mind that he did not really have an interest in the Piping Rock, but under the normal understanding of the English language and the law, having the staff from your nightclub in New York City work summers at the Piping Rock and, taking a cut of the gambling profits for nearly a decade from the place, certainly sounds an awful lot like an "interest" in the place.

When Meyer Lansky went before the committee, he was asked several questions regarding his connection to Saratoga Springs. A small sampling of his responses should suffice to highlight the absurdity of his answers for the reader:

Question: "Have you ever been in Saratoga Springs, NY?"

Lansky: "I decline to answer on the ground that it may tend to incriminate me."

Question: "Were you ever in the premises of the Arrowhead Inn at Saratoga Springs?"

Lansky: "I decline to answer on the ground that it may tend to incriminate me."

Question: "Did you ever hear of the Arrowhead Inn at Saratoga Springs?

Lansky: "I decline to answer on the ground that it may tend to incriminate me."

Of course, Lansky had been coming to Saratoga and gambling there for years. He first came to work for Arnold Rothstein at the Brook, out Church St, along with other up-and-coming gangsters Lucky Luciano and Dutch Schultz. It was well known that he was running the Arrowhead throughout the 1940's. He was clearly not a stranger in town.

When the committee called Joseph Doto, alias Joe Adonis, they probably could have assumed that they would get the same response from him as they did from Lansky. And they were right.

Question: "Is it not a fact that you were partners in the Piping Rock Casino at Saratoga Springs from 1941 to 1942?"

Adonis: "I decline to answer."

Chairman Kefauver: "You are directed to answer."

Adonis: "I decline to answer on the ground that it would or might tend to incriminate me."

Question: "Have you ever been in Saratoga Springs?"

Adonis: "Yes, sir."

Question: "Have you ever been at the Piping Rock Casino?"

Adonis: "Yes, sir."

Question: "Did you ever see gambling in progress at the Piping Rock Casino?"

Adonis: "I decline to answer."

Chairman Kefauver: "You are directed to answer."

Adonis: "I decline to answer on the ground that it might tend to incriminate me."

And on and on it went with Joe Adonis. Of course, we cannot blame the likes of Costello, Lansky, and Adonis for asserting their right not to incriminate themselves. After all, they were in the organized crime business and they, like everyone else, have certain constitutional rights.

But police and public officials are not supposed to be in the business of aiding hoodlums or failing to act to stop them from committing crimes within their jurisdiction. When Jim Leary testified before the committee, he managed to avoid making any incriminating statements, while avoiding invoking his right against self-incrimination. He was much smoother than the gangsters in his answers. The testimony of Saratoga Springs Police officers was a different story.

Police Chief Rox testified that he had known several of the men involved in the inquiry for many years, particularly the local men: Louis "Doc" Farone, Matty Byrnes, and Gerard King. Yet, he could not specifically say what each of the men did for a living.

Rox did say that he earned a salary of $3700 per year and supplemented that income with a job using his own personal car to transport the nightly receipts from the Saratoga Raceway (harness track) to the banks for $10 per night.

Chief Rox admitted to the committee that he knew that some of his men were transporting money for some of the casinos but that he thought it was better than having a stick up. He never told his men to do it, and he never told them to not do it.

He also explained that his men had difficulty closing down the horse rooms in town because the operators of those joints employed counter surveillance measures and his men were rarely able to catch any of them in the act. With a small police force, they simply did not have the resources to put a stop to the horse rooms.

As for the night clubs and lake houses, Rox told Kefauver's panel that he did receive complaints about the gambling being carried on there and that, in response, he always sent out Detective A'Hearn or another officer to investigate. They always came back and reported that they could find no evidence of gambling.

Similarly, Saratoga County Sheriff Frank S. Hathorn informed the committee that he also had received complaints about the lake houses, and he dispatched two deputies to cooperate with the city police officers in the investigation of those places. They too, always came back with a report that gambling was nowhere observed.

While Rox claimed that he had never visited any of the places under consideration by the committee, he did say that each year he attended the Turf Writer's Ball at the Arrowhead Inn during August, but never saw gambling there.

He lamented the fact that neither Detective A'Hearn, nor the State Police, had ever reported to him that they had uncovered gambling, because if they had, he would have gone out with his men on a raid and closed the places down.

Detective Walter F. "Bolly" A'Hearn, for his part, explained that he only ever went into the lobby of each of the gambling places, so he never actually saw gambling. He assumed that if he went any further and caused trouble that something would have happened to him, the implication being that he would have been out of a job. He also admitted that he never received any orders to not properly investigate the gambling houses. He just knew enough not to be too diligent because he had seen the repercussions suffered by other officers who enforced the law too closely in the past.

A'Hearn summed up his approach to the gambling situation this way, "the less you know, the better you are off."

One wonders where A'Hearn learned such police work. Could it have been from Chief Rox, who testified back during the Heffernan Investigation that he knew many of the gamblers in town but never actually saw gambling and wouldn't even know gambling equipment if he saw it? It was the testimony that Justice Heffernan labeled as perjured. Or was it the same Patrick Rox, then a detective in 1939, who was charged with bringing four roulette wheels back from the Piping Rock Club, but only managed to bring back one? Wherever could Detective A'Hearn have learned such police procedures? Perhaps we will never know.

Walter A'Hearn did have one good point. He said that there were more gangsters in Saratoga during August than there were in Miami in the winter. As the pages of this book have detailed, he probably wasn't wrong.

Being a local man, A'Hearn would have known how many times the same men were elected to head the police department who obviously had connections to those very same gangsters and which the public apparently had no problem with. A'Hearn knew how often criminal charges had been brought against gamblers, but either the grand jury failed to indict, or the obviously guilty escaped justice with an acquittal at trial. A'Hearn certainly realized the economic importance of the summer season, and that a large portion of the townsfolk did not mind the gambling being wide open.

Perhaps it was a little unfair to place all the blame for the conditions at Saratoga on the public officials. As Superintendent Gaffney had said, everyone knew what went on at Saratoga and everyone had to know, as did Senator Tobey, that Saratoga had become a rich harvest for the underworld. But it had to come to an end, didn't it?

Yes, it did and when it did, there were no dynamic raids. No chases or shootouts with police. Only the steady, painstakingly detailed work of a special prosecutor's office and the accompanying grand jury.

The Kefauver hearings exposed the situation at Saratoga and forced Governor Thomas Dewey to act. On April 2, 1951, Governor Dewey appointed an Extraordinary and Special Term of the Supreme Court to be presided over by Supreme Court Justice Leo Hagerty.

To run concurrently with the term of the Supreme Court was a special session of the Grand Jury charged with investigating the gambling situation and political corruption in Saratoga County with a special prosecutor assigned to head up the investigation and present the cases to the grand jury. The Special Assistant Attorney General in Charge of the Saratoga County Investigation was John Minton. Paul Williams took over for Minton in January of 1952 and led the investigation until he was himself appointed a Supreme Court Justice in September 1953, when Arthur Christy was appointed to replace him.

The scope of the investigation was three-fold. First, the probe was to center on the extent of gambling in Saratoga County from 1946-1949. Next, the grand jury was to investigate the breakdown of policing in the county and finally, the probe was to examine the conspiracy between gamblers, law enforcement, and politicians who protected the gambling operations in the County.

With the stage set, the Special Prosecutor got to work and immediately realized there were going to be obstacles to justice in Saratoga County.

It was discovered that the Saratoga County Commissioner of Jurors, a Leary ally, had not been properly choosing grand jurors. In fact, during the period of 1946-1950, out of a total of over ten thousand potential grand jurors that could have been called, the list of names prepared by the Commissioner of Jurors who could have been called for grand jury duty contained only 455 names. Of those names, 78 were either dead or otherwise ineligible to serve on a grand jury, and the investigation found that many of the names on the list had been called repeatedly for grand jury service over the years. The presumption here would be that they would know how to "properly" vote in the grand jury room.

Of the 152 names pulled for the Extraordinary Term, fifty-five were either political office holders, family, or close personal associates of political office holders in Saratoga County. Eleven had already served on the grand jury during the same year, making them ineligible to serve again.

Given Saratoga County's history of failing to hold gamblers to account for their criminal activity, is it any wonder that the illegal filling of the grand jury pool was going on in Saratoga?

Naturally, the Commissioner of Jurors resigned his post, which he had held for the previous seventeen years, immediately before the Extraordinary Term of the Grand Jury was empaneled.

The investigation also had to battle through the prevailing public opinion that wide open gambling was necessary for the economic well-being of the town and that many people in Saratoga benefited from the gambling facilities in town.

In addition, since the investigation was looking at the time period of 1946 through 1949, much of the gambling evidence uncovered would not lead to any chargeable offense, since the statute of limitations on misdemeanors, like gambling, was only two years. By 1951, any misdemeanors uncovered prior to 1949 could not be charged, and after Kefauver's hearings started in

1950, the gambling, even in Saratoga Springs, had been limited to the horse rooms around town. The big places near the lake had virtually shut down gambling operations in 1950.

Nevertheless, the investigation began and found that, while the lake houses themselves were often owned by local people, the gambling interests were mainly controlled by national organized crime figures and the gambling was where the major profits lay.

The grand jury met for forty-four months, taking over 13,000 pages of testimony, hearing from almost five hundred witnesses, and costing taxpayers well over half a million dollars. Twenty-four indictments were brought against sixty-six defendants and six corporations. Most of the defendants pled guilty. Only three went to trial and several indictments were dismissed.

For the sake of clarity and brevity, we shall focus our attention on the major organized crime figures indicted by the Saratoga County Grand Jury, specifically Meyer Lansky and Louis "Doc" Farone, as well as long time Commissioner of Public Safety Arthur "Doc" Leonard and Republican political boss James Leary. Relatively minor players in the gambling scene at Saratoga will be mentioned for historical accuracy.

While the investigation was able to link organized crime syndicates from Miami, Rochester, Las Vegas, and New York to lake houses operating in Saratoga Springs, the investigation could not find sufficient evidence to charge either Joe Adonis or Frank Costello, despite what was learned about them and their Saratoga connections during the Kefauver hearings.

Meyer Lansky, pal of Charles "Lucky" Luciano and Benjamin "Bugsy" Siegel, finally had the law catch up with him in Saratoga. In September 1952, Lansky was indicted for various charges related to the operation of the gambling at the Arrowhead Inn in 1947. Specifically, Lansky (and five others) were charged with conspiracy to gamble, being common gamblers, forgery, tax evasion, and making false statements. The indictment alleged that Lansky, "...was in daily attendance at the restaurant and gave instructions to the bookkeeper, steward, and head waiter."[8]

Meyer Lansky soon decided to plead guilty rather than face a jury and on May 2, 1953, he was sentenced to three months in jail, the only jail term he ever served, by Justice Haggerty. He was fined $2500 as well for running the Saratoga night spot.[9]

Lansky biographer Dennis Eisenberg, in his book, *Meyer Lansky: Mogul of the Mob*, quoted Lansky as saying, "...I was sent to prison, but it was only a gambling charge. I could gamble legally in Nevada and Florida but not Saratoga. But everybody knew there was gambling up there. The place was full of casinos."

He lamented the fact that he had bad timing since, he believed, the only reason authorities made any move on his interests in the Arrowhead and Piping Rock was because Governor Dewey had been embarrassed by the revelations in the Kefauver hearings about Saratoga, a mere thirty miles from the governor's mansion in Albany.

According to his obituary in the *New York Times*, Maier Suchowljansky, Lansky's given name, was once the director of the feared Murder Inc. gang of hired gunmen. He became fabulously wealthy through his gambling interests in Miami, Cuba, and Las Vegas, and was one of the few top Mob bosses who retired and died peacefully. He passed away in 1983 in Miami.

While he never did employ a gang of professional assassins like Meyer Lansky, Louis "Doc" Farone did run a bootlegging and gambling kingdom in and around Saratoga and, as we have seen, he was not averse to defending his turf with gunplay if necessary. His influence and connections extended north to the Canadian border, south through Schenectady, and west along the Mohawk River to Utica and its environs.

Unlike Meyer Lansky, Doc Farone decided to take his case to trial. The prosecution had charged him with sixteen counts of various offenses related to operating the gambling at Riley's Lake House, The Brook, and Smith's Interlaken.

During his four-week trial in early 1953, Doc Farone was confronted with no less than twenty witnesses against him, many of whom were bettors at his various casinos, but none of whom could say definitively that they had seen Doc at any of the places they gambled. Although, one bettor did write a check to cover his gambling losses to the Modern Appliance Company, a company owned by Doc Farone.

During the trial, it was established that the payoff amount for Riley's Lake House ran to $8,000 per week.[10] In addition, the amount of "ice" required for the Brook to open was $3500. When the Brook was late in opening its doors one summer, there was no leniency and police made sure the place did not open that year until the full $3500 was paid. By way of comparison, horse rooms might be required to pay as little as $100 per week to remain open, and a lump sum of $3,000 for the month of August.

With such a heavy price to pay for graft, it was a good thing that Doc Farone made over $500,000 over the course of the four summers from 1946 through 1949 from his gambling operations. He might have been friendly with the police and local officials, but graft was graft, and, in order for Doc to operate, he had to pay, just like everyone else.

Farone was represented by James Carroll, who pointed out that the survey made by Inspector LaForge back in 1947 made no mention of Louis "Doc" Farone at all. He claimed that Farone was the "scapegoat" for the investigation and that the prosecution, "…to build up the case, has twisted and turned the laws inside and out to act against Farone." [11]

Unfortunately, Farone's own accountant testified that an "S" in a ledger stood for a gambling syndicate (Farone's) that loaned $27,000 to the Brook to cover expenses. [12] That, along with other damning evidence, was produced for the jurors to consider when they pondered Doc Farone's fate.

On February 24, 1953, the jury came to a decision in the first trial of the Extraordinary Term of the Grand Jury and determined that Louis J. Farone was guilty on fourteen of the sixteen counts against him.

At his sentencing on May 2, 1953, (the same day as Meyer Lansky) Farone received a sentence of nine months in prison and a $7,000 fine. Justice Hagerty, in sentencing Farone, said, "The court regards these events significant. They may be interpreted as indicating a determination on the part of the people of Saratoga County themselves to rid their community of illegal gambling and its attendant evils." He went on, "...the jury, in the opinion of the court, decided that you were a so-called big-time operator and that you had violated and flaunted the law of the State of New York in wholesale fashion in all probability for many years."

Hagerty, while pointing out that the court could have sentenced Farone to one year and a $500 fine for each count, considered Farone's family, current business activities, and the situation in Saratoga relative to gambling dating back decades, in passing the relatively light sentence. [13]

Farone's lawyers appealed his conviction and were successful in getting a reduction in the amount of the fine and a couple of the original charges dismissed, but he had to do the time, which many people in town thought was a travesty of justice. Farone, despite his involvement in the vice conditions at Saratoga for over thirty years, was still well liked in town.

Another of the most popular men in town was facing a trial of his own. James Leary had been indicted by the grand jury for perjury. Of course, the grand jury investigated James Leary for his connections with underworld figures and associated payoffs from said gangsters, but he was not charged with any acts of corruption.

While the grand jury did not find any gambler or gangster putting money directly into the hands of James Leary, the grand jury did find that Leary engaged in a thirty-year conspiracy to conceal his wealth and his ownership of stock in the Saratoga National Bank. Presumably this was because the source of his wealth was the ill-gotten gains he received from all manner of criminals, from Doc Farone to Arnold Rothstein and Meyer Lansky.

Specifically, the grand jury alleged that Leary, "...for upwards of 30 years had been engaged in a plan and scheme and course of conduct, in which he was aided by...the co-conspirator Herbert Stone, and many others, pursuant to, and in which the defendant Leary conducted most of his varied and numerous businesses and business transactions and affairs in the names of a multitude of dummies, tools, agents, fictitious names and nominees, for the purpose, among others, of concealing his wealth and the true nature and character of his said business and other transactions..." [14]

To boil it all down, the prosecution alleged that James Leary owned stock in the Saratoga National Bank that was held by a man named Herbert Stone in order to conceal Leary's ownership of the stock. He then lied about it to the grand jury to avoid having to disclose how he came upon the money to buy the stock in the first place.

The bank stock in question was originally purchased in the early 1920's, which a more jaded observer might connect with the arrival of Arnold Rothstein and his opening of the Brook. Now we must be careful to point out that Leary was never charged with accepting any money as graft from Arnold Rothstein or anyone else.

We also should point out that as James Leary's trial approached, Herbert Stone, the principal witness against Leary, vanished without a trace.

Herbert Stone was a television repairman from Gloversville who once worked at a horse room in Gloversville. How he ended up holding 688 shares of Saratoga National Bank stock for James Leary is anyone's guess, yet there he was, a television repair man holding a controlling interest in a bank. He would remain missing throughout Leary's trial.

Stone had been missing for about a year when Leary went to trial. Represented by E. Stewart Jones, Leary's defense was that he was not being prosecuted, but persecuted. After all, as his attorney pointed out, the investigation had cost over six hundred thousand dollars, called more than fifty witnesses against Leary and produced some seven hundred exhibits. All for a ten-week trial about who owned stock in a bank, unrelated to any gambling or corruption, which is what the entire investigation was supposed to be about anyway.

As Jones said, "Someone in Albany, after fifty years, suddenly thought there might be gambling in Saratoga County."

Despite the fact that two potential jurors were removed for making false statements while trying to get onto the jury (usually people try to get out of jury duty), and the fact that the court felt there was some evidence that there were attempts made to influence and interfere with the Leary jury, the jurors nevertheless took an honest, sober look at all the evidence and declared James Leary, "NOT GUILTY."[15]

One week after the acquittal of James Leary, Justice Hagerty addressed the grand jurors. He reassured them that they had done good work thus far and that the Leary acquittal was not based on the evidence that was presented in court. Hinting that there was some other factor involved in the jury's decision to free Leary, Justice Hagerty classified the verdict as, "...a gross miscarriage of justice and therefore can only be characterized as a distinct dis-service to the people of Saratoga County and the State of New York."

His displeasure at the verdict mattered little to the citizens, who had packed the courtroom and cheered when the not guilty verdict was read aloud. Apparently, many of the citizens of Saratoga Springs had a different definition of justice than Leo Hagerty.

Six months after the Leary trial closed, Leary's law partner, Michael Sweeney, showed up in Monroe County where Herbert Stone's mother was recovering from an operation in a Rochester hospital and paid a judgement owed by Herbert Stone to Monroe County in the amount of $7,417 for her medical care.[16]

It appears that Herbert Stone, prior to going missing, had applied for public assistance to help pay for his mother's medical care. Because he met the income requirements for assistance, the Monroe County Welfare Department picked up her medical bills. When they found out that Stone owned a controlling interest in a bank in Saratoga Springs, they naturally sought reimbursement. They obtained a judgement against Stone (paid by Sweeney), who was still missing six months after the close of the trial.

Three years later, although officially still considered missing, Herbert Stone's name appeared in court papers when a Leary associate filed a mortgage discharge in Saratoga County Court in Ballston Spa bearing Stone's signature, indicating that at that time, Stone was clearly alive and living back in Gloversville.[17]

Jim Leary, whose law and political career in Saratoga spanned more than three decades despite the constant and well-founded rumors of connections to major organized crime figures and corruption, managed to escape the law in 1953. He remained a political force in Saratoga County until his death in October 1963.

Now we come to long-time Public Safety Commissioner Arthur "Doc" Leonard.

Doc Leonard, who in the 1920's, the reader will recall, ordered the seizure of the coal cars at the railroad depot and resigned from his post as Commissioner of Public Safety rather than waive immunity before the grand jury after the Heffernan investigation.

Doc Leonard, who once put his chauffeur on the police department payroll as a patrolman, even though the man was not an officer.[18]

Doc Leonard, whose brother was a manager at Riley's Lakehouse.[19]

Doc Leonard, who during the Great Depression, when the Federal Civil Works Association had welfare jobs available in Saratoga, used his influence to get the jobs for men politically connected to him (including gamblers, men already employed, and his own democratic committee delegates), even though men out of work with families to support applied for the very same jobs. [20]

Doc Leonard, who put Patrick Rox in charge of the police department, even after Rox had been labeled a perjurer by Justice Heffernan, and again after Rox "lost" roulette wheels he was supposed to bring back to the police station and was fired.

Doc Leonard, who was the man one needed to see in Saratoga Springs for one of those jobs at the casinos that were part of the graft deal with the major hoodlums hanging around during the summer tourist season.

Doc Leonard, who once again, when faced with a subpoena to testify before the grand jury in July 1951, resigned his post and, once again, was reelected by the good folks of Saratoga Springs the following fall.

Doc Leonard, who, when faced with yet another subpoena to appear before the special grand jury in January of 1952, resigned once more, for the final time, rather than face the grand jury without immunity. For those who like to keep score of such things, Leonard's final resignation in January 1952 was the third time in his storied public career that he resigned under fire, during a grand jury investigation, in order to avoid testifying.

Yes, it was that Doc Leonard, who on April 30, 1952, was indicted on seventeen counts of conspiracy, taking bribes, obstruction of justice, and accepting unlawful fees. Specifically, the indictment claimed that Leonard, "...was part of the conspiracy that (Leonard) should hold and continue to hold the office of Commissioner of Public Safety of the City of Saratoga Springs and see to it that the gambling operations of the casino (Piping

Rock) were not interrupted, interfered with or molested by the Saratoga Springs city police."

It was also found by the grand jury that monies from the operations of the Piping Rock casino were, "…used to pay public office holders and other political henchmen" that appeared on a list provided to the gamblers annually by Leonard and his Deputy, Peter Hofsses.

Eight men were charged with paying bribes to Doc Leonard, while several of his associates were accused of, but not charged by the grand jury, with being part of the conspiracy to accept graft from the Piping Rock Casino. These unindicted co-conspirators included Jeal Smith, an employee of the Public Safety Department and Democratic Committeeman; Leonard's Deputy Commissioner of Public Safety, Peter Hofsses; Charles McTygue, the Commissioner of Public Works; and Detective Walter A'Hearn. [21]

It took three years to resolve the case against Leonard, not because the evidence wasn't strong or the prosecution was not ready to proceed. It wasn't even that Leonard's attorney was effective in delaying the trial. No, 73-year-old Doc Leonard was simply sick with a heart ailment. When two different doctors testified that Leonard would not survive the rigors of a trial for his freedom and even if he did, would never survive a prison term, the charges against him were simply dropped.

So Justice Hagerty dismissed the indictments against Leonard as, "the only sensible thing to do under the circumstances" and set Leonard free.[22] Hagerty did note, however, that all eight of the men who had been indicted for paying bribes to Leonard had pled guilty to the charge and therefore left no doubt that had Leonard gone to trial, he would certainly have been found guilty.

Leonard, relieved that he would not face a jury trial, remained out of public office for the rest of his life. A Saratoga native, born in 1897, the legendary Doc Leonard, having won election thirteen times for the office of Commissioner of Public Safety, died on October 21, 1959.

And so, it all came to an end, without any fireworks or spectacular gambling house raids. There were no broken-down doors, shootouts with law men, or chases through the streets of Saratoga. No lengthy prison terms were meted out. No mob war broke out between rivals looking for the spoils of the smashed vice market at the Spa.

The dismissed indictments of charges against Doc Leonard essentially closed the Extraordinary and Special Term of the Supreme Court; the casinos and lake houses were never to be reopened on the historical scale that they had reached in bygone days.

The curious reader may wonder what happened to the smaller fish that were caught up in the investigation, as well as the lawmen who were not indicted or charged with any crimes. So, as a point of historical accuracy, the following mention is made of some of the lesser players in this drama.

Both Detective Walter A'Hearn and Police Chief Rox resigned from the police force at the outset of the investigation. Although they both admitted to the Kefauver Committee to irregularities in their conduct, they both likely were judged to be incompetent in the eyes of the grand jurors, rather than criminally responsible for their actions.

Although the Kefauver investigators had the names of several police officers who were rumored to be bag men for Leonard and Leary, it is unlikely that anyone could actually put money in the hands of any officer acting as the go-between for the gamblers and public officials; otherwise charges would surely have been brought.

By the close of the investigation there had been 47 guilty pleas by forty defendants. There were three trials, during which only Doc Farone was found guilty. James Leary and Victor Urquhart were both acquitted of the charges against them.

Of the 47 men who pled guilty to the charges against them, we have already mentioned Meyer Lansky from New York City. Cassius Pond and James "Piggy" Lynch of New York and New Jersey both paid a $2500 fine. Herman Weiner and George Brown, gangsters out of Miami, paid $2500 fines as well. Joe "Doc" Stacher from California got fined $10,000. Samuel Gold and

Harry Samuels were from the Rochester mob and both were assessed $500 fines.

Saratoga men who paid fines ranging from $500 to $1,000 were: Gerard and John King (Gerard served 30 days in jail with Lansky), Alfred Pepper, James and George White, John Brophy, George Smaldone, Robert Duval, Malcolm and Joseph Cherry, John and Edward McEwen, and Constable "Gus" DeMatteo.[23]

All the gambling equipment that the investigators managed to get their hands on during the three-year investigation was burned at the Ballston Spa village dump. The value of the various devices, including roulette tables, bird cages, money wheels, blackboards, and craps tables seized from the various storage barns, casinos, and horse rooms throughout the county was put at about $65,000.

The investigators assigned to the investigation had rented the Kessler Mansion in Ballston Spa as their headquarters. In the spring of 1955, they cleaned out their desks and locked the doors for the last time. While there would be minor raids during the next few years, the days of wide-open gambling in Saratoga Springs were over.

From the founding of the village in 1826 to the close of the Special Investigation in 1955, it had taken only 129 years for the lid to finally be clamped down on the gambling situation at Saratoga. As Special Prosecutor Arthur H. Christy wrote in his letter to Attorney General Jacob K. Javitz at the close of the investigation,

"I respectfully call your attention to that part of the Presentment of the Grand Jury which states that gambling has been effectively eliminated from Saratoga County."

Endnotes

Chapter 11

[1] Unless otherwise noted, the information contained in this chapter is derived from the gambling file in the Saratoga Room of the Saratoga Springs Public Library in which is a collection of hand written notes and memorandums written by New York State Police personnel who conducted a survey of the gambling in Saratoga in 1947, transcripts of the Kefauver Committee investigation which can be located at several websites and at the Saratoga Springs Public Library, and the Report of the Saratoga County Investigation written by Arthur H. Christy, Special Assistant Attorney General in Charge, which can be located in the Office of the City Historian in Saratoga Springs.

[2] Abadinsky, Howard. *Organized Crime*. Nelson-Hall. Chicago. 1990.

[3] Kefauver, Estes. *Crime in America*. Greenwood Press, New York. 1968.

[4] "Thomas J. Leonard." *Amsterdam Evening Record*. April 23, 1946.

[5] Armstead, Myra. *Lord, Please Don't Take Me in August: African-Americans in Newport and Saratoga Springs, 1870-1930*. University of Illinois Press, Chicago. 1999.

[6] "Mrs. Weiss Launches Suit to Close 'Gambling Houses;' Doyle Sees Political Motive." *The Saratogian*. August 20, 1949.

[7] "Complainant's Husband has Police Record." *The Saratogian*. August 20, 1949.

[8] "Luciano Pal Faces Spa Court on Conspiracy Count." *The Saratogian*. September 10, 1952.

[9] "Farone Gets 9 Months in County Jail, $7,000 Fine." *The Saratogian*. May 2, 1953.

[10] "Payments Went to Officials, Spa Jurors Hear." *The Saratogian*. February 12, 1953.

[11] "Farone Defense to Call Rudolf Halley." *The Saratogian*. February 5, 1953.

[12] "Witness Outlines Gambling Policies." *The Saratogian*. February 13, 1953.

[13] "Spa Jury Finds Farone Guilty." *The Saratogian*. February 25, 1953.

[14] "Jury Reindicts Leary on 1 Count." *The Saratogian*. September 8, 1953.

[15] "Jury Acquits Leary on Both Charges." *The Saratogian*. December 10, 1953.

[16] "Leary Aide Pays $7,417 for Support of Stone's Mother." *The Saratogian*. May 19, 1954.

[17] "Missing Stone's Name Pops Up In Court Paper." *The Saratogian*. May 23, 1957.

[18] "Finley Protests Leonard Employee on City Payroll." *The Saratogian*. February 2, 1927.

[19] "Thomas J. Leonard." *Amsterdam Evening Recorder*. April 22, 1946.

[20] "Names Given by Miss St. John to Back Accusations." *The Saratogian*. January 15, 1934.

[21] "Leonard is Indicted in Saratoga Probe." *The Schenectady Gazette*. May 1, 1952.

[22] "Leonard Indictments Dropped, Farone Gets Stay for Appeal." *The Saratogian.* March 29, 1955.

[23] "Saratoga Investigators Moving Out of Old Kessler Mansion." *The Saratogian.* April 26, 1955.

It almost seems that somehow, the story shouldn't end here. Time and time again, the gamblers and gangsters returned to Saratoga after they had been ousted. The order to close was always just temporary. Grand Juries would always fail to indict after wholesale arrests had been made. Everything always seemed to go back to the old way, except after Kefauver, it didn't.

A good percentage of the Saratoga population had always assumed that the city would fall into economic ruin if the gamblers were run out of town. They could always stomach the likes of Arnold Rothstein, Meyer Lansky, Lucky Luciano and Joe Adonis hanging around town, as long as the crowds continued to come and enough money rolled in to keep the town afloat until the next summer. When the gambling came to an end, they were almost proved correct as several years of desperate economic conditions plagued the city.

But by the 1950's, times were changing. The police were moving toward more professionalism and the public was growing tired of gang wars and mob hits. Gambling, had it continued to be run by gentleman gamblers, like John Morrissey or Richard

Canfield and not notorious hoodlums, like Meyer Lansky and Lucky Luciano, might have had a chance to come back, but alas, illegal gambling had become so much a part of the mafia's portfolio that a classy, independent fellow like Richard Canfield would find no room in the field by the time Kefauver started poking around the organized crime rackets.

To be sure, gambling on a small scale continued in Saratoga Springs well past the days of Lansky and Adonis. Occasional raids would be executed, and local men would find themselves behind bars for a little while or, if the they were a young first-time offender, with an offer from the judge to enlist in the military. Candy stores, delis, cigar shops, and newsrooms all continued to offer gambling around back, only now Luciano and Lanksy were not taking such a large cut of the much smaller Saratoga pie. One never did need to actually visit the track to bet on a horse.

With all the shoot outs, fixed horse races, gunmen and hoodlums throughout this story, one almost hopes for a cataclysmic end. A desperate fight in the streets as the good guys do battle with the bad guys over supremacy in the City. But organized crime rings and cultural changes don't always come with a bang.

For organized crime, the end often comes when the government unseals indictments and their investigation is painstakingly laid out over months of court proceedings. The battle is in a courtroom, rather than a street corner.

For a community like Saratoga, the end often comes when the hypocrisy becomes too much to bear. When the average citizen can no longer live with an ends justifies the means approach to running a town. When their support for gangsters and corrupt officials is laid bare in a court of law and cannot be denied or explained away. Change comes when outside reformers are no longer needed because the people of the town have decided that they have had enough.

Today, we can look back and appreciate our history without condoning it. There might be a small part of us that would like a little bit of the old days to come back. To make life a little more colorful. To provide a little bit more entertainment and drama to the summer scene.

Yet to open the lid just a little would invite someone to pull the lid off entirely. There is no such thing as bringing back a little bit of the old days, lest Saratoga ends up once again, A Gangster's Paradise.

Index

A

Adelphi Grill, 228, 229
Adelphi Hotel, 58
Adinolfi, Nicholas, 107
Adler, Polly, 192, 193
Adonis, Joe (Joespeh Doto), 2, 4,
135, 297, 299, 301, 302, 308, 315,
319, 321, 322, 330, 348
A'Hearn, John, 291
A'Hearn, Walter (Bolly), 311, 325,
340, 342
Anderson, Robert, 230
Andrew Hall, 182
Andrus, Charles, 10, 15, 16, 41, 67
Arena, 223
Arena, Salvatore, 222, 224, 237
Armstrong, John, 104, 105, 106,
108, 110, 111, 119, 174, 177
Arrowhead Inn, 12, 31, 56, 157, 276,
281, 295, 296, 299, 311, 314, 319,
321, 324, 330
Arvin, George, 148
Ashton, Edward B., 21

B

Baggatta, Carlo, 178
Ballou, Charles, 227
Banque d'Hochelaga, 217
Barrie, Peter, 162, 163, 164, 165
Bascom, Waymon, 67
Beefsteak Charlie's, 72, 77, 286
Bennet, Louis, 286
Bitz, Irving, 185, 186, 245
Bleeck, John, 277
Bly, Nellie, 8, 14
Bootleg Trail, 37, 125, 196
Boutwell, Alfred, 99

Brackett, Edgar, 67
Brophy, Jack, 316
Brophy's, 70, 71, 77, 80, 83
Brown, Rachel, 14, 34, 85
Bryant, Frederick H., 249
Buchalter, Louis, 187
Burdo, Joseph, 80
Burns Detective Agency, 110
Burns, Matthew, 263
Byrne's, 72, 78, 79, 80
Byrnes, Matthew, 79

C

Cahill, Matty, 296
Callahan, Frederick, 174, 176, 177
Canfield Casino, 6
Canfield, Richard, 10, 8, 10, 12, 34,
62, 271, 301, 349
Capone, Al, 30, 121, 132, 184, 248
Carey, Officer, 61
Carfano, Anthony (Little Augie
Pisano), 245, 285, 286, 287, 288,
289, 290
Carroll, Edward, 18, 21
Cavanaugh, Jesse, 100
Cherry, Joseph, 343
Cherry, Malcolm, 343
Chicago Club, 34, 72, 128, 191, 192,
255, 257, 263, 309, 316
Circular Street, 45, 227, 285
Cito, 142, 143
Clark, Lefty, 2, 314
Cleroux, Henri, 218
Coakley, John (O.K.), 296
coal shortage, 20
Codigotto, Atteiro, 56
Cokes, Herbert, 174
Coll, Peter, 133, 246
Coll, Vincent "Mad Dog", 115,
133, 136, 246, 247

Coll-Schultz War, 247
Comstock, Anthony, 7, 8, 67
Condon, James, 59
Conn, Belmont, 149, 150, 152
Cook, Charles, 283
Cook, Harold, 48
Cook, Leslie, 47, 48
Costello, Frank, 2, 4, 135, 173, 289, 297, 299, 301, 302, 308, 319, 320, 322, 330
Crannell, Scott, 314, 316
Cromie, William, 98, 299, 300
Crooks, Morris, 107
Crosby, Bing, 272, 302
Cummings, James, 108, 284

D

Dannemora Prison, 43, 86, 210
Davis, James H., 102
Davis, Leo, 222, 224
Deitz, Courtney, 193, 194, 195, 196, 197, 198
Delorenze, Ceylon, 211
DelVecchio, Officer, 118, 127
Dematteo, Gus (Dynamite), 36, 60, 191, 210, 211, 212, 343
DeMatteo, Louis, 18, 211, 212, 256, 257, 263, 265
Department of Justice (USDOJ), 52, 185
DeRossi, Alphonse, 59
Dewey, Thomas, 184, 187, 326
Diamond, Jack (Legs), 30, 115, 121, 123, 128, 131, 132, 133, 134, 135, 136, 186, 187, 196, 197, 198, 243, 245, 246, 274
Doherty, Joseph, 85, 291, 293, 294
Dominick, Frank "Funny", 210, 212
Dominick, Joseph (Crazy Joe), 179, 180, 181, 182, 229
Donivan, Roy, 39
Donohue, Officer, 214, 215, 255, 256, 258
dope sheet (dope book), 271

Dorsey, Hugh, 40, 82, 104, 193
Doyle, John, 226, 227, 231, 232, 233, 234
Dugout, 215, 216, 217
Dunn, Matthew (Matty), 56, 272, 277, 278, 282, 287, 290, 293
Dunnigan, John, 138, 140
Duval, Alfred, 47, 49
Duval, Robert, 50, 343
dying declaration, 231, 234, 235

E

Eastman, Monk, 183, 187
Eddy, Spencer B., 70, 72
Einstein, Isadola (Honest Izzy), 54, 56, 58
Elizabethtown, 37, 49
Elliot, James, 56
Ellis, Norman, 181

F

Faets, John (Don Petes, Peets), 311, 312, 313
Farone, Alfred, 126
Farone, Louis (Doc), 25, 26, 27, 121, 122, 123, 125, 128, 129, 131, 132, 135, 136, 253, 254, 255, 259, 261, 315, 331, 333, 334, 342, See
Farone, Paul, 208, 209
Fennell, James, 177, 296
Fennell, Thomas, 61
Fennell's, 77, 80, 83
57 Congress Street, 55
Finley, Peter, 67, 68, 70, 74, 77, 78, 81, 88, 94, 98, 100, 101, 102
Fisher, Reverend Harry B., 77, 78, 80, 81, 98
Fitzgibbons, Denis, 78
Flat Rock Holding Company, 300
Formel, Jules, 74, 75, 76, 77, 78, 85, 86, 87, 88, 89
40 High Rock, 59
41 Nelson Ave, 75
42 Beekman Street, 179

42 Phila Street, 72
449 Broadway, 58, 82
46 Congress Street, 105
493 Woodlawn Ave, 119
Frank, Tony (The King), 221, 222

G

Gaffney, John, 19, 309
Gallant Fox, 147
Gambino, Frank, 220, 221, 222, 223, 225
Garant, Frank, 210
Gordon, Vivian, 192
Gordon, Waxey, 183, 184, 185
Grand Union Hotel, 254, 308
Greenberg, Max (Big Maxey), 183
Grennan, Patty, 280
Gunn, Marjorie, 202
Gylfoyld, Agent, 53

H

Hagerty, Justice Leo, 326, 333, 336, 337, 341
Halfway House, 36
Hall, Andrew, 146
Hankard, William, 40
Harrison, Harry (Harry the Jew), 256, 257, 259, 265
Harry Carter's Pig Farm, 256
Haupt, George, 40, 41, 42, 43, 44
Hayes, Theodore, 167
Heffernan, Christopher (Justice), 6, 66, 69, 70, 71, 72, 73, 74, 75, 77, 78, 79, 80, 81, 82, 83, 84, 85, 87, 88, 89, 90, 91, 92, 93, 97, 98, 99, 100, 102, 103, 104, 107, 109, 112, 174, 290, 293, 325, 338
Higgins, Charles (Vannie), 186
Hirsch, Trooper, 39, 40
Hofsses, Peter, 313, 314, 340
Home of the Good Shepherd, 126
Hoover, J. Edgar, 153, 187, 248, 299

I

Ingram, Robert, 80
Izzy and Moe, 55, 56, 57, 58, 270, 282, 298

J

Jock's Lunch, 228
Johnson, Elijah, 146, 147
Josephson, Joseph, 158, 159, 160

K

Karpis, Alvin, 152, 153, 188, 189, 190
Kefauver Committee, 1, 3, 5, 20, 297, 299, 316, 319, 342
Kefauver, Estes, 307
Kelly Gang, 33, 34, 35, 36
Kenny, Lenny, 278, 280
Kentucky Club, 317
Kilmer, Clarence, 20
King, Gerard, 280, 315, 323
King, James, 12
King, John, 343
King, William, 44
Knapp, Clarence, 54, 57, 59, 100, 270, 282, 288
Kummer, Clarence, 141

L

LaCoppa, Tony, 208
Ladana, 155, 156, 161
Lafayette Street, 33, 35
LaForge, Charles, 2, 25, 309, 310, 316, 319, 332
Lake Lonely, 56, 68, 70, 271, 280
Lally, Daniel, 47, 48, 49
Lansky, Meyer, 2, 4, 13, 14, 30, 31, 135, 184, 225, 297, 299, 301, 308, 314, 319, 320, 321, 322, 329, 330, 331, 333, 334, 342, 343, 348, 349

Leary, James (Jim), 11, 14, 15, 16, 17, 18, 19, 27, 53, 70, 71, 72, 73, 76, 77, 81, 85, 86, 87, 88, 93, 103, 173, 191, 272, 274, 310, 313, 314, 319, 322, 327, 329, 334, 335, 336, 337, 342
Leonard, Arthur (Doc), 18, 68, 215, 290
Leonard, Thomas, 215, 293
Lewis, Truman, 120, 121, 123, 129
Lido Venice, 299, 300
Lindbergh, Charles, 185, 186
Lober, Agent, 53
Lombardo, Anthony (Hawk-Eye-Tinny), 280, 315
Lucas, Officer William, 104, 105, 203, 235
Luciano, Charles (Lucky), 4, 13, 14, 30, 31, 135, 140, 173, 190, 191, 192, 200, 225, 289, 309, 320, 321, 330, 348, 349
Lutz, John, 117
Lynch, James (Piggy), 314, 342

M

MacMahon, Carl, 70
Madden, Vincent (Owney), 308
Maginn, Officer, 61
Mahedy, William, 8
Manilla, Christine, 232
Manning, James (Joseph Davis), 151, 152
Manny, Charles, 296
Martin, Jules, 244
Martino, Angelo, 181
Martino, George, 181
Mason, Detective George, 209, 211
Matilda Street, 5
Matthews Garage, 37
Mayone, Annette, 285
McCarthy, Dan (Deafy), 249
McGirr, Officer, 284, 285
McKelvey, Lawrence B., 288
McNeary, Winifred, 211
McNulty, Mayor James, 20

McTygue, Judge Michael, 281
Meader, Abbie, 49
Meadowbrook Casino, 315
Meehan, James "Jimmy", 157, 158, 159, 160, 161
Mellefont Café, 55, 58
Mellefont, Richard H., 56, 58
Millett's Hotel, 111
Mitchell, Caleb, 8, 9, 10, 11, 17, 299
Modern Appliance Company, 262, 332
Morel, Louis, 221, 222
Moreland Act, 69, 90, 93
Morrison, William (Scotchy), 303, 315
Morrissey, John, 5, 6, 7, 13, 62, 139, 165, 172, 348
Morrissey, Trooper, 39
Murphy, Ms. Ann, 49

N

Natale, Frank, 181, 182
New Commercial Garage, 32, 215
New York State Police, 1, 2, 38, 227, 233, 309, 312
Newman, Henry, 274, 275, 276, 277
Newman's Lake House, 274, 275, 277, 280, 282, 311
Nieri, Ciro, 220, 221, 222, 223, 224, 237

O

O'Neill, Thomas, 285, 286, 287, 288
O'Brien, Frank (Skinny), 42, 44, 46
overnight race, 156
102 Congress Street, 55, 208, 209
107 Catherine Street, 122, 125, 127, 128, 129

P

painting horses, 162
Palace Chop House, 136, 253

Paletto, James, 208
Panetian, 148, 149, 150, 151, 152, 154, 157
Parillo, Adam (Eff, Effie), 203, 206, 208, 210, 213, 214, 215, 217, 221, 223, 225, 226, 228, 230, 231, 232, 235, 236, 237, 238, 267, 312
Patneaud, A.J. (Charlie Blues), 31, 32, 33, 34, 35, 36, 37
payoff man, 158
Peck, Henry C., 101
Pelletier, Officer Isreal, 219, 220
Pepper, Alfred (Allie), 280, 315, 316, 317, 343
Pinkertons, 145, 149, 150, 152, 154, 163, 166, 196, 197
Piping Rock Club, 299, 300, 301, 302, 314, 320, 325
Pompay, Anthony (Sonny), 129, 228, 234
Pompay, Augustus, 80
Pompay, Genaro, 213
Pullman, Gladys, 285

R

Railroad Place, 20, 61, 70, 77, 229, 317
Rancocas Stable, 155, 156
Ranney, Charles, 234, 235
Rasmussen, Corporal, 40, 42
Red Front, 82
revenue racket, 179
Ricket's Farm, 256
Riley, Ben, 295, 296, 297
Riley, James, 280, 281, 295
Riley's Lake House, 280, 291, 293, 294, 295, 297, 310, 315, 331, 332
Roberts, Marion (Kiki), 196, 197, 198
Rose, Harry (Walter Mosler), 51
Rothstein, Arnold, 12, 13, 15, 16, 28, 30, 31, 34, 62, 76, 115, 135, 140, 141, 144, 157, 159, 160, 165, 183, 186, 190, 225, 243, 245, 281, 296, 308, 321, 334, 335, 348

Rox, Patrick, 2, 4, 11, 16, 22, 23, 47, 83, 84, 104, 145, 166, 193, 255, 285, 290, 294, 297, 309, 325, 338
Russo, Stanley, 25, 312
Ryan, Judge Andrew, 234

S

Sabino, Bartholomew, 256, 257, 265
Salvinsky, Matthew, 40, 41, 42, 43, 44, 47
Saratoga Clubhouse, 6, 7, 9
Saratoga Coal Company, 21
Saratoga National Bank, 334, 335
Saratoga Springs Taxpayers Association, 67, 78
Saratoga Way, 11, 12, 27, 212, 295, 307
Savard's Clothing Store, 53
Schultz, Dutch, 13, 30, 31, 115, 128, 131, 132, 133, 134, 135, 136, 193, 242, 243, 244, 245, 246, 247, 248, 249, 250, 251, 252, 253, 259, 260, 267, 321
Scott, Clarence, 102
Scott, James, 105
Searing's Alley, 8, 116, 182
Serafini, Giuseppe, 220, 289
Shady Acres Farm, 256, 258, 263
Shapiro, Jacob (Gurrah), 187
Sheridan, Charles, 150
Sherman, Chink, 246
Sherman, Richard, 20, 288
Siegel, Benjamin (Bugsy), 330
Silvo, Frank, 79
6 Railroad Place, 316
64 Beekman, 59
66 Beekman Street, 206
66 South Franklin Street, 206
69 Jackson Street, 205
Skipit, 167
Smaldone, George, 213
Smaldone, Thomas, 208
Smith, Alfred (Governor), 68
Smith, Attorney John, 233

Smith, George (Moon), 152, 153, 313
Smith, Jeal, 73, 340
Smith, Moe, 55
Smith's Interlaken, 272, 302, 303, 315, 317, 331
South Franklin and Ash, 256, 257, 258
Spencer, Albert, 7, 8
Spitale, Salvatore (Salvy), 185, 186, 245
Spratt, Harold, 80
Squealer's Gash, 208
St. Vincent de Paul prison, 225, 236
Stacher, Joseph (Doc), 2, 297, 314, 342
Stevens, George, 106
Stone, Harry, 220, 225
Stone, Herbert, 334, 335, 337
Sullivan, Dr. Eugene J., 88
Sullivan, James, 81, 104
Sun Mission, 146, 147, 148, 152
Sweeney, Commissioner Edward, 6, 97, 104, 105, 106, 107, 109, 110, 111, 120, 129, 130, 174, 177, 337

T

Tabbano, Paul, 210
Taylor, Frank, 155
Taylor, Marie, 52, 53
Tennes, Monte, 34
The Brook, 12, 68, 76, 331
35 Caroline Street, 210, 214
36 Beekman Street, 60
38 Circular Street, 13
39 Ash Street, 153
39 Phila Street, 318
three-card monte, 166
Tobey, Senator Charles W., 1, 2, 326
Towne, Scott, 203
Trask, Spencer, 7, 67
Travers, Arthur, 40

Trooper Morrissey, 41
Tucker, Sophie, 272, 302
Turf Inn, 208
20 Phila Street, 316
21 ½ Marvin Street, 206
24 Caroline Street, 316
29 Caroline Street, 316
22-26 Railroad Place, 111
210 South Broadway, 13, 14, 15, 18, 22, 76, 157

U

Ullman, Joe, 34
Urquhart, Victor, 80, 314, 316, 317, 342

V

Valentino, Mike, 222, 224, 226
Van Rensselear, Stanley, 25
Volpe, Joe (The Fox), 256, 257, 261, 262, 263, 265
Volstead Act, 24, 29, 55, 62, 282

W

Waite, Alfred, 49
Walbridge, John, 100
Walker, John (Boob), 158, 159, 193
Weinberg, Abraham, 71, 72, 73, 74, 78
Weiss, Phillip, 253, 317, 318, 319
Welch, James, 56, 296
White, Almeron F., 78, 79
Willow Walk, 8, 116
Wilmot, Arthur G., 67, 70, 71, 75, 81, 88, 91, 93, 94, 98, 99, 102, 103
Winship, Officer Theodore, 203, 204, 205, 227, 229, 230, 235
Wolley, James, 127
Woodlawn Avenue, 5, 72, 77
Woods, Earnest (a.k.a. N.K. Pumphrey), 174

Greg Veitch is a fifth generation Saratogian, lifelong resident, and retired Saratoga Springs Chief of Police. Greg holds a Master's Degree in Leadership from SUNY Plattsburgh and teaches in the Criminal Justice program at SUNY Adirondack. He attends New Life Fellowship Church in Saratoga where his wife, Jennifer is Director of Family Ministries. Greg and Jen have five children, Rebekah, Rachel, Elizabeth, Luke and Nathan.

CPSIA information can be obtained
at www.ICGtesting.com
Printed in the USA
BVHW080952070921
616221BV00011B/1108